What Is Mental Illness?

What Is Mental Illness?

Richard J. McNally

The Belknap Press of Harvard University Press

Cambridge, Massachusetts, and London, England • 2011

Library of Congress Cataloging-in-Publication Data

McNally, Richard J.
What is mental illness? / Richard J. McNally.
Includes bibliographical references and index.
ISBN 978-0-674-04649-8 (alk. paper)
1. Mental illness.   2. Mental illness—United States.   I. Title.
RC454.M326   2011
616.89—dc22   2010035456

FOR DONNA, WIFE AND FRIEND

Contents

What Is Mental Illness?

1

Nearly 50 percent of Americans have been mentally ill at some point in their lives, and more than a quarter have suffered from mental illness in the past twelve months.[1] Madness, it seems, is rampant in America.

These startling conclusions emerged from the National Co-morbidity Survey Replication (NCSR), a study involving psychiatric interviews with a sample of more than nine thousand adults. Studies in other countries, for their part, seem to confirm the high level of mental illness in America. Consider two recent psychiatric surveys done in China and Nigeria. Both indicated that about 4–5 percent of the population had a mental disorder during the previous year, compared with 26 percent of people in the United States.[2] Remarkably, Americans seem more vulnerable to breakdown than people in impoverished, often chaotic regions of the globe. Does affluence somehow breed mental disorder?

The NCSR surveyors interviewed adults, not children. But they did ask subjects when their problems began. They found that half of those who had suffered from mental illness developed their disorder before the age of fourteen, and three-quarters of them had fallen ill by the age of twenty-four.[3] Mental disorders, then, strike much earlier in people's lives than many would have guessed.

The NCSR also found that most people do not receive treatment in a timely fashion, if at all.[4] For example, for those with mood disorders, the delay from illness onset to first professional contact ranged from six to eight years. For those with anxiety disorders, it ranged from nine to twenty-three years. The reasons for delay are unclear. Some people may fail to recognize their problems as symptoms of treatable mental disorders, whereas others may worry about the stigma of being labeled "crazy." Furthermore, among people who had a mental disorder during the previous year, 59 percent went untreated. The NCSR researchers interpreted these findings as indicating a "profound unmet need for mental health services."[5]

Yet strangely enough, despite the vast number of untreated individuals, nearly one-third of all mental health visits involve problems too mild to meet criteria for any psychiatric disorder.[6] So in addition to the many cases of unmet need, we seem to have many cases of "met un-need," as the psychiatric epidemiologist William Narrow called it.[7] This would seem to imply that distressed people experiencing ordinary problems of living are consuming scarce resources needed by those with serious problems such as schizophrenia and depression. If so, then we have the worst possible situation: those most in need of treatment do not receive it, whereas those least in need do.

Of course, not all psychological troubles signify mental disorder. Mental health professionals often provide helpful guidance to people whose distress arises from difficulties in everyday life. People seek counseling for relationship problems, difficulties at work, or loneliness. Moreover, people whose mental illness has gone into remission may still require counseling to ensure sustained recovery. For example, therapists can help patients with a history of bipolar disorder adhere to medication regimens and cope with life stressors that might otherwise trigger a relapse into depression or mania. In this sense, not everyone who sees a therapist necessarily counts as a case of met un-need.

The NCSR interviewers also asked subjects who did seek help about the kind of treatment they received. The results were disturbing. A mere one-third had received pharmacological or psychological treatments of demonstrated efficacy. That is, only a minority had received treatments that controlled clinical trials had shown were actually better for reducing psychiatric symptoms than a pill placebo or no treatment at all.[8] Few received an antidepressant drug for serious depression or cognitive-behavior therapy (CBT) for panic disorder. In fact, nearly one-third of all mental health visits involved spiritual healers, practitioners of "alternative" medicine, and others offering nonmainstream treatments such as past-life regression therapy. As Thomas Insel, the director of the National Institute of Mental Health (NIMH) put it, "mental health care in America is ailing."[9]

So we've heard the claims that half of America has suffered from *mental disorder,* but what exactly do we mean by the term? Nearly all clinicians and researchers today follow the definitions and diagnostic guidelines of the American Psychiatric Association (APA) as outlined in the *Diagnostic and Statistical Manual of Mental Disorders* (DSM).[10] According to the DSM, mental disorders are behavioral or psychological syndromes, clusters of co-occurring symptoms, which cause significant distress or interfere with a person's ability to function in everyday life, or both. Symptoms of mental disorders arise from a presumptive dysfunction within the mind (or brain). That is, something has gone wrong within the person. Normal emotional distress arising from ordinary difficulties of living, such as anxiety about losing one's job in an economic downturn, does not signify mental disorder. Likewise, behavioral problems that conflict with social norms, such as criminal activity, do not indicate mental disorder. Although some criminals are mentally ill, committing crimes is insufficient to justify a diagnosis of mental illness. Very few murderers are insane. People can be bad without being mad.

Mental disorders vary greatly in terms of type and severity. Schizophrenia, for example, involves a psychotic "break with reality," marked by hallucinations, delusions, and difficulty functioning in everyday life. For example, a man with paranoid schizophrenia who has delusions that his coworkers are plotting to poison him is likely to have difficulty functioning at work. Other disorders, such as snake phobia and alcohol abuse, produce less suffering and impairment. A woman with a snake phobia may avoid camping outdoors but otherwise experience minimal interference in her family or work life. The DSM-IV provides explicit criteria for objectively diagnosing each mental disorder. Therefore, when epidemiologists announce that half of America has suffered from mental illness, they're playing by the rules. The problem, however, is that the rules themselves may be faulty. Does our system of diagnosing mental disorders fail to distinguish normal human suffering from genuine mental illness? Or are we really getting sicker?

Consider major depressive disorder. People with this condition suffer from unremitting sadness, an inability to experience pleasure, or both. They also typically lose their energy, appetite, and ability to sleep or concentrate on daily tasks. Suffering from guilt and hopelessness about the future, they often contemplate suicide. When depressed people also have a hard time controlling their impulses or suffer from unrelenting, intense anxiety, they are at high risk for attempting suicide.[11]

Evidence indicates that major depressive disorder has been striking an increasingly larger proportion of each successive generation.[12] This implies that Generation Xers are at greater risk than are Baby Boomers, who, in turn, are at greater risk than those born during the Great Depression or earlier. Perhaps younger cohorts are less resilient to ordinary life stressors than are older cohorts, who lived through the Depression and World War II. Younger groups may be more psychologically minded and more willing to admit symptoms than older ones. Of course, some members of older cohorts may have forgotten previous episodes of depression. Some depressed members of older cohorts may have died prematurely, perhaps by suicide. These factors would diminish the apparent rate of depression in older versus younger segments of the population.

Yet clinical researchers believe that these factors cannot explain the rising incidence of depression over time; the phenomenon appears genuine.[13] The increase is so dramatic that it strains credulity to imagine that it is entirely due to faulty memory and other artifactual causes. Indeed, only about 2–3 percent of people born before 1915 developed the disorder, despite having lived through the Great Depression and World War II.[14] In contrast, about 20 percent of those born between the late 1950s and the early 1970s have had depression.[15] During the past century, depression has been striking people at increasingly younger ages.

But why? Social trends in recent decades may have increased stressors while diminishing the capacity of people to cope with them. Our society has become increasingly individualistic; we are now more likely to be "bowling alone" than with others.[16] Loosening of social bonds, aggravated by increased geographical mobility, may diminish the support systems vital for coping with the problems of everyday life. Social relationships may not be sufficient to ensure emotional health, but they are a necessary part of it.[17] Factors that disrupt these relationships may foster depression, especially among people genetically at risk for the disorder.[18]

Anxiety also has been increasing across generational cohorts. The psychologist Jean Twenge noted that researchers have administered the Taylor Manifest Anxiety Scale to groups of college students for many decades.[19] This questionnaire asks respondents whether statements such as "I feel anxious about something or someone almost all of the time," and "I am a very nervous person," apply to them. For each generation, Twenge calculated the median score (that is, the score dividing the top 50 percent of the students from the bottom 50 percent). She found that the typical college student in the 1990s was more anxious than 71 percent of college students in the 1970s and more anxious than 85 percent of college students in the 1950s. In other words, students scoring at the median (50th percentile) in the 1990s would have scored at the 71st percentile had they attended college in the 1970s and at the 85th percentile had they attended college in the 1950s. The typical college student in the 1990s would have looked neurotic in the 1950s. Similarly, the average schoolchild in the 1980s scored higher on standardized measures of anxiety than did the average child psychiatric patient in the 1950s.

Twenge believes that people born in the 1970s, 1980s, and 1990s encounter stressors seldom experienced by those born earlier.[20] About half of them come from broken homes, and many never knew their fathers. Younger cohorts work more hours, deal with higher housing costs, and experience far more geographic mobility, which, in turn, erodes stable networks of social support.

Studies of clients in university counseling centers are consistent with this trend. The proportion of students seeking help for complex clinical problems has increased since the late 1980s, and the number of suicidal students has tripled.[21] There has been an "extraordinary increase in serious mental illness on college campuses today," says Richard Kadison, chief of mental health services for students at Harvard University.[22] He cited a 2001 survey of directors of university counseling centers in which 85 percent reported an increase in "severe" psychological problems over the course of the previous five years. Kadison warned parents that nearly half of students today will experience a depression so serious that they will be unable to function, and that about one in ten will become suicidal. Between 25 and 50 percent of students in campus counseling centers take antidepressants.[23] This high rate of medication use is consistent with the kinds of problems students encounter today. The challenges that students of earlier generations faced, such as adjusting to being away from home, confusion about future careers, and conflicts with roommates, no longer dominate the picture. Serious depression, preoccupation with committing suicide, and self-injurious behavior, such as cutting and burning oneself, are far more common than in the past.

A major survey published in 2008 confirms the observations of Kadison and others. The National Epidemiologic Study on Alcohol and Related Conditions (NESARC) involved face-to-face psychiatric interviews with a representative sample of more than 40,000 Americans. In one NESARC report, the authors focused on subjects aged nineteen to twenty-five.[24]

In this sample, 2,188 subjects attended college and 2,904 did not. Among college students, 46 percent had at least one mental disorder during the previous twelve months. Twenty percent of the college students met criteria for either alcohol abuse or dependence, and about two-thirds of these problem drinkers were dependent on alcohol. More than 10 percent had suffered from a mood disorder during the previous year, usually major depression or bipolar disorder. Anxiety disorders occurred in nearly 12 percent of college students. The NESARC interviewers diagnosed personality disorders—severe, longstanding interpersonal problems—in nearly 18 percent of the college population. Less than 20 percent of students with a mental disorder had sought treatment during the year prior to the survey.

Young people who are not attending college are not doing any better than their peers in school. Forty-eight percent of this group suffered from a mental disorder during the previous twelve months. For the most part, the same illnesses afflicted this group as afflicted the college students. Moreover, similar factors influenced risk for psychiatric disorder in both groups. Being foreign-born or a member of a racial or ethnic minority group lowered risk, whereas disruption in social relations, including romantic disappointments, increased risk. As the NESARC researchers observed, this finding underscores the powerful impact of social relationships in the lives of young people. The popularity of Facebook, text messaging, and continual cell phone contact may partly arise to counteract trends for increasing social isolation.

Could this increase in mental illness among students be due to the fact that more young people than ever before are attending college, including those whose mental health troubles would have prevented them from doing so before psychiatric drugs became so widely prescribed? Even though medication may enable them to finish high school and enroll in college, the stress of university life may nevertheless unmask preexisting vulnerabilities.

All these studies imply that mental illness is a public health crisis of staggering proportions. But is the epidemic genuine? Not everyone thinks so. As Paul McHugh, former chair of the Department of Psychiatry and Behavioral Sciences at Johns Hopkins University, remarked, "Fifty percent of Americans mentally impaired—are you kidding me? Pretty soon we'll have a syndrome for short, fat Irish guys with a Boston accent, and I'll be mentally ill."[25]

In fact, recent figures for annual and lifetime prevalence rates for mental disorders seem implausibly high. How could it possibly be true that nearly half of Americans have been mentally ill? If that many citizens were "going crazy," how could society function at all? The problem here is our understanding of what it means to be mentally ill. When most people think of mental illness, they think of schizophrenia. Schizophrenia is a psychosis characterized by auditory hallucinations, delusions, social withdrawal, and apathy. Most people with this diagnosis experience severe impairment in occupational and interpersonal settings. Yet only a minority of individuals with psychiatric illness have schizophrenia; its lifetime prevalence is only about 0.5 to 1 percent.[26] It constitutes only a tiny fraction of the number of individuals who develop mental disorder. Most suffer from mood disorders, anxiety disorders, and substance abuse or dependence. These problems are serious enough, but with few exceptions, such as bipolar disorder or psychotic depression, they seldom involve a loss of contact with reality.

If we consider, then, that mental illness occurs on a spectrum of severity, the high rates don't seem quite so improbable. Why should mental illness be rare when physical illness is not? After all, nearly everyone catches the flu or develops tooth decay at some point in their lives, and hypertension, diabetes, and obesity are anything but rare in contemporary America. Physical illness runs from the common cold to cancer, and disorders within a medical domain vary in severity, impairment, and need for intervention. Imagine the incredulity provoked by headlines announcing that epidemiologists have discovered that (only!) 50 percent of Americans get sick at some point during their lifetimes. When we lump all mental (or physical) illnesses together, we should not be surprised at high rates. Some mental illnesses are the equivalent of "psychiatric hangnails," as Ronald Kessler, the head of the NCSR, put it.[27] Phobic fear of heights, speaking in public, or flying in airplanes might count as examples of these common but less disabling disorders. Hence, public skepticism about an epidemic of mental illness arises partly because laypeople have a much narrower concept of "mental illness" than do mental health professionals. For the latter, "mental illness" means much more than just "psychosis."

Rates of mental illness might also be so high because epidemiologists are better at diagnosing disorders in the general population today than in the past. Detecting these illnesses has always been challenging. They have long been a source of shame and stigma, motivating sufferers to conceal their problems. "The mass of men lead lives of quiet desperation," Thoreau said in 1854.[28] Yet despair and its variants are more visible today than ever before, partly because of advances in psychiatric epidemiology.

Epidemiologists have two main missions. In contrast to clinical researchers, who study patients in treatment, epidemiologists study large, representative samples from the population in an attempt to obtain unbiased, generalizable knowledge about the incidence, prevalence, and risk factors for disease. Epidemiologists can also provide valuable information about the need for treatment. Without accurate estimates of how many people need services, health care policy becomes little more than guesswork.

Then there's the question of cost. How can we possibly manage to pay for treating all these people? Advocates for the mentally ill argue that psychiatric disorders are just as real and no less deserving of health insurance coverage than are physical disorders. To be sure, debate abounds regarding insurance coverage for nonpsychiatric illnesses, too. But that controversy concerns the type and extent of coverage, not whether the condition is, indeed, a genuine medical illness deserving of *any* coverage.

These arguments convinced Congress. The Paul Wellstone and Pete Domenici Mental Health Parity and Addiction Equity Act of 2008 requires group health care plans involving more than fifty employees to provide insurance coverage for all mental disorders at a rate no less than that for other medical conditions.[29] It updates the previous Mental Health Parity Act of 1996 by extending coverage to substance abuse and dependence disorders. If a health care plan pays 80 percent of the cost of nonpsychiatric medical costs while the patient pays the rest, then the law requires the plan to pay for 80 percent of the cost of treatment of a mental disorder, too.

But there is a downside: claims that mental disorders are both common and serious may provoke backlash. On the one hand, advocates stress the equivalence of mental and physical disorders, arguing that schizophrenia, bipolar disorder, and other mental illnesses are biologically based diseases of the brain, and at least as devastating as cancer, heart disease, and other uncontestable medical diseases. On the other hand, they cite alarming statistics confirming the very high prevalence of mental disorder in the population, underscoring the extent of unmet need. When those who foot the bill consider these two points together—severity and prevalence—a backlash seems inevitable, especially in a climate of shrinking health care dollars. As the psychiatrist and epidemiologist Darrel Regier pointed out, "Some major media commentators identified such high rates as indicating a bottomless pit of possible demand for mental health services."[30]

Health care plans provide coverage for *medical* conditions, and psychiatric disorders qualify as medical disorders. Yet these plans provide coverage only when there is "medical necessity." Can it be, then, that many disorders in the community are insufficiently severe and do not require professional treatment? Perhaps epidemiologists have counted people whose conditions are so mild that treatment is unnecessary. If so, then the prevalence data overestimate the magnitude of treatment need. If epidemiologists were to count only clinically significant disorders when they estimate prevalence, would this reduce widespread skepticism about implausibly high rates as well as provide a more realistic guideline for health care planning?

Let's look at major depressive disorder. To be diagnosed with this disorder a person must experience either sadness or loss of pleasure for most of the day for only two weeks in addition to reporting four other symptoms (for example, fatigue, sleep disturbance, concentration problems, and diminished appetite). Most people who seek professional help for depression have been suffering far longer than only two weeks. In contrast, those who have experienced recent hardships, such as the loss of a loved one, may wind up qualifying for a diagnosis of major depression even though their condition is expectable and may abate over time without need of any professional intervention.

William Narrow, Darrel Regier, and their colleagues revisited large epidemiological data sets to investigate this issue.[31] They counted cases of disorder only when the person's condition met criteria for "clinical significance." They defined a case as "clinically significant" only if the person told the interviewer that he or she had mentioned the problem to a health care professional, took medication for the problem, or said that it had interfered with life "a lot."

These criteria are not ideal. It is tough to know what subjects might have meant when they said the problem interfered with their lives "a lot." The social context is missing. Unfortunately, these are the questions asked in the original research, and Narrow had to have some systematic way of distinguishing between disorders with and without clinical significance.

Not surprisingly, prevalence rates dropped when they counted only cases that were clinically significant. Subjects in this category were more likely to be suicidal and to report impairment in fulfilling their everyday responsibilities, such as missing days from work because of the disorder, relative to cases without clinical significance. Clinically significant disorders are those most likely to qualify as needing treatment under the medical necessity rule.

Even though these criteria revised prevalence estimates downward, the numbers were still quite high.[32] If the demand for services is anywhere near the prevalence rate, then "the mental health system would have to expand enormously to meet this need, with attendant increases in workforce deployment and overall costs," as Narrow and his colleagues observed.[33]

This attempt to reduce prevalence rates by counting only clinically significant disorders met with vigorous opposition from others in psychiatry and epidemiology. Why should we confine psychiatric disorders only to their most severe expressions if the same restriction does not hold for other medical specialties?[34] Dermatologists treat everything from warts to melanoma. Why should matters differ only for psychiatry?

Ronald Kessler agreed that resources for mental health are woefully inadequate to cope with treatment need.[35] Yet he criticized Narrow and colleagues for trying to limit the scope of mental disorder. Identifying treatment-worthy problems as only the most severe expressions of mental illness does not solve the problem of unmet need; it merely amounts to an attempt to define it out of existence. Mild problems, he asserted, deserve reimbursable, professional treatment.

To emphasize why, Kessler examined data from a follow-up study of subjects assessed in his original National Comorbidity Survey (NCS).[36] Kessler showed that mild problems identified in the original NCS often predicted the emergence of severe ones later. Thus a person who barely qualified for depression at time one wound up suffering from severe depression at time two. Providing early treatment for individuals with mild conditions might prevent the emergence of devastating illnesses down the road. This approach would be cost-effective as well as humane. Among people with recurrent depression, later episodes may be more resistant to treatment than first episodes.[37] Because depression may alter the brains of its victims, it is important to intervene early, before the person develops immunity to otherwise effective medications. Kessler also pointed out that many mental illnesses occur on a continuum with no clear, natural boundary between nondisorder and disorder.

By intervening early, doctors can prevent a condition from developing into a full-blown, potentially intractable disorder. If we wait before a mild condition reaches the severity of "clinical significance," costs, let alone suffering, might be higher than they would otherwise have been. Similarly, doctors treat precancerous cells before full-blown cancer develops, and they treat high blood pressure to prevent stroke and heart attack. Why not the same for psychiatry? This argument, however, presupposes that mild psychiatric conditions seldom remit without treatment, and that most are destined to get worse. How often this cancerlike model applies to mental disorders is an open question.

Prevalence rates for mental disorder might be so high because lay interviewers overdiagnose mental disorders. Epidemiologists usually hire survey interviewers, not expensive psychiatrists, to conduct standardized, structured interviews. These interviews do not permit clinical judgment to enter the diagnostic process. Hence even highly trained lay interviewers might mistake normal emotional problems for symptoms of mental illness, inadvertently inflating prevalence rates. They might diagnose shyness as social phobia or sadness in response to life's disappointments as major depressive disorder.

Kessler, however, has dismissed this objection. He points to studies showing that lay judgments and those of mental health professionals usually agree. In some cases, the psychiatrists actually diagnose disorder more often than do trained lay interviewers. If anything, lay interviewers may miss disorders rather than overdiagnose them. This seemingly implies that epidemiologic surveys underestimate the true prevalence of mental illness.

Perhaps the criteria for diagnosing disorders are themselves flawed. In addition to identifying the truly disordered, they may also pick up false positives—people whose "symptoms" are merely transient emotional responses to the difficulties of everyday life. Even if lay interviewers apply the criteria properly, they may wind up overdiagnosing disorder if the criteria themselves are too inclusive. Indeed, psychiatrists developed diagnostic criteria for distinguishing among mental disorders in clinics and hospitals, not in the community. As Regier and colleagues observed, "The human organism has a limited repertoire of response patterns to various physical, biological, and emotional stresses. Transient changes in blood pressure, pulse rate, body temperature, anxiety, or mood are not always indicators of pathology but of appropriate adaptive responses."[38] As people try to cope with the difficulties of everyday life, their behavior, thoughts, and emotions vary, sometimes in distressing ways. Yet not all of these changes indicate that something is wrong with their mind. No one is happy all the time.

Narrow aimed to estimate the need for professional mental health treatment, not the true prevalence of mental illness in the community. To determine the prevalence of mental disorders independent of treatment seeking is why epidemiologists conduct their studies in the general population in the first place. Moreover, diagnostic status is conceptually unrelated to treatment seeking: many people who do not have a mental disorder seek help from mental health professionals, and many people with a mental disorder do not seek help. Ascertaining the rates of mental disorder and estimating treatment need are related, but distinct, issues. As Jerome Wakefield and Robert Spitzer argued, Narrow's approach to recalibrating prevalence rates—calling something a disorder only when it has clinically significant consequences—fails to solve the real problem afflicting the field: distinguishing mental disorders from emotional problems that do not signify psychopathology.[39] Not all forms of suffering, including intense suffering, signify mental illness. Grief in response to the sudden loss of a loved one does not suggest mental illness on the part of the bereaved person. Evolution has not designed people to be eternally happy, and mental distress is not equivalent to mental illness. The concept of mental disorder implies that something internal to the person's psychobiology is not functioning properly. Yet our way of diagnosing disorders today ignores the context of suffering, focusing on symptoms, and thereby increasing the risk of classifying people as disordered whose suffering does not arise from mental illness at all.

The problem may lie in the DSM itself. Continuing a tradition inaugurated in 1980 with the appearance of the third edition of the psychiatric "bible," the current version defines each discrete disorder by its symptoms, not by its causes. Although this approach has been immensely successful in many ways, some experts believe that this purely descriptive approach to defining mental disorders has outlived its usefulness and may be blocking further progress.[40] Yet there are good reasons that the descriptive approach took over the field, its now-apparent limitations notwithstanding. It emerged in response to a crisis of legitimacy that struck psychiatry in the 1960s and 1970s.

The debate about the apparent epidemic of mental illness could not have occurred had the APA not entirely transformed diagnostic practice in 1980 with its publication of DSM-III.[41] The third edition of the diagnostic manual specified explicit diagnostic criteria for each disorder, essential for the conduct of objective, structured interviews integral to modern epidemiology. The first two versions of the DSM provided only brief, narrative descriptions of mental disorders, not explicit descriptions of symptoms and the number needed for a person to qualify for a diagnosis.

Consider the DSM-II definition of *inadequate personality disorder.* According to DSM-II, "This behavior pattern is characterized by ineffectual responses to emotional, social, intellectual and physical demands. While the patient seems neither physically nor mentally deficient, he does manifest inadaptability, ineptness, poor judgment, social instability, and lack of physical and emotional stamina."[42] Given this vague description, how could we ever be sure whether someone truly suffered from inadequate personality disorder? As it turns out, the DSM-III committee didn't even try to provide a specific, objective set of criteria for this one. A victim of its own terminal vagueness, inadequate personality disorder was consigned to the dustbin of psychiatric history.

Few psychiatrists worried very much about diagnostic disagreement in the years prior to DSM-III's publication. Interest in scientifically rigorous diagnostic criteria was minimal. The subfield of psychiatric diagnosis was an intellectual backwater that attracted little professional attention, and for good reason. Until the discovery of drugs effective against psychotic symptoms, doctors could do little more than provide custodial care for patients by confining them to large asylums and experimenting with physical interventions, such as prefrontal lobotomy.[43] Getting the correct diagnosis becomes important only given the availability of specific treatments that are more effective for one disease than for another. If nothing seems to work, diagnosis does not count for much. The discovery of effective medications for treating psychotic symptoms, such as hallucinations and delusions, and for treating mood disturbances changed things. Once phenothiazines became available for schizophrenia and lithium for manic-depressive illness, diagnosis began to matter because it suddenly had treatment implications.

The hegemony of psychoanalysis during psychiatry's postwar pinnacle of prestige likewise acted to downgrade the importance of diagnosis. During the 1940s and 1950s, increasing numbers of psychiatrists worked outside the asylum, treating troubled individuals in long-term psychodynamic psychotherapy. Under the sway of Freud, therapists regarded symptoms as idiosyncratic symbols of unconscious conflicts, not straightforward indications of specific illnesses. Because the meaning of a symptom varied from patient to patient depending on the individual's psychic conflicts, diagnosis was irrelevant. The goal was to understand and treat the unconscious source of the problem, not to assess symptoms to arrive at a correct medical diagnosis. Moreover, if psychoanalytic psychotherapy were the treatment of choice for anyone who sought help, getting the diagnosis right would have no bearing on treatment.

Psychoanalysis may have been a part of modernism's cultural avant-garde in the 1920s, but it had long become the core of mainstream outpatient psychiatry by the 1960s. As with so many other established bastions of authority, psychiatry received fierce criticism. Even members of the discipline attacked its legitimacy as a medical specialty. "Antipsychiatrists" such as David Cooper and R. D. Laing held that seriously mentally ill people were undergoing an inner voyage of discovery. As Laing put it, "We can no longer assume that such a voyage is an illness that has to be treated."[44] He regarded psychosis as more of a breakthrough than a breakdown. The antipsychiatrists viewed schizophrenia as an expectable, adaptive response to an insane world, often blaming the patient's family as the source of the disturbance. Psychiatric disorders were not medical diseases but consequences of unjust social, political, and economic conditions.

From the perspective of the twenty-first century, these views seem quaint and naïve, and they never gained much traction within psychiatry itself. However, they did manage to foster suspicion about the medical credentials of the field within American society. Indeed, the belief that psychiatry did not treat real diseases diminished its capacity to flourish. The popularity of the acclaimed film *One Flew over the Cuckoo's Nest* indicated just how widespread negative views of the field had become by the 1970s.

The psychiatrist Thomas Szasz has long sought to undermine

psychiatry's legitimacy as a medical specialty.[45] Proclaiming that mental illness is a myth, not a disease, he argues that conditions such as schizophrenia fall outside the jurisdiction of medicine. People called "schizophrenic," he acknowledges, may behave oddly, but their behavior reflects problems in living, not symptoms of a disease. He argues that the concept of mental illness is an oxymoron because illness can only affect the body, not the mind. If scientists were to discover that brain pathology causes schizophrenia, then that would qualify the disorder as a neurological disease, not a mental illness.

Contrary to what many people think, Szasz is not an antipsychiatrist. He does not object to contractual psychotherapy whereby clients voluntarily seek help and advice from psychiatrists when they experience problems in day-to-day life. Rather, he objects to the loss of liberty associated with involuntary hospitalization and treatment. Like the antipsychiatrists, however, Szasz has had little impact within psychiatry itself other than raising awareness about the ethics of involuntary treatment. Indeed, the evidence that schizophrenia is associated with brain pathology is undeniable.[46] Yet psychiatrists have not concluded that schizophrenia no longer counts as a mental disorder whose treatment should be the responsibility of neurology. Psychiatrists are not dualists who consider their province to be treatment of a disembodied mind unrelated to dysfunction of the brain.

Social scientists likewise challenged the medical legitimacy of psychiatry in the 1960s and 1970s. The sociologist Thomas Scheff held that people who get labeled "mentally ill" begin by breaking certain unwritten rules in public settings.[47] There is no law against mumbling to oneself in public, but doing so violates implicit social norms and counts as a kind of rule breaking. Those who violate such rules are labeled mentally ill, and their behavior gradually conforms to the label imposed on them. In this regard, social forces transform minor deviance into full-blown "mental illness." Again, society is the main culprit, not some disease process within the person.

Scheff popularized the view that what counts as a mental disorder varies according to social circumstances. Yet he had little impact on mainstream psychiatry. He was never very clear about the social norms whose violation earns someone a label of mental illness. Although psychotic behavior surely violates norms, there is more to psychosis than merely mumbling in public.

Psychiatry's crisis as a legitimate medical specialty culminated in a controversy ignited by the social psychologist David Rosenhan's provocative article in *Science* in 1973 titled "On Being Sane in Insane Places."[48] Rosenhan and seven other psychiatrically normal individuals got themselves admitted to inpatient psychiatric units at twelve different hospitals. Each complained of a single symptom: auditory hallucinations of a single word: "thud," "hollow," or "empty." During the intake interview and their inpatient stay, averaging nineteen days, the pseudopatients behaved normally and complained of no further symptoms. One received a discharge diagnosis of schizophrenia, whereas the others received a discharge diagnosis of schizophrenia in remission. The failure of the psychiatrists to detect the sanity of the pseudopatients led Rosenhan to conclude, "We now know that we cannot distinguish insanity from sanity."

Rosenhan's study implied that social context was far more important than symptoms themselves in the diagnostic process. An insane context, such as an inpatient psychiatric unit, drastically colored how staff interpreted the behavior of patients. Rosenhan's study amounted to a critique of the *validity* of psychiatric diagnosis. Valid diagnostic criteria correctly identify those with the disorder and exclude those without the disorder. Validity, in turn, requires diagnostic *reliability*. If the diagnostic criteria for a disorder are reliable, then two clinicians who interview the same patient should arrive at the same diagnosis. If the diagnostic criteria are vague, rendering them subject to idiosyncratic interpretation by different doctors, then they will be unreliable. The validity of a diagnosis presupposes its reliability. We must be able to measure phenomena reliably before we can investigate their causes and treatments. Reliability, by contrast, does not presuppose validity. Indeed, the reliability of the discharge diagnoses in the Rosenhan study was remarkably high. Seven of the eight pseudopatients received a diagnosis of schizophrenia in remission, whereas the other received a diagnosis of schizophrenia. But the validity of the diagnoses was abysmal; none of the pseudopatients actually had schizophrenia.

Many other studies on the reliability of psychiatric diagnosis conducted during the 1960s and 1970s were not encouraging. In one study, American and British psychiatrists who viewed videotaped interviews with patients differed dramatically in the diagnoses they assigned.[49] The same patient might receive a diagnosis of schizophrenia from one doctor, a diagnosis of manic-depression from another, and a diagnosis of personality disorder from a third doctor. Worse yet, disagreement occurred even at the level of symptoms. For example, after viewing one of the videotaped interviews, 67 percent of American psychiatrists noted that the patient had delusions, whereas only 12 percent of British psychiatrists did so. Not only were the diagnoses vague, but the criteria for identifying symptoms were, too.

The strangest episode leading to the diagnostic revolution embodied in DSM-III was the disappearance of homosexuality as a psychiatric diagnosis by democratic vote of APA members.[50] In DSM-II, homosexuality appeared among "sexual deviations"—a category including syndromes such as necrophilia, pedophilia, and sexual sadism. Psychoanalytic doctrine held that homosexuality was rooted in unconscious infantile conflicts induced by a cold, reject-

ing father and an overprotective mother. Helping the patient uncover and resolve these conflicts would presumably cure his homosexuality.

Gay activists strongly objected to this characterization, and
they began to stage protests at APA meetings in the early 1970s. At
the 1970 meeting, activists disrupted a session on the treatment of
homosexuality, seizing the microphone and denouncing aversive
techniques for altering sexual orientation. Disruptions occurred
the following year, and activists demanded the removal of homosexuality from the DSM-II. To placate the activists, the APA sched-
uled sessions to allow gay speakers to present their point of view.
Dr. Anonymous, a hooded and cloaked gay psychiatrist, gave
the most riveting presentation. He revealed that more than 200
APA members were homosexual, and that this group, the Gay Psychiatric Association, met secretly each year at the annual APA conference.

In the fall of 1972, the Columbia University psychiatrist Robert
Spitzer attended the annual conference of the Association for Ad-
vancement of Behavior Therapy (AABT). Behavior therapists had
developed Pavlovian conditioning techniques designed to help homosexual patients who sought to change their sexual orientation.
One method involved showing the patient pictures of men en-
gaging in homosexual activity and then delivering painful electric
shocks to the patient's forearm as he fantasized about the men in
the pictures.[51] Another method, orgasmic reconditioning, required
patients to masturbate in the privacy of their homes while engag-
ing in homosexual fantasy and then switch to heterosexual fantasy
prior to orgasm. Behavior therapists have long ceased any attempt
to "treat" homosexuality, influenced by the AABT president Gerald
Davison, who criticized the ethics of the practice in his 1974 presi-
dential address.[52] Yet in 1972, attempts to change sexual orientation
were still occurring, and for this reason, more than one hundred

gay activists caused a disruption at the conference. After the protest, Spitzer lingered behind to speak with the organizer of the demonstration. They discussed their respective views on homosexuality as a form of mental illness. The conversation ended with Spitzer promising to arrange a meeting between the activists and the APA's Committee on Nomenclature and to schedule a panel on homosexuality at the next APA convention.

The panel included a gay activist as well as psychiatrists on both sides of the debate regarding the APA's position on homosexuality. Spitzer also received an invitation to attend the secret meeting of the Gay Psychiatric Association at APA. He was impressed by these high-functioning psychiatrists, individuals who were not at all distressed by their sexual orientation. The obvious mental health of the gay psychiatrists convinced Spitzer that homosexuality per se was not a mental disorder.

Spitzer soon spearheaded the movement to remove the diagnosis from the next printing of the DSM-II. After several APA committees approved the change, the association's Board of Trustees voted unanimously in favor of declassifying homosexuality as a mental disorder.

Traditional psychoanalysts were enraged. They mobilized their colleagues to support a referendum to decide whether the decision should be reversed. Although both sides of the debate couched their arguments in terms of science, democracy prevailed. The APA voted to determine whether homosexuality is a mental disorder. The poll of APA members indicated that 58 percent favored eliminating homosexuality from the DSM, whereas 37 percent opposed the move.[53] Formal democratic procedures seldom answer classification questions in science. Indeed, until astronomers recently voted to kick Pluto out of the planetary solar system, the APA vote to decertify homosexuality as a mental disorder may have been the only instance in modern times. Doctors are disinclined to resort to democracy when considering whether something counts as a disease.[54]

The declassification of homosexuality as a mental disorder pleased political progressives and angered political conservatives. But the democratic process by which the APA resolved the controversy did nothing to encourage the view that psychiatry was a scientific discipline. In fact, it showed that psychiatry had no principled basis for distinguishing mental disorders from other aspects of human functioning. When gay activists challenged psychiatry to explain why homosexuality was a form of mental illness, the field had no good answer.

Treaty obligations with the World Health Organization (WHO) determine when the APA revises its diagnostic manual, and the process for revising DSM was about to begin as Spitzer was successfully resolving the embarrassing public controversy over homosexuality. His interest in diagnosis, his energy, and his skill at mediating bitter disputes in the field earned him the chairmanship of the task force to revise DSM. As the leader of the DSM-III process, he wound up transforming the field of psychiatry.

Spitzer was among a small cadre of psychiatrists, many from Columbia University and Washington University, who were dissatisfied with the abysmal state of diagnosis and with psychiatry's marginal status in modern scientific medicine. If psychiatrists cannot reliably decide who has what disorder—or whether a person has a disorder at all—it is impossible to conduct the research necessary to ascertain the causes and cures for mental illness.

Fortunately, psychiatric researchers at Columbia and Washington Universities had already elucidated "operational" criteria for defining discrete mental disorders as an essential prelude to conducting research on the course of illness, family history, causes, and so forth.[55] The operational emphasis entailed careful description of the signs and symptoms of mental disorder, unencumbered by psychoanalytic assumptions about their causes. This descriptive approach precluded speculation about why a person had a disorder. It drew inspiration from Freud's contemporary Emil Kraepelin, whose pioneering work with psychotic inpatients had been eclipsed by the glamour of psychoanalysis.

For assistance revising the manual, Spitzer recruited psychiatrists keen to overhaul the DSM, placing it firmly on a descriptive neo-Kraepelinian basis. DSM-III represented a radical break from tradition, and it encountered stiff resistance from many groups, especially psychoanalysts.[56] The new approach, though, promised many benefits. By providing clear, explicit descriptions of diagnostic criteria, it allowed clinicians and researchers of diverse theoretical persuasions—psychodynamic, cognitive, behavioral, and biological—to agree, at least in principle, whether someone qualified for a certain diagnosis, even if they could not agree about its causes. DSM-III promised to solve the reliability problem; whether it consistently did so remains a matter of debate.[57] Suffice it to say, clinicians and researchers could diagnose reliably, as many studies have shown, even if they sometimes failed to do so.

DSM-I and DSM-II did not contain a definition of mental disorder, thereby fostering confusion about the professional bailiwick of psychiatry, as critics noted. To rectify this omission, Spitzer wrote a working definition of mental disorder that appears, with minor modifications, in the current manual:

In *DSM-IV*, each of the mental disorders is conceptualized as a clinically significant behavioral or psychological syndrome or pattern that occurs in an individual and that is associated with present distress (e.g., a painful symptom) or disability (i.e., impairment in one or more important areas of functioning) or with a significantly increased risk of suffering death, pain, disability, or an important loss of freedom. In addition, this syndrome or pattern must not be merely an expectable and culturally sanctioned response to a particular event, for example, the death of a loved one. Whatever its original cause, it must currently be considered a manifestation of a behavioral, psychological, or biological dysfunction in the individual. Neither deviant behavior (e.g., political, religious, or sexual) nor conflicts that are primarily between the individual and society are mental disorders unless the deviance or conflict is a symptom of a dysfunction in the individual, as described above.[58]

Importantly, this definition answers critics who claimed that psychiatrists classify mere social deviance as mental illness. It specifies that the problem must originate within the person, placing it in the domain of mental health rather than of law enforcement, for example. Moreover, the internal dysfunction must cause the individual suffering or harm. This proviso would presumably justify the exclusion of homosexuality on the grounds that gays comfortable with their sexual orientation suffer no harm other than homophobic discrimination.

Spitzer chaired an interim revision of the manual, DSM-III-R, which appeared in 1987. Allen Frances replaced him as chair of DSM-IV, which appeared in 1994. Another edition of DSM-IV came out in 2000, but this one chiefly updated the accompanying text; it contained few changes to diagnostic criteria.[59]

By enabling reliable diagnosis, the atheoretical, descriptive tradition inaugurated by DSM-III has transformed the study and treatment of mental disorders throughout the world. It has spurred the growth of psychiatric epidemiology, basic research on the cognitive, behavioral, and biological aspects of mental illness, and it has paved the way for the development and evaluation of new psychological and psychopharmacological treatments. As a diagnostic lingua franca, DSM-III and its successors have provided the indispensable foundation for progress.

Yet all is not well in the field of mental health, and the descriptive approach of the DSM may be part of the problem. In other areas of medicine, doctors identify a disease not only by its symptoms but also by its causes (etiology) and the resultant bodily dysfunction (pathophysiology). Symptoms of fever, weakness, and a persistent cough are consistent with the presence of many diseases, and doctors must probe further, conducting additional tests to confirm a diagnosis. In contrast, doctors dealing with mental disorders have traditionally lacked laboratory tests that can illuminate etiology and pathophysiology. However, information about the context of the symptoms and their course can sometimes help distinguish mental disorders from normal emotional reactions. Knowing that a person reporting symptoms of depression has suddenly lost a loved one, for example, provides important context for the practitioner.

Skepticism about the epidemic arises partly from the increase in the number of mental disorders recognized by psychiatry. In a seminal 1972 article that inspired the DSM-III revolution, John Feighner and his colleagues provided explicit criteria suitable for advancing research.[60] They listed a mere 14 syndromes for which they believed there was good scientific evidence. DSM-III greatly expanded the number of syndromes, coding for 211 discrete mental disorders. DSM-IV further expanded the number to 341 disorders. Has psychiatry actually discovered 327 new forms of mental illness unknown to doctors in 1972?

There are several reasons for the growth in the number of diagnoses. Professional and economic factors required that the discrete entities appearing in DSM-III cover the kinds of problems that psychiatrists routinely encounter in their clinical practice.[61] If the DSM-III were to recognize only the short list of syndromes deemed validated by Feighner and colleagues, then many people treated in outpatient settings would fall outside the scope of reimbursable practice. Something had to change.

Differentiation within existing categories likewise multiplied the number of discretely coded diagnoses. For example, the DSM-III committee divided the DSM-II diagnosis of phobic neurosis into simple phobia, social phobia, and agoraphobia. The DSM-IV committee changed the name of simple phobia to specific phobia, further dividing it into subtypes (for example, fear of fainting at the sight of blood; animal phobia; situational phobia, such as fear of enclosed spaces). In this case, doctors did not discover new disorders so much as make new distinctions within one subtype of an established diagnosis.

More controversial, however, are cases of problems that now fall under the rubric of mental illness but seem rather far removed from prototypical mental disorders such as schizophrenia and major depression. Among these are relatively trivial problems, such as caffeine-induced sleep disorder. Even more controversial are the seemingly expanding boundaries of mental disorders that underscore the problem of distinguishing between the normal range of human emotions and disorder. Critics worry that we are medicalizing more and more of human life. Are we, for example, medicalizing normal sadness, confusing it with the disease of depression? Are we now diagnosing shy people as suffering from social anxiety disorder?

Then there's the question of just who benefits from expanding the definition of mental disorder. The pharmaceutical industry, for one. Mental health professionals, psychotherapists as well as psychopharmacologists, also stand to benefit from an expanded scope of reimbursable disorders. There is money in madness. In contrast, managed-care companies and others responsible for paying the bill favor restricting the scope of disorder.

Money aside, if our diagnostic criteria fail to distinguish between the truly disordered and the normally distressed, studies on the efficacy of treatment will be invalid. For example, clinical trials on major depressive disorder have yielded placebo response rates that range from 12.5 percent to 51.8 percent.[62] As many as 50 percent of people recover from depression by swallowing sugar pills for a few months. Given this number, we have to wonder if the diagnostic criteria for this illness are so broad that they wind up including people whose symptoms do not signify the presence of the depressive disease. The diagnostic criteria for major depressive disorder may capture an extremely heterogeneous group of people whose problems have diverse etiologies and pathophysiologies.

Similar problems occur with posttraumatic stress disorder (PTSD). The original diagnostic criteria described a syndrome arising from extreme life-threatening events, such as combat. Current criteria enable individuals to qualify for PTSD who have been horrified by *learning about others* who have been trauma-exposed. For example, citing survey data, one research group argued that about 4 percent of Americans developed PTSD after watching televised coverage of the terrorist attacks occurring on September 11, 2001.[63] Yet it is implausible that individuals whose "PTSD" was caused by television have much in common with people whose PTSD arose from personal trauma. Regardless of the PTSD symptoms they acknowledged on a survey, the first group is unlikely to share a psychobiology with the survivors of terrorist attacks themselves.

In this book I evaluate current attempts to clarify the boundary between mental disorder and mental distress. Unlike other medical issues, psychiatric problems uniquely strike at our very sense of self. As the perimeter of what counts as mental illness continues to expand, people worry more than ever about whether their emotional difficulties signify a serious psychiatric condition, and, if so, what to do about it. Many critics, for their part, accuse mental health professionals of pathologizing normal emotional responses to the stressors of everyday life.

Consider depression. As the psychiatrist Peter Kramer has observed, there is a left-wing perspective and a right-wing perspective on the disorder.[64] Both express reservations about treating depression, but for different reasons. From the perspective of the left, depression indicates refined intellectual and aesthetic sensibilities. To this way of thinking, treating depression runs the risk of destroying the source of creativity. Would antidepressant medication have blunted the genius of van Gogh, Beethoven, and Virginia Woolf? Less dramatically, others worry that giving pills to poor, disadvantaged people who suffer from depression only masks the social and economic causes of understandable emotional suffering.

From the perspective of the right, people should maintain a stiff upper lip as they struggle against life's adversities. Reliance on medication and psychotherapy runs the risk of undermining the mental toughness and moral fiber of our nation. The upshot is that forces outside as well as inside the mental health field tug at the boundary between mental distress and mental disorder, and, by implication, affect the decision to initiate treatment.

As this book will show, there is no infallible boundary separating mental distress from mental disorder. This does not mean, however, that "mental illness" is nothing but an arbitrary social convention. Far from it. Clinical scientists have provided abundant psychological and biological data that go a long way toward answering the question "What is mental illness?" The results of their labors show that cases of mental illness possess many properties lacking in cases of mental distress. Yet because the boundary between the two is a fuzzy one, social, political, and economic factors often prove decisive when it comes to deciding whether ambiguous cases count as mental illness or mental disorder (I use these terms interchangeably). Decisions about cases straddling the boundary between distress and disorder are not merely semantic quibbles.

They have consequences. Whether someone secures treatment for their suffering often turns on how these matters are decided.

It has become fashionable to trash psychiatry and to bash its "bible," the DSM. I am not a DSM-basher. I am a clinical psychologist and experimental psychopathologist who served on the PTSD and specific phobia committees of the DSM-IV. I currently serve as an external advisor to the groups responsible for revisiting and revising the diagnostic criteria for panic disorder and for PTSD. I am often critical of trends in psychiatry, but I'm a friendly critic, one who's keen to make constructive suggestions about the direction of the field and how we understand and treat mental disorders.

2

The APA has launched the revision process that will culminate in DSM-5 (note the change from roman to arabic numerals). If all goes well, we'll have a new diagnostic manual in 2013. Presumably, DSM-5 will describe psychopathology more accurately than its predecessors did. Successive revisions of the DSM should get progressively closer to capturing the truth about mental disorders.

Not everyone buys this line. Skeptics regard it as either naïve or disingenuous. They see the process as one of invention, not discovery. As the British psychiatrist Derek Summerfield asserted, "Psychiatric categories are manufactured constellations emerging from DSM or ICD [International Classification of Diseases] committee decisions. That is indisputable, so why do we treat them as if they were facts of nature identifiable 'out there,' as is, say, a tree or a broken leg?"[1] Similar sentiments appear in books titled *Creating Mental Illness; The Harmony of Illusions: Inventing Post-Traumatic Stress Disorder; Creating Hysteria: Women and Multiple Personality Disorder;* and *Making Us Crazy: DSM: The Psychiatric Bible and the Creation of Mental Disorders.*[2] If mental disorders are products of social processes, not natural ones, then we cannot carve nature at its joints because there are no natural joints to carve.

Occasionally the critics exemplify what the sociologist Karl Mannheim called "the unmasking turn of mind."[3] An unmasking critique does not refute a theory by identifying its errors or its lack of empirical support. Rather, it demolishes it by exposing its hidden ideological agenda and the political and economic interests it serves.

Unmaskers question whether psychiatry is fundamentally a scientifically based medical discipline devoted to the study, treatment, and prevention of mental illness. They question whether its mission is really the disinterested pursuit of truth in the service of reducing the suffering of humanity. Summarizing the standard unmasking critique, the medical anthropologist Allan Young noted how often historians and anthropologists have embraced the following ideas: "Psychiatric institutions and practices have, in the past and the present, promoted hegemonic cultural perspectives and social interests. Psychiatric diagnosis blames and stigmatizes victims for their misfortunes. Today, hegemonic psychiatry's most powerful instruments are its biological etiologies, therapeutic interventions (psychopharmacology) and its research programs. Through biological reductionism, these instruments desocialize and dehumanize distress, naturalize social and economic inequities, silence the voices of suffering and resistance and eliminate the possibility of agency."[4]

Behind-the-scenes accounts of the politics of DSM-III do little to undermine this critical view.[5] One iconic image depicts Robert Spitzer and his neo-Kraepelinian colleagues sitting around a table, formulating new diagnostic categories on the spot, while Spitzer taps out the defining criteria on his typewriter.[6] Of course, most DSM-III disorders did not have such a spontaneously improvisational origin. Nevertheless, the majority of new diagnoses appeared in DSM-III only after influential clinicians, invoking their expertise, advocated vigorously for their inclusion. It is not as if overwhelming scientific evidence compelled their inclusion.

In fact, had the DSM-III committee required prior scientific support, very few disorders would have qualified for inclusion in the new manual. As Spitzer later acknowledged, if solid science had been a prerequisite for creating a new diagnosis, then the DSM-III committee would have been unable to "include over 200 categories—most of which were included on the basis of expert clinical judgment (face validity) alone." Among these were multiple personality disorder, posttraumatic stress disorder, and passive-aggressive personality disorder. Commenting on the then-ongoing DSM-IV revision process, Spitzer predicted that final decisions would "still be based primarily on expert consensus, rather than on data, as was the case with *DSM-III* and *DSM-III-R*."[7] His frank admission that clinical opinion, however expert, drives the revision process seems unsettlingly incongruent with the standard view of how scientific medicine should operate.

Further ammunition for skeptics comes from the expanding size of the DSMs and the frequency of the manual's revision.[8] DSM-I appeared in 1952; it had 128 pages and 106 diagnoses. DSM-II appeared in 1968; it had 134 pages and 182 diagnoses. DSM-III appeared in 1980; it had 494 pages and 265 diagnoses. DSM-III-R appeared in 1987; it had 567 pages and 292 diagnoses. DSM-IV appeared in 1994; it had 886 pages and 365 diagnoses, and its text revision (DSM-IV-TR), which appeared in 2000, has 943 pages. But does the increase in diagnostic categories represent genuine scientific progress? Has psychiatry truly discovered this many new disorders, somehow missed by otherwise astute clinicians in the past?

In defense of the DSM, the increase in the number of diagnoses often reflects newly recognized subtypes of older diagnoses. In addition, increased knowledge of prevalence, risk factors, and course of illness requires longer explanations accompanying each disorder, thus accounting for the growing girth of the manual. In DSM-III, the skimpy text accompanying most disorders was little more than an admission of ignorance about such matters, limited to educated guesses.

Nevertheless, some critics see the expansion of the DSM as indicative of psychiatry's attempt to extend its professional hegemony by either claiming authority over problems previously considered nonpsychiatric or pathologizing more and more of everyday life.[9] DSM-IV includes mathematics disorder, stuttering, developmental coordination disorder, caffeine intoxication, and the jet-lag subtype of circadian-rhythm sleep disorder. Clinicians have speculated that Internet addiction, compulsive shopping, and racism may merit inclusion in DSM-5.[10] Others have argued that obesity is a brain disorder and thus deserves consideration as a mental illness in DSM-5.[11] They argue that people whose obesity arises from heightened motivation for food have a psychiatric disorder akin to drug dependence. The trouble is that food is essential for survival, whereas cocaine, for example, is not.[12]

DSM-III became a worldwide best-seller, generating massive revenue for the American Psychiatric Association.[13] All mental health professionals use the manual, not just psychiatrists. Its diagnostic categories provide the classificatory framework for everything from undergraduate abnormal psychology textbooks to insurance reimbursement. Clinicians need to provide a DSM diagnosis if they wish to receive payment for their services from third-party insurers. Moreover, when a new edition appears, everyone must purchase a copy. Psychiatrists themselves have wondered about the role of revenue in the ever-shortening revision cycle. A national survey indicated that 20 percent of American psychiatrists believe that profit motive was a key factor in the APA's production of DSM-IV.[14]

Although there is no convincing evidence that the pharmaceutical industry had a role in DSM-III, which appeared in 1980, the industry's subsequent influence on psychiatry has been profound and undeniable.[15] Critics claim that it imperils the credibility of the profession. Newspaper reports appearing in 2006 revealed that every member of the DSM-IV committees on schizophrenia and mood disorders "had financial ties to the pharmaceutical industry, and more than half of those working on the remaining disorders had similarly compromising ties."[16]

Both drug company officials and psychiatrists argue that preventing the leaders of the field from serving as industry consultants would choke off a vital source of expertise, thereby impeding the progress of clinical psychopharmacology. The psychiatric consultants themselves downplay the risk of bias, often emphasizing that they consult for many companies whose products compete for the allegiance of doctors and patients. Receiving income from so many companies supposedly cancels out any bias that they might otherwise have in favor of any one company or product. Such pharmacologic evenhandedness would not, however, counteract a bias in favor of drugs versus cognitive-behavioral interventions, which often possess equal or greater efficacy than medication.[17]

Financial ties to industry affect whether drug studies appear in the medical literature. An analysis of clinical trials published in three prestigious psychiatry journals revealed that those funded by drug companies are less likely to report negative findings than are studies funded independent of industry (for example, by an NIMH grant).[18] Among those funded independently, 36 percent reported negative findings, whereas among those funded by industry, only 15 percent reported negative findings. However, the presence of an employee of the company, including shareholders and paid consultants, among the authors of a study was an even better predictor of study outcome. Studies with positive results were far more likely to have been cowritten by a company employee than were studies with negative results.

An investigation of randomized controlled trials (RCTs) of antidepressant medication found strong evidence of selective publication depending on the results of the study.[19] The authors located seventy-four clinical trials registered with the Food and Drug Administration (FDA), and they checked to see which ones appeared in the medical literature. Of the thirty-eight judged by the FDA to have a positive outcome, thirty-seven got published. Of the thirty-six judged by the FDA to have either a negative or a questionable outcome, fourteen saw the light of day, but eleven of these were presented in a way that made the results appear positive, not negative or ambiguous. The upshot is that 94 percent of the published trials were positive, whereas the FDA regarded only 51 percent of trials as positive. If doctors appraise the value of antidepressant medications by reading the published literature, they will come away with a more (unjustifiably) positive view of their efficacy than if they were privy to the full FDA database.

Other meta-analytic studies of antidepressants have concluded that these drugs are seldom more effective than placebos, at least for mild to moderately depressed people. In one meta-analysis, the superiority of drug over placebo was clearly apparent only for patients suffering from very severe depression.[20] Another meta-analysis of the relatively new selective serotonin reuptake inhibitors (SSRIs, such as Prozac) showed a modest advantage of drugs only for patients with very severe depression.[21] This occurred not because medication was more effective for these very ill patients but because placebos were less effective for them.

How can we square these results with the widespread clinical opinion regarding the effectiveness of these drugs? The meta-analyses provide the answer. Patients receiving the drugs do experience very significant improvements in their mood. Yet with few exceptions, those receiving placebos experience equally dramatic improvements. Because practicing clinicians only prescribe active drugs, they never witness the improvements that follow administration of placebos.

Psychiatry's ties to the industry may influence diagnostic considerations as well as judgments about treatment efficacy. Consider the use of psychiatric drugs in pediatric patients. In recent years, there has been a massive upsurge in the use of powerful antipsychotic medications for children diagnosed with bipolar disorder, a condition historically diagnosed in adults. One especially unsettling article in the *New York Times* concerned a congressional investigation on industry ties to medicine. The authors reported that Joseph Biederman, a renowned professor of child psychiatry at Harvard Medical School and an influential advocate of diagnosing bipolar disorder in children, had received at least $1.6 million in consulting fees from companies manufacturing these medications, but had failed to disclose much of this income to officials at Harvard.[22] Reports like these fuel concerns about how potential conflicts of interest might distort diagnostic and prescribing practices.

Of course, drug companies are in business to make money, and it's hardly surprising that they try to influence doctors and the public at large. Companies sponsor continuing education symposia at professional conferences, provide financial support for patient advocacy groups whose biomedical orientation is congruent with pharmacologic treatment, and use direct-to-consumer advertising urging viewers to request their products ("Ask your doctor whether Viagra is right for you"). These advertisements often oversimplify matters to the point of tendentiousness.[23] One ad pitching a drug to combat social phobia claimed that it "works to correct the chemical imbalance believed to cause the disorder."[24] Although such drugs do influence brain chemistry by blocking the reuptake of serotonin, there is no evidence that medication corrects any pre-existing chemical imbalance, let alone that the conjectured imbalance "causes" social phobia.[25] Just because aspirin relieves headaches doesn't mean that the cause of headaches is a deficiency of aspirin.

Even more worrisome is evidence suggesting that chronic psychoactive medication may prompt compensatory responses by the brain, making it difficult for patients to withdraw from medication following their recovery without resurgence of symptoms.[26]

Insurance companies, too, are partly responsible for the trend toward prescribing medication. HMOs may more readily authorize reimbursement for psychopharmacologic treatment than for psychotherapy, assuming that the former is less expensive and more effective than the latter. This is sometimes true. Yet for many disorders, cognitive-behavioral psychotherapy is at least as effective as medication, and more cost-effective over time.[27] In some cases, third-party payers reimburse for psychotherapy sessions only if the patient has agreed to take medication as well.

When forced to choose between medication and psychotherapy for treatment of a disorder that is equally likely to respond to either approach, some patients may prefer psychotherapy yet feel pressured into taking medication so that insurance will pay the bill. Doctors, for their part, may prescribe defensively. They may fear legal accusations of negligence, for example, should they fail to prescribe medication for a depressed patient who subsequently commits suicide.

THE BOUNDARY PROBLEM

Critics complain that psychiatry is expanding the boundary of mental disorder, inappropriately pathologizing everyday life by classifying normal variations in emotion, behavior, and cognition as disorders. One version of this critique holds that doctors, serving as agents of social control, affix psychiatric labels to social deviants to justify medicating them into obedience. Exemplifying this perspective, the psychiatrist Peter Breggin objects to nearly all use of psychopharmacology.[28] He claims, for example, that diagnosing children with attention deficit hyperactivity disorder (ADHD) and medicating them with Ritalin amounts to doctors labeling exuberant kids as disordered and drugging them into submission. The interests of parents, schoolteachers, doctors, and the pharmaceutical industry all converge to the detriment of children. Seeing no virtue in psychopharmacology, Breggin melodramatically claims that "all psychiatric drugs disable the brain and none improve its function."[29]

There are a few grains of truth buried in Breggin's hyperbole. Severely agitated people in the grip of psychosis often do cause social disturbances, and medication can help quell their turmoil. Psychoactive medications, by definition, affect the brain, and most have side effects whose importance patients and doctors must evaluate relative to their therapeutic benefits.

Yet Breggin overlooks important details. He ignores the benefits of psychoactive drugs, and the fact that many grateful patients regard them as life-saving. More important, many patients request medication from their doctors rather than having doctors forcing drugs on them.

In fact, the apparent eagerness of many people to solve their problems with a pill is the focus of yet another critique of the boundary issue. According to this view, the public has wholeheartedly colluded in the invasion of psychopharmacology into everyday life. People have grown increasingly intolerant of emotional distress and have reached too readily for medicine as a quick fix for the normal problems of day-to-day living. In fact, as the sociologist David Karp suspects, "a necessary condition for widespread psychiatric drug use is a culturally induced readiness to view emotional pain as a disease requiring medical intervention."[30]

Consumption of psychiatric drugs has increased dramatically. In 2001, Americans spent more than twelve billion dollars on antidepressants alone. This is the equivalent of spending $43.85 per person in the United States.[31] As of 2005, 11 percent of American women and 5 percent of American men were taking antidepressants, and antidepressant use in the United Kingdom increased by 234 percent in the decade up to 2002.[32]

This trend partly signifies that people suffering from mental disorders are finally getting the help they need. Some experts suspect, however, that we are becoming a nation of wimps, unable to tolerate the vicissitudes of everyday life without relying on mental health professionals.[33] In fact, the psychiatrist Peter Kramer wondered whether "cosmetic psychopharmacology" might be the wave of the future, whereby healthy people consume medication to remake their personality so they can become "better than well."[34]

The philosopher Christina Sommers and the psychiatrist Sally Satel worry that America is now becoming "one nation under therapy."[35] Sommers and Satel suspect that the expanding boundary of mental disorder presupposes excessive psychological fragility and an assumption that the ordinary stressors of everyday living are traumas that will have devastating emotional consequences unless mental health professionals are there to intervene. "Therapism," as they call it, may unwittingly undermine people's autonomy, responsibility, and resilience.[36]

Karp, Sommers, and Satel do not endorse a "pharmacological Calvinism" that would deny drug treatment (or psychotherapy) to people suffering from genuine mental disorders.[37] Nevertheless, they do worry about the potentially adverse consequences of psychological or pharmacological therapism. As Karp put it, "With the growth of the therapeutic professions and the efforts of pharmaceutical companies to market solutions for every imaginable discomfort, the line between normal life pain and genuine pathology has become seriously blurred. The effort to secure personal happiness has become a social mandate, if not a moral obligation."[38]

In fact, our expectations for acceptable emotional health are moving closer to the ambitious aspirations of the World Health Organization. The WHO defines health as "a stage of complete physical, social, and mental well being and not merely the absence of disease or infirmity."[39] Although no one will complain about achieving "complete" (!) mental well-being, does failure to reach this lofty state call for professional intervention? Does distress at falling short of this psychic nirvana betray intolerance of life's inevitable disappointments and limitations?

Then there is the stigma. People diagnosed with a psychiatric disorder often experience shame and social rejection. Although public education campaigns have likely diminished the stigma of mental illness in America, accepting that one has a psychiatric disorder and that one must see a "shrink," especially for medication, is difficult for many people. Few people embrace the role of psychiatric patient and the need for medication without ambivalence.[40] To be sure, receiving a diagnosis and thus an explanation for one's troubles can be a source of relief. Naming the problem can be the first step toward solving it. Nevertheless, taking psychiatric medication is not quite the same as taking insulin for diabetes. Abnormalities in metabolizing sugar do not strike at the core of a person's sense of self in the way that abnormalities in thought, feeling, and behavior do.

Improvements in the treatment of mental disorder may reduce stigma further. Yet when health care professionals can do little or nothing to restore normal functioning, stigma can persist. Euphemisms are sometimes used in an attempt to diminish the shame associated with intractable conditions. Consider mental retardation. Today's readers are startled to find references to imbeciles, morons, and idiots in medical literature of the early twentieth century. Once these technical words migrated into everyday language as terms of abuse, professionals replaced them with words that had not yet acquired such pejorative connotations.

Social, economic, and political factors affect where we draw the line between mental distress and mental disorder. Yet merely because these influences affect the boundary problem, we cannot conclude that all solutions are arbitrary and devoid of scientific support. Indeed, some mental health professionals believe that science unencumbered by these other factors can draw a principled distinction between normal suffering and suffering arising from mental illness. As the cases below make clear, however, value judgments continually resurface, implying that science alone lacks the resources to solve the boundary problem.

In the sections that follow, I show how these issues are playing out with regard to sexual dysfunction, depression, social anxiety disorder, and PTSD arising from exposure to horrific images in the media. Each of these cases illustrates how factors other than science affect the way clinical psychopathologists work to resolve disputes at the border between distress and disorder.

Sexual Dysfunction

During the 1970s and 1980s, doctors distinguished between organic and psychogenic sexual problems by ascertaining, for example, whether a man's erectile dysfunction resulted from performance anxiety or from vascular insufficiency of the penis caused by diabetes. Although patients commonly expressed anxiety about their problem in either case, doctors referred them for psychological treatment only after they had ruled out organic causes. At that point they often saw cognitive-behavior therapists specializing in the sex-therapy methods pioneered by William Masters and Virginia Johnson.[41] If the problem was physical, patients were referred to medical specialists, usually urologists.

On the basis of Masters and Johnson's work, the DSM-III committee included specific diagnostic categories for sexual dysfunctions that affected the stages of sexual desire, sexual arousal, and orgasm. The DSM recognition notwithstanding, the sexual dysfunction field remained a small, underfunded area of clinical research until the 1990s.

Viagra changed everything. It eclipsed sex therapy as the primary treatment for erectile dysfunction and motivated drug companies to market their wares for other sexual problems as well. Viagra and similar drugs cause erections by increasing blood flow to the penis, regardless of whether the man's problem is organic or psychogenic. No longer did a man troubled by performance anxiety require sex therapy. He could circumvent his anxiety by taking a pill that ensured an erection.

The commercial success of Viagra sparked tremendous interest among pharmaceutical companies in sexual dysfunction. Suddenly, industry-sponsored conferences, research funding, and professional interest in the pharmacologic treatment proliferated. Industry was especially keen to create a version of Viagra for women.

The search for a quick pharmacologic fix for women has provoked sharp criticism.[42] One early industry option was to market Viagra to women as a treatment for the DSM-IV disorder of female sexual arousal disorder, the counterpart to erectile dysfunction. Clinical trials, however, were disappointing, and so industry reconceptualized the target as the DSM-IV condition of hypoactive sexual desire disorder. The pharmaceutical campaign amounted to a solution in search of a problem. Rather than identifying a dysfunction and looking for an effective treatment, we have a treatment for male erectile dysfunction and a search for a female problem—any problem—for which the same or a similar drug might work.

Sparking industry enthusiasm, one widely publicized survey uncovered high rates of apparent male and female sexual dysfunction in the general population.[43] The investigators interviewed American men and women, aged eighteen to fifty-nine, asking them whether they had experienced one of several problems during the previous twelve months: (1) lack of desire for sex; (2) difficulty with either lubrication or achieving erections; (3) inability to achieve orgasm; (4) anxiety about sexual performance; (5) reaching orgasm too quickly; (6) physical pain during intercourse; and (7) lack of pleasure during sex. If a respondent replied "yes" to any one of these questions, he or she qualified as dysfunctional.

The results indicated that a whopping 43 percent of women and 31 percent of men met these criteria for sexual dysfunction during the previous twelve months. The authors cautioned, however, that these survey data are not equivalent to a clinical diagnosis of a sexual disorder. Nevertheless, they suggested that the figures might actually underestimate the true magnitude of the problem. Many respondents in the study, they argued, may have been too embarrassed to reveal their sexual problems to the interviewers. The survey seemingly uncovered a hidden epidemic of sexual disorders ripe for pharmacologic treatment.

Gaining less media attention than the shocking prevalence rates were clues to an alternative interpretation of the data. For example, socioeconomic stress, as indexed by declining household income, was associated with erectile dysfunction in men and with all sexual problems in women. Moreover, sexual dysfunction in women was strongly associated with low feelings of emotional and physical satisfaction and low levels of happiness. Men who reported problems with low sexual desire and erectile problems mentioned low quality of life.

These correlations are insufficient to determine causal direction. Does low quality of life diminish sexual desire and erectile functioning or vice versa? These data do imply that many sexual difficulties may result from chronic economic and social stressors, especially those arising in intimate relationships, rather than originating in a psychobiological abnormality that can be corrected with medication. If this is the case, then medication would amount to little more than a pharmacological Band-Aid, incapable of addressing the source of the problem.

Patterns of help-seeking further suggest that the authors may have overestimated the rate of true disorder in the population. Only about 20 percent of dysfunctional women and 10 percent of dysfunctional men sought medical consultation for their sexual problems. If people seeking help are deemed those most likely to have a genuine disorder, then the annual prevalence of sexual disorder in women would be about 9 percent (not 43 percent) and in men about 3 percent (not 31 percent). Annual prevalence estimates of 9 percent and 3 percent for disorder are not trivial, but they are much lower than the rates publicized by drug companies.

Research on sexual problems underscores the importance of the boundary problem and suggests clues to its solution. Problems that arise from social stressors do not necessarily involve dysfunction in the psychobiological mechanisms that mediate desire, arousal, and orgasm. These seem to fall outside the boundary of psychiatric illness. For example, we should not expect a woman who fights constantly with her husband to experience much sexual desire for him. Diagnosing her with hypoactive sexual desire disorder locates the problem in the wrong place. Likewise, are women whose desire has waned because they are exhausted from caring for small children while pursuing a demanding career mentally ill, suffering from hypoactive sexual desire disorder? Similar stressors can undermine sexual functioning in men as well. In these cases, we have a causal (but not medical) etiology, and we have no pathophysiology at all.

Some sexual problems do arise from internal dysfunction. Men with diabetes often experience erectile difficulties, as do those who drink too much alcohol, whereas others suffer from performance anxiety that impairs functioning. The first group has problems that fall within the domain of urology, not psychiatry, and the second group has a focal social phobia, not sexual dysfunction per se. In the absence of distinctive biology detectable by medical science, the boundary between normal and abnormal sexual functioning will rest heavily on an individual's circumstances.

Depression

Allan Horwitz and Jerome Wakefield published a penetrating analysis of the boundary problem in their book *The Loss of Sadness*.[44] Horwitz is a medical sociologist and Wakefield is a clinical social worker who also has a doctorate in philosophy. They argue that defining depression by its symptoms without reference to its causes blurs the distinction between normal sadness and disease. In addition to picking out true positives—people suffering from the disorder—the criteria also pick out false positives. That is, a person can now receive a diagnosis of depression whose symptoms do not arise from dysfunction in the psychobiological mechanisms that presumably mediate mood.

The false-positive problem seldom arises in inpatient settings, where anyone meeting criteria almost certainly suffers from the disorder. Things become more ambiguous in outpatient clinics, where those seeking help include people experiencing intense but normal emotional responses to life's stressors as well as people suffering from depressive disease. Matters may become seriously ambiguous, though, once epidemiologists apply the criteria in general community samples. A similar problem may arise in primary care medical settings where patients complete screening questionnaires for detecting major depression. When researchers apply the symptom-based, context-free criteria in the community, the result is skyrocketing prevalence estimates for major depressive disorder.

Horwitz and Wakefield question claims about a hidden epidemic of depression and a massive amount of unmet need for psychiatric treatment. They argue that disregarding the social context of depression increases the odds of misclassifying people as mentally ill whose emotional distress signifies a normal response to adversity. When we misclassify normal sadness as disease, we overestimate the cost of genuine depression.

As Horwitz and Wakefield observe, the DSM does permit consideration of context when it comes to bereavement. Recent bereavement is an exclusion criterion for assigning the diagnosis of major depression; that is, a woman whose depressive symptoms follow the death of her husband is not mentally ill. Her heart may be broken, but her mind is intact.

Horwitz and Wakefield believe that a similar exclusion criterion should apply to other major losses such as divorce or unemployment. Why, they ask, should only bereavement qualify as an exclusion? Failure to consider the context for other losses further obscures the difference between normal sadness and depression, increasing the false-positive rate.

To gauge the extent of this problem, Wakefield and his colleagues reanalyzed data from the National Comorbidity Survey.[45] They recalculated the rates of depression after extending the bereavement exclusion to other major losses. They found that lifetime prevalence dropped from 14.9 percent to 11.3 percent, and current (previous year) prevalence dropped from 8.6 percent to 6.5 percent. In other words, about 25 percent of cases of major depression in the community are due to normal responses to loss.

Not everyone shares Horwitz and Wakefield's concern about inflation in the diagnosis of major depressive disorder. As outlined in the DSM, the nine symptoms of a major depressive episode are: depressed mood most of the day, nearly every day; markedly diminished interest or pleasure in nearly all activities most of the day, nearly every day (anhedonia); loss of appetite or significant weight loss or gain; insomnia or hypersomnia nearly every day; observable psychomotor agitation or retardation; fatigue nearly every day; inappropriate guilt or feelings of worthlessness; difficulty concentrating nearly every day; and recurrent thoughts of death or suicidal ideation, or suicide attempt.[46]

Many experts regard even mild forms of depression as lying on a continuum of severity with severe depression. Although a person must have at least five symptoms to qualify for major depression, some experts believe that even people who report only two to four of the nine symptoms of depression suffer from the disease.[47] Indeed, impairment gets increasingly worse with the number of depressive symptoms a person experiences. The more symptoms people reported, the more likely they were to seek professional help, take medication, or say that symptoms interfered with their lives "a lot." Some epidemiologists argue that we cannot dismiss minor depression as merely a normal response to life stressors or a transient drop in mood.[48]

In fact, people in the community who endorse only a *single* symptom of depression exhibit more impairment than do those who report no depressive symptoms at all.[49] The psychiatrist Lewis Judd and his colleagues wrote that "even one current depressive symptom may be clinically 'significant' and associated with some psychosocial dysfunction or risk."[50] Accordingly, Judd suggested that minor depression and major depression may constitute different points on a continuum of illness severity, and any symptomatic manifestation may indicate that the "disease process is present, active and should be considered for treatment."[51]

If depression truly lies on a continuum of severity, then a categorical approach to diagnosis that distinguishes the depressed from the nondepressed on the basis of a symptom count will underestimate the prevalence of depression. Moreover, if degree of functional impairment in everyday life increases as a function of symptom number, then we have further justification for classifying people with subthreshold numbers of symptoms as truly ill and in need of treatment.

Another argument against defining disorders such as depression more stringently is that people with mild cases are at increased risk for developing severe disorders later.[52] If we treat mild disorders early, perhaps we can reduce the likelihood that people will develop more severe, more costly, and potentially more intractable disorders down the road. Once we recognize minor depression as a disease, we realize that a serious, hidden public health problem is crying out for attention.

Not everyone with mild symptoms, of course, is doomed to get worse in the future. But distinguishing between people whose mild symptoms will remit without professional treatment and people whose mild symptoms are a harbinger of serious depression is no easy task. Only the second group needs early intervention.

Horwitz and Wakefield acknowledge that mild conditions can sometimes predict full-blown disorders. But merely because something is a risk factor for disorder does not make it a disorder itself. Moreover, they acknowledge that continuously varying dimensions may underlie variation in symptomatic expression, and they realize that DSM symptom thresholds are to some extent arbitrary cutoffs.

However, they argue against defining depression downward. Regarding every point along a continuum of symptom severity as indicative of disorder conflates normal sadness with sadness arising from dysfunctional mechanisms of mood regulation. Although symptoms of depression in the general population may increase smoothly with no natural breakpoint demarcating disorder from nondisorder, a dimensional construal of depression still fails to consider the cause of symptom emergence. Whether a person reports few symptoms or many, we still cannot know whether the symptoms reflect dysfunction in psychobiological mechanisms regulating emotion in response to loss without considering the context.

Moreover, it's not surprising that impairment worsens as a function of the number of symptoms a person experiences. But this alone does not confirm that all points along a continuum of depression signify disorder. Consider a teenager dumped by his girlfriend. He's likely to experience at least a few symptoms suggestive of depression, along with social withdrawal, difficulty concentrating on his homework, and other indicators of functional impairment. Merely because indicators of impairment correlate with symptoms of sadness does not mean that he suffers from a "minor depression," a mental illness that may signify progression to full-blown major depressive disorder and risk for suicide. Indeed, both the emotional and the functional consequences of the romantic break-up indicate that mechanisms regulating emotional response to loss are functioning just fine.

As Horwitz and Wakefield emphasize, conceptualizing depression dimensionally on a continuum is not "a substitute for the distinction between disorder and nondisorder."[53] At any point on this continuum, a practitioner must go beyond mere symptoms and consider contextual factors to arrive at a judgment of disorder. We must think about etiology and pathophysiology: two issues that transcend the atheoretical, descriptive approach to diagnosis inaugurated by DSM-III.

Scrutinizing context to identify clues to pathophysiology is not always reliable. Most people with mood disorders can identify a trigger for their first episode (say, divorce). Yet the connection between stressors and later episodes often becomes more obscure over time. Episodes either erupt without apparent cause or become uncoupled with stressors that do occur.[54] Does this mean that the first, stressor-induced episode reflects normal sadness and only the later, autonomous episodes reflect genuine, harmful dysfunction?

Does this imply a revival of the now-discredited distinction be-tween reactive depressions and endogenous depressions?[55] This old distinction presupposed that some depressions occurred in re-sponse to environmental stressors, whereas other depressions char-acterized by neurovegetative signs, such as appetite loss, early morning awakening, and psychomotor agitation, were "biological" and arose independent of stressors. The distinction collapsed when it became apparent that even endogenous, "biological" depressions often had stressful antecedents. In fact, the clinical psychologist Scott Monroe has emphasized that the onset of major depressive disorder nearly always erupts following exposure to a severe life stressor.[56]

But how can we be sure that a stressor really is the cause of a depression? People tend to link their emotions to events, and yet merely because a stressor precedes an episode of depression doesn't mean that it caused it. It could have emerged for entirely unrelated reasons. For example, the psychiatrist Ronald Pies notes that a pa-tient who attributes his depression to his girlfriend's abandon-ing him may fail to realize that his dysphoria began prior to the breakup.[57] In fact, his chronically low mood may have caused the breakup. Pies also points out that people often experience de-pression after suffering a stroke. Is this a real depression? How can we determine whether the syndrome results from neuroana-tomical damage, endocrine disturbance, or a normal psychological response to the stressor of suffering a stroke and rationally worry-ing about its likely impact on daily functioning? Pies's example il-lustrates how difficult it can be to determine exactly what caused an episode of depression.

Horwitz and Wakefield's approach to depression has seem-ingly paradoxical treatment implications, as the clinical psycholo-gist Gregg Henriques observed.[58] Consider an impoverished, unem-ployed, single mother living in a high-crime neighborhood. Her bleak socioeconomic circumstances seem unremitting. What should a clinician or epidemiological interviewer conclude if she reports enough symptoms to qualify for major depression? Should they defend her dignity and refuse to "medicalize" her misery by refusing to label her mentally ill, noting that nearly anyone would feel as she does in such circumstances? Indeed, the mechanisms calibrating response to loss and stress seem to be operating normally. Would offering her medication amount to providing her with a pharmacological band-aid, numbing her to inequitable and unjust social circumstances? Or would medication jumpstart her motivation, enabling her to take steps to overcome the social and economic obstacles that trap her in a demoralizing environment?

Now consider another woman, this one with a loving, supportive husband, wonderful children, close friends, and a lucrative, satisfying career. Despite her circumstances, she sees her world as empty and wonders whether there isn't more to life. She, too, meets symptomatic criteria for a major depressive episode. Anyone would be puzzled at why someone so fortunate is feeling so miserable. She has sustained no major loss that could explain her unhappiness. Something seems seriously awry with her mood-regulation mechanisms.

Of these two women, who suffers from a genuine mood disorder? Horwitz and Wakefield's approach suggests that only the second woman has a disorder. The first woman's mood-regulation mechanisms appear to be working. Nothing internal to her seems broken, her intense suffering notwithstanding. Lacking a DSM diagnosis of major depression, the first woman would be out of luck when it comes to receiving reimbursable treatment.

Further complicating matters, even people whose depression does not seem to arise from internal dysfunction may still benefit from treatment, as the psychiatrist Kenneth Kendler pointed out. In a review of Horwitz and Wakefield's book, he described one of his cases to illustrate this point.[59] His patient became depressed after receiving a diagnosis of cancer. The context of her depression makes the episode expectable, reasonable, and warranted. Therefore, we might conclude that nothing is wrong with her emotion-regulation mechanisms. Yet Kendler treated her anyway, and antidepressant medication lifted her depression despite the continued presence of her cancer.

In fairness to Horwitz and Wakefield, they emphasize that their approach does not immediately have treatment implications.[60] Other factors, in addition to the presence of disorder, affect treatment decisions. At the very least, doctors who would treat the first person would be fully aware of what they were doing: medicating a normal reaction to life stressors, not treating a real disease. Horwitz and Wakefield's aim is to conduct a conceptual analysis, informed by data, to help us distinguish genuine mood disorder from nondisordered sadness. Their aim is not to dictate treatment options, nor to distinguish those who deserve reimbursable treatment from those who do not. Yet if their analysis provides only conceptual clarification, can it offer much guidance for clinical practitioners?

Social Phobia (Social Anxiety Disorder)

People with social anxiety disorder fear and avoid activities and situations where they risk embarrassment or negative evaluation by others. Believing that others will regard them as ridiculous, weak, and incompetent, they become intensely anxious in social situations. They blush, tremble, sweat, and become tongue-tied and inarticulate. Their extreme self-consciousness about others' noticing these symptoms exacerbates their misery.

Any situation with the potential for critical scrutiny can be very difficult for people with social phobia. As a result, they may avoid doing things in front of others, such as eating, drinking, or signing checks, for fear that their trembling may betray their anxiety. Most people with social phobia fear a wide range of situations, not merely public speaking. Many dread asking someone for a date, conversing with strangers, or attending parties.

Longing for connection with others yet fearful of rejection, people with social phobia often suffer from aching loneliness. Their fears can seriously interfere with their academic, occupational, and social lives. DSM-III described social phobia as "apparently very rare."[61] Unfortunately, the DSM-III committee based this guess on clinical experience with help-seeking populations; no good epidemiological estimates were available. Yet according to recent surveys, the disorder afflicts between 12.1 and 18.7 percent of the population at some point in their lives.[62]

A disorder this common was bound to attract the attention of the pharmaceutical companies. SmithKline Beecham marketed its antidepressant Paxil as a treatment for social anxiety disorder.[63] Direct-to-consumer advertising included television commercials characterizing sufferers of social anxiety disorder as allergic to other people. The ads urged viewers to ask their doctor whether Paxil might be right for them. Drug companies sponsored professional symposia on social phobia and provided financial support for patient advocacy organizations aiming to raise public awareness about the condition.

Such marketing campaigns send a mixed message to the public. On the one hand, sufferers appear to be attractive people who are clearly not "crazy" but who have a very common problem. On the other hand, this common problem is a serious disorder supposedly caused by a chemical imbalance in the brain calling for drug treatment.

Discovery of this hidden epidemic has prompted claims that psychiatry is now pathologizing people who are merely shy by temperament.[64] Renaming social phobia as social anxiety disorder complicates matters. So when does shyness shade into disorder? How can we validly distinguish between genuine disorder and extreme but normal shyness?

Wakefield, Horwitz, and Schmitz think they have an answer.[65] They believe that social anxiety is a disorder only when there is a dysfunction in the psychobiological mechanisms governing anxiety in social groups. They argue that the capacity to experience social anxiety is an adaptation that enabled our ancestors to function smoothly in small hunter-gatherer bands, allowing them to pursue status and related goals (for example, successful mating) without provoking retaliation from others of higher status. The capacity for experiencing social anxiety enabled them to find their place within a hierarchy, making it easier to cooperate yet also compete successfully and safely for valued resources without risking ejection from the group and certain death.

Wakefield and his colleagues argue that we can plausibly infer dysfunction when debilitatingly high levels of social anxiety cause interference in species-typical contexts and tasks, such as interacting with safe, familiar people, or being in settings where critical scrutiny is unlikely. For example, they suggest that the diagnosis might apply to a college student who becomes intolerably anxious while sitting among hundreds of other students in a lecture hall because he or she is unlikely to be the focus of critical scrutiny in that setting. In contrast, anxiety in the instructor might not qualify as social phobia because he or she is the focus of scrutiny of hundreds of strangers. Fear in the latter case constitutes a mismatch between a contemporary setting and the hunter-gatherer context in which our capacity to experience social anxiety evolved.

People vary in their degree of shyness, and a person whose social anxiety merely reflects the temperamental extreme of normal variation does not have a disorder, according to Wakefield, regardless of how uncomfortable the person might be in certain settings. It is not enough that someone's anxiety is extreme, undesired, and impairing in some social roles.

Some experts object to confining ascription of dysfunction to serious anxiety in social contexts having antecedents in the hunter-gatherer stage of human evolution.[66] Although it may be true that our distant ancestors never had to address a large audience of strangers in a lecture hall, the fact that people today can experience crippling anxiety in public-speaking situations has clinical relevance. Whether we call this a disorder or not, people will seek treatment to help them speak comfortably in front of large groups. If these people do not receive a diagnosis, they fail to receive reimbursable treatment.

Indeed, Wakefield, Horwitz, and Schmitz acknowledged that intense but normal shyness can cause much suffering, and that it might call for compassionate attempts to help the person become less shy. We should not, however, confuse such efforts with treating a disorder.

Where does that leave us? Is there any way to distinguish pronounced shyness from social anxiety disorder other than by speculating about the social lives of our hunter-gatherer ancestors and then basing inferences about dysfunction on these speculations?

The psychiatrist Donald Klein proposed a method for differentiating between social phobia and normal shyness.[67] If the former arises from dysfunction in a social threat–detection system, then pharmacological intervention should correct this dysfunction without helping people who are simply shy. Monoamine oxidase (MAO) inhibitors, such as phenelzine, benefit people with social phobia. Unlike benzodiazepines, these drugs are not available on the street, implying that they do not brighten mood or alleviate anxiety in people without disorder. If social phobia were merely the endpoint on a continuum of shyness, that is, if it were not a disorder, then providing MAO inhibitors to the moderately shy would diminish their shyness. On the other hand, if there is a qualitative distinction between normal shyness and social phobia, then MAO inhibitors would not help the normally shy become less shy. They would, however, reduce the anxiety of those with social phobia.

Unfortunately, Klein's proposal requires that phenelzine be more consistently effective in alleviating social phobia than it actually is. About one-quarter of patients with the diagnosis do not benefit from this drug.[68] Are we then to conclude that these nonresponders do not have social phobia after all, despite being otherwise indistinguishable from those who do benefit from the drug? Or do we conclude that the drug is inconsistently effective for many patients with social phobia? If the latter is true, then Klein's method will not reliably distinguish shyness from social phobia. Moreover, no one has yet tested whether phenelzine benefits the moderately shy.

Posttraumatic Stress Disorder of the Virtual Kind

Posttraumatic stress disorder is an anxiety disorder that sometimes arises after a person is exposed to a traumatic event. PTSD consists of three clusters of symptoms: (1) recurrent recollection of the trauma (intrusive images, nightmares), (2) avoidance of reminders that may trigger disturbing recollections and emotional numbing (difficulty experiencing positive emotions, loss of interest in formerly pleasurable activities), and (3) heightened arousal (exaggerated startle, insomnia, irritability).

PTSD, as originally conceptualized in DSM-III, could only result from exposure to a restricted class of overwhelmingly terrifying, often life-threatening, events such as combat, rape, or confinement to a concentration camp. These extreme stressors were usually far outside the realm of everyday life. Regardless of the symptoms people reported, they could receive the PTSD diagnosis only if they had been exposed to a stressor that qualified as sufficiently traumatic. A person whose distress was embodied in PTSD-like symptoms would be denied the diagnosis if he or she had experienced an insufficiently traumatic stressor.

Concerns about excluding suffering people from receiving the diagnosis and reimbursable treatment motivated a kind of conceptual bracket creep in the definition of trauma, ratified in subsequent versions of the DSM.[69] No longer must one directly experience an extreme stressor to qualify as trauma-exposed. Experiencing helplessness, intense fear, or horror upon merely receiving news about the misfortunes of other people now qualifies one as a trauma survivor oneself, and thus eligible for a diagnosis of PTSD.

The DSM-IV definition of trauma recognizes three types of trauma survivors. One group includes those who are direct recipients of serious threat or harm, such as victims of rape or survivors of combat. A second group includes people who have personally witnessed trauma suffered by others, such as bystanders present at a drive-by shooting. The third group, new in DSM-IV, includes those who are "confronted with" information about threats to others, such as a mother who learns that her child has just died in an automobile accident.

On these terms, nearly everyone is a trauma survivor today. Applying DSM-IV criteria, the epidemiologists Naomi Breslau and Ronald Kessler found that 89.6 percent of adults in southeastern Michigan had survived at least one trauma during their lives.[70] The broadened range of potentially PTSD-causing events resulted in an increase in the rate of trauma from 270 events per 100 persons to 430 events per 100 persons. This represents an increase of 59.2 percent in the "total life experiences that can be used to diagnose PTSD," as the authors observed. These newly qualifying traumatic events accounted for 37.8 percent of the total number of PTSD cases in the survey.

The DSM-IV does not require that survivors have a personal connection to direct trauma victims, as in the case of the bereaved mother. In the wake of the September 11, 2001, terrorist attacks, traumatologists—professionals who study and treat victims of trauma—realized that indirect exposure to dangers experienced by others could occur via the media.[71] Accordingly, horrified citizens throughout America who saw televised coverage of the attacks—from the comfort of their living rooms—qualify as trauma survivors just as do those who managed to escape the twin towers. The realization that televised images of trauma now qualify as PTSD-causing stimuli inspired an entire research field on what Allan Young wryly calls "posttraumatic stress disorder of the virtual kind."[72] Today, a person no longer needs to be physically present at the scene of a trauma to qualify as a trauma survivor.

In the first major study on virtual PTSD, the RAND Corporation surveyed 540 American adults during the weekend following the attacks. They asked the subjects whether they had experienced any of five symptoms of PTSD, and if so, how severe the symptoms were on a five-point scale ranging from one ("not at all") to five ("extremely").[73] The researchers concluded that 44 percent of Americans "had substantial symptoms of stress." They wrote, "Clinicians should anticipate that even people far from the attacks will have trauma-related symptoms," ominously warning that these symptoms "are unlikely to disappear soon."

To qualify as one of the 44 percent of Americans deemed "substantially" stressed, a subject merely had to score a four ("quite a bit") on only one of the five symptoms. For example, anyone who experienced "quite a bit" of anger at the terrorists counted as substantially stressed. This is akin to saying that someone with a cough has a "symptom" of bacterial pneumonia.

In a web-based epidemiological survey, William Schlenger and his colleagues had a representative sample of American adults complete a PTSD questionnaire on symptoms related to events of September 11.[74] They found that 4 percent of the population outside the attacked cities reported enough symptoms to qualify for probable PTSD. These data imply that television caused millions of cases of PTSD in America.

Yet there are good reasons to doubt that an epidemic of virtual PTSD erupted throughout the land.[75] Even in New York City, the evidence for an epidemic of PTSD is unconvincing. Interviewing residents living south of 110th Street in Manhattan five to eight weeks after the attacks, Sandro Galea and his colleagues found that 7.5 percent had developed apparent PTSD.[76] Yet when they conducted another survey six months later, they found that only 0.6 percent of Manhattan residents still had PTSD related to the attacks.[77] A rapid 92 percent drop in the prevalence of PTSD strongly implies that the surveys may have been detecting normal, transient distress reactions, not symptoms of disorder. Indeed, the New York surveys did not require that symptoms interfere with a person's ability to function in everyday life. Moreover, many symptoms of PTSD are nonspecific and not uniquely associated with the disorder. One need not have PTSD to have difficulty sleeping or concentrating on work, or to experience irritability or loss of interest in activities.

Expecting an epidemic of PTSD and related mental health problems, authorities in New York prepared for a flood of people seeking mental health services.[78] Yet most of the funds earmarked for this purpose went unspent; few New Yorkers sought treatment. Among those identified in the surveys as having either depression or PTSD, 86 percent were already in treatment before the terrorist attacks occurred.[79]

In support of the claim that watching television can cause PTSD, researchers have pointed to the correlation between amount of self-reported viewing of coverage of the terrorist attacks and self-reported PTSD symptoms.[80] This correlation, of course, does not confirm causation. High levels of preexisting neuroticism are likely to foster anxious preoccupation with viewing coverage of the attacks as well as proneness to report distress, including apparent symptoms of PTSD.

The assertion that millions of otherwise healthy adults across the United States developed PTSD by watching televised coverage of 9/11 is one of the most glaring examples of conceptual bracket creep in the definition of trauma. Grouping actual survivors of the World Trade Center attacks with those who merely witnessed the events on TV and claiming that they are equally trauma-exposed and suffering from the same mental disorder is outlandish. Other such examples of supposed PTSD include people diagnosed with the disorder after having given birth to a healthy baby following a routine, uncomplicated delivery or after exposure to rude sexual jokes in the workplace.[81] One group of researchers reported that some people develop PTSD symptoms after having a wisdom tooth extracted.[82] No one would argue that these experiences are pleasant. Yet whether the distress experienced is the same as that suffered by rape victims and torture survivors is preposterous.

Some traumatologists suspect that concerns about bracket creep are exaggerated. Dean Kilpatrick, a psychologist and former president of the International Society for Traumatic Stress Studies, wondered whether "it is a pseudoproblem that sounds worse than it is and is primarily of interest to a few academics and others with forensic agendas."[83] After all, a person exposed to trauma must still exhibit sufficient symptoms of PTSD to qualify for the disorder; exposure to trauma does not automatically cause PTSD. Should we deny the diagnosis to a person who meets symptomatic criteria merely because the stressor was seemingly too mild?

Nevertheless, bracket creep does cause problems. First, it dras-

tically increases the heterogeneity among people potentially qualifying for PTSD, making it very difficult to elucidate the psychobiological mechanisms mediating symptom expression. Television
viewers in California, for example, reacting with horror to the terrorist attacks would seem to have little in common with people
who survived Auschwitz. Yet both now qualify as victims of trauma.
The psychobiology of survivors of television trauma and Nazi
trauma is likely to differ dramatically.

Second, the more we expand the concept of trauma, the less
plausibly we can attribute causal significance to the stressor itself,
and the more we must emphasize vulnerability factors in the emergence of PTSD. Of course, risk factors are important for any disorder, including PTSD. Yet one consequence of bracket creep is a
background-foreground inversion whereby risk factors dominate
the causal foreground, and the stressor itself recedes into the background. If almost all the variance in outcome is attributable to
neuroticism or preexisting mental disorder rather than to the objective severity of the stressor itself, then the justification for having
a diagnosis of PTSD disappears. It makes more sense to attribute a
highly anxious person's PTSD triggered by a minor fender bender
to the person's anxious temperament than to the accident itself.

Third, by regarding increasingly more of the stressors of everyday life as potentially causing PTSD, we may wind up undermining resilience in the face of adversity. If nearly every unpleasant
event that provokes a reaction of horror, helplessness, or intense
fear counts as a trauma, then *trauma* has lost whatever distinctive
meaning it originally had.

Commenting on our current preoccupation with trauma, the
historian of military psychiatry Ben Shephard asked, "Will psychiatrists have the sense to realize that by medicalizing the human response to stressful situations, they have created a culture of trauma
and thus undermined the general capacity to resist trauma?"[84]

Shephard, however, concluded that it is probably too late to fix things, now that the concept of trauma "has been vectored into the wider society by the law and the media" and that so many mental health professionals make a living off it.

The boundary problem in the PTSD field consists of two subproblems: the boundary between traumatic and nontraumatic stressors, and the boundary between normal and abnormal stress reactions. We can solve the first problem by restricting traumatic stressors to those involving direct exposure or personal witnessing of the event. That is, a person should be physically present at the scene of the trauma to qualify as a trauma survivor. We can partly solve the second problem by eliminating nonspecific symptoms, such as irritability, difficulty sleeping, concentration impairment, and loss of interest in activities, while retaining those specific to PTSD, such as nightmares and intrusive recollections about the trauma, avoidance of reminders of the trauma, and emotional numbing.[85]

DSM'S ATTEMPTS TO SOLVE THE BOUNDARY PROBLEM

Our current symptom-based, context-free approach to diagnosis makes it difficult to distinguish disorder from distress. Unlike doctors in other specialties, psychiatrists can't order a lab test to determine whether someone has a certain disease. But it's not as if psychiatry has ignored the boundary problem. In fact, DSM-IV-TR incorporates several features into diagnostic categories that represent attempts to distinguish distress from disorder. Unfortunately, each of these safeguards has significant limitations.

First, most diagnoses require that symptomatic criteria be met for a minimum duration of time before authorizing a diagnosis. Consider major depression. In addition to fulfilling the minimum symptom count, a person must have experienced either sadness or a loss of pleasure in previously enjoyable activities for much of the day nearly every day for at least two weeks. People in clinical settings usually meet the duration requirement. Many have suffered for months before finally seeking help. This does not necessarily hold in epidemiological surveys, however. That is, the duration requirement classifies someone who has been depressed for two weeks in the same category as someone who has been depressed for two years.

Yet even among those people who have been sad for longer than two weeks, not all suffer from major depression, even if they satisfy the requisite three additional symptoms. Some may be responding to chronic stressors, such as demoralizing unemployment, or to other losses. In such cases, merely satisfying the duration requirement does not signal mental illness.

Second, many diagnoses require that symptoms must produce either significant distress or significant impairment in everyday life. Only if a person's problems satisfy at least one of these two criteria will a mental health professional assign the diagnosis. For PTSD, symptoms must cause "clinically significant distress or impairment in social, occupational, or other important areas of functioning."[86] Unfortunately, the first clause is subject to two interpretations, and neither solves the boundary problem. One interpretation results in clinically significant distress being entirely redundant with symptom severity. A person with many severe symptoms is almost by definition someone suffering clinically significant distress. In fact, revisiting major depression data from the National Comorbidity Survey Replication, Wakefield and his colleagues found that 97.2 percent of respondents who reported persistent sadness or its equivalent said they experienced distress, thereby confirming its redundancy with symptoms. As they concluded, "The regular association of distress with sadness renders the distress criterion all but useless in distinguishing normal sadness from major depression."[87]

The other interpretation of the clause is that it implies a kind of metadistress or distress about one's distress (symptoms). A person might fulfill criteria for social anxiety disorder, for example, but fail to worry much about it. Such an intensely shy person might conclude, "This is just the way I am," and thus not meet criteria for the disorder. Another shy person distressed about failing to be the life of the party would have a mental illness.

Requiring distress about symptoms would seem odd in other areas of medicine. Consider an elderly, stoic person who develops inoperable cancer and who regards his disease as God's will. Few oncologists would shrug and say, "We cannot diagnose cancer because the patient does not appear distressed about the situation." Finally, people with certain conditions, such as antisocial personality disorder, do not necessarily experience distress about their behavioral abnormalities unless they run afoul of the law, for example. The best solution to the problem of the distress clause would be for the DSM-5 committee to dispense with both versions of it.

The functional-impairment clause does a better job of distinguishing between normal distress and mental disorder. When people cope sufficiently well that their symptoms do not interfere with their ability to get along with others, to complete schooling, and to earn a living, then there is less justification for calling the person mentally ill.

The importance of functional impairment is most evident in epidemiological surveys. Prevalence estimates for mental disorder can vary dramatically depending on the level of impairment needed to assign the diagnosis. According to the National Vietnam Veterans Readjustment Study (NVVRS), 30.9 percent of all men who served in the war developed PTSD, and 15.2 percent still had the illness in the late 1980s.[88] This high percentage puzzled historians and other scholars deeply familiar with military psychiatry because only between about 12.5 and 15 percent of all men who served in Vietnam did so in a direct combat role.[89]

There are many hypotheses for why the NVVRS rates were so high, but one possibility pertains to impairment.[90] The NVVRS researchers used the then-current DSM-III-R criteria for diagnosing PTSD, which did not require that symptoms result in significant functional impairment (or distress). Therefore, some veterans receiving the PTSD diagnosis may have been experiencing nonpathological distress, not a disorder calling for treatment.

Bruce Dohrenwend, a social psychologist and epidemiologist, and his colleagues reanalyzed the NVVRS data, using another measure of functioning before counting diagnosed cases as true instances of PTSD.[91] They also excluded cases whose traumatic histories were not corroborated by archival records and cases with prewar onsets of PTSD. These adjustments resulted in both the lifetime and current (late-1980s) estimates of PTSD dropping by 40 percent, thereby confirming the suspicions of the historians that the NVVRS had overestimated the rate of PTSD.[92] In fact, a slightly more stringent definition of impairment, and one approximating the level of clinical impairment that might require treatment, resulted in the prevalence dropping by 65 percent.[93] Thus, the current (late-1980s) prevalence estimates for PTSD dropped from 15.2 percent (NVVRS) to 9.1 percent (Dohrenwend) to 5.4 percent (clinical impairment), depending on how one defines impairment. Likewise, a study of Dutch veterans who served in the war in Iraq indicated that prevalence estimates for PTSD ranged from 4 to 21 percent depending on factors such as the level of impairment and method of diagnosis (interview versus questionnaire).[94]

These studies show that prevalence estimates for war-related PTSD fluctuate wildly when investigators use different criteria for impairment. The same happens in civilian epidemiological samples, too.[95]

In sum, the DSM-IV-TR attempts to solve the boundary problem by stipulating that symptoms must be present for a minimal duration, and that levels of distress, metadistress, or impairment must be present. None is an infallible method of discriminating normal distress from mental disorder. None directly provides insight into the presence of dysfunction in psychobiological mechanisms governing cognition, emotion, and behavior.

In the next chapter, I consider an influential attempt to solve the boundary problem by appealing to evolutionary biology and psychology. This approach promises to provide a nonarbitrary, objective, and naturalistic route to distinguishing mental distress from mental disorder.

Can Evolutionary Psychology Make Sense of Mental Disorder?

3

According to Masters and Johnson, women who have never had an orgasm under any circumstance suffer from primary orgasmic dysfunction. This disorder may afflict as many as 20 percent of women, making it "a clinical problem of considerable magnitude," as the psychologist Barbara Andersen observed. Fortunately, it is among the most treatable conditions in the field of mental health. Dispelling myths about sexuality and teaching patients to masturbate produce cures—that is, an orgasm—in 92 to 100 percent of cases.[1]

These spectacular success rates beg the question, did these women even have a disorder in the first place? According to Jerome Wakefield, the Masters and Johnson diagnosis "overpathologizes women" by presupposing that the absence of orgasms, or anorgasmia, signifies a defective capacity to experience them.[2] It implies that something internal to the woman is not working properly.

As Wakefield argues, many factors may contribute to anorgasmia, including lack of sexual opportunities, unfamiliarity with masturbation, or strict religious beliefs. In some cases the focus, duration, and frequency of sexual stimulation may be insufficient to produce orgasm. For women with partners, relationship problems may be to blame.

To be sure, Masters and Johnson were well aware of these factors. Yet they saw them as causing a dysfunction in the woman, whereas Wakefield sees them as providing a basis for ruling out a dysfunction. Only when clinicians confirm the absence of these external factors should they conclude that something internal to the woman is failing to function as designed. Only then, he believes, should we assume dysfunction in the psychobiological mechanisms mediating orgasm.

The distinction is neither trivial nor merely semantic. Being told that you suffer from orgasmic disorder is likely to be much more devastating than learning that there's nothing wrong with your capacity to achieve orgasm that some information and sexual practice can't fix.

Wakefield's concern that diagnosing women with primary orgasmic dysfunction overpathologizes them is a tacit recognition of the persistence of stigma associated with certain mental health conditions. The extraordinarily high cure rates for this condition are insufficient to erase the stigma associated with the label primary orgasmic dysfunction.

THE HARMFUL DYSFUNCTION ANALYSIS OF MENTAL DISORDER

Wakefield's critique of the Masters and Johnson diagnosis of primary orgasmic dysfunction inspired him to formulate his harmful dysfunction analysis (HDA) of mental disorder.[3] The HDA promises to provide a principled basis for solving the boundary problem, enabling us to distinguish mental disorders from other forms of mental distress and problems of everyday life. It captures the intuition, shared by doctors and laypersons alike, that mental disorder implies that something internal to the person has gone wrong. The HDA provides substance to this intuition by asserting that what has gone wrong is an evolved psychobiological mechanism of the mind. As Wakefield expressed it, "a disorder exists when the failure of a person's internal mechanisms to perform their functions as designed by nature impinges harmfully on the person's well-being as defined by social values and meanings."[4]

Disorder is a hybrid concept that straddles the natural world of scientific facts and the socially constructed world of values. It has two components. The factual component specifies the mechanism that is failing to function properly. The value component specifies the harms that result from the dysfunction. Harms can include personal suffering, increased mortality risk, inability to work, and difficulty getting along with other people.

Dysfunction implies unfulfilled function. Specifying the function of a hammer, a pen, or other artifacts created by human beings is usually straightforward. All we need to do is identify the object's purpose, the reason someone made it. A dysfunctional pen is one that no longer writes, for example.

Specifying the function of natural objects is more complicated because no one has designed them with a purpose in mind. Consider the heart. It does several things, including pumping blood and making sounds useful for medical auscultation. According to the selected effects or etiological perspective favored by Wakefield, its natural function, however, is the effect it has that explains why hearts exist today.[5] To identify pumping blood as the heart's natural function requires reference to evolutionary theory as providing the only nonteleological basis for conceptualizing the purpose, and therefore the natural function, of the heart. To speak of the heart's "purpose" or its being "designed" for pumping blood is merely a shorthand way of denoting its evolved, natural function. Evolutionary "design" does not imply a "designer."

Evolutionary theory shows how certain effects of a psychobiological mechanism account for its presence today. Natural selection favored mechanisms whose effects fostered reproductive success in members of ancestral populations, ensuring their presence in future generations. To account for a psychobiological mechanism in terms of its evolutionary purpose, its design, or its natural function is an elliptical way of causally explaining it in terms of natural selection.

According to Wakefield, evolutionary theory underlies all correct ascriptions of natural functions, and therefore underlies the concept of disorder as harmful dysfunction. However, natural science alone, including evolutionary theory, cannot provide a value-free basis for accomplishing this task. For example, the psychiatrist Robert Kendell defined disease as any condition that decreases fertility or increases mortality.[6] Schizophrenia and pedophilia are two conditions that satisfy the diminished fertility criterion. Depression shortens life and therefore satisfies the early mortality criterion, mainly by impairing immune and cardiac function, but also by suicide.[7] Some conditions, by contrast, diminish fertility without being disorders, and some disorders have no discernible effects on fertility or mortality. To count as a disorder, a dysfunction must also directly cause suffering for the person or result in other harms as defined by prevailing social norms and values. Consider a man who gets a vasectomy. He can no longer transmit his genes, so technically he now has an evolutionary dysfunction. Yet he desires his sterility and suffers no distress or other harms as a result of it. Hence, he does not have a disorder.

Likewise, statistical deviance alone fails to identify disorders. Not all disorders are rare (think the common cold or tooth decay), and rare conditions, such as very high intelligence, are not disorders. Moreover, statistically deviant, negative reactions do not necessarily signify disorder. For example, the intensity and duration of normal grief reactions vary considerably; some individuals will experience unexpectedly marked reactions yet their response need not reflect derangement in any psychobiological mechanism.

Just as natural science alone cannot provide a principled basis for conceptualizing disorder, there is more to mental disorder than merely violation of social norms. The argument that the concept of mental disorder is nothing but a label that we impose on socially deviant behavior fails; it cannot distinguish between disorders and other socially disvalued conditions. Although people with mental illness may be poor, illiterate, or criminal, poverty, illiteracy, and criminality per se do not signify mental illness. There is something more to the concept of mental disorder than social deviance. That something is dysfunction in an evolved psychobiological mechanism that causes socially disvalued conditions, personal suffering, or both.

Furthermore, intense grief following the death of a loved one may look like major depression, but it's not mental illness. Indeed, the mechanisms mediating the emotional response to loss are working precisely as designed. Grief causes suffering and hence harm, but it does not arise from dysfunction. Sadness, crying, sleep disturbance, loss of appetite, and loss of interest in pleasurable activities characterize both grief and depression. If a grieving person still satisfies the symptomatic criteria for a major depressive episode two months after the death of his or her loved one, then that person will be eligible for a diagnosis of major depression. In addition, if the grieving person experiences psychotic symptoms, suicidal ideation, feelings of worthlessness, psychomotor retardation, or marked functional impairment, then a diagnosis of major depressive episode is appropriate, even if two months have not elapsed.[8]

The HDA accommodates dysfunction at either the biological or the psychological level of analysis. Consider panic disorder. According to the psychiatrist Donald Klein's suffocation false-alarm theory, spontaneous panic attacks arise from dysfunction in an evolved suffocation alarm system.[9] A defect in the system incorrectly signals increasing levels of carbon dioxide, thereby producing intense breathlessness, hyperventilation, and terror. The evolved dysfunction lies in the brain circuits mediating respiration.

In contrast, the psychologist David Clark's cognitive theory of panic situates the dysfunction at the psychological or information-processing level of analysis.[10] According to Clark, panic results from catastrophic misinterpretation of certain bodily sensations. For example, misconstrual of benign palpitations as harbingers of impending heart attack increases fear, which worsens palpitations, thereby seemingly confirming the person's catastrophic belief. The vicious circle of sensation, misinterpretation, and fear spirals upward, culminating in full-blown panic. Debate persists about whether people must misinterpret bodily sensations as an impending heart attack, psychosis, or similar emergency for panic to occur.[11] At least some patients dread these bodily sensations not because they believe they're about to die but merely because they detest the experience of panic. They correctly interpret the sensations as impending panic, yet they still panic.

My point in citing Clark's theory is to illustrate how easily it fits within the HDA scheme. The HDA applies to dysfunctions in psychological mechanisms as well as in biological mechanisms. To speak of psychological mechanisms as distinct from biological ones does not entail Cartesian dualism whereby the former reside in the ethereal realm of the mind and the latter in the physical body. Rather, it concerns mechanisms describable at different levels of analysis. In Clark's theory, faulty computation of threat occurs in a postulated threat-appraisal system that exists at a psychological level of description. Although instantiated in the brain, it is not expressible at a neural level of description. The dysfunction lies in the brain's "software," not in its "hardware." Panic meets the HDA's criteria for disorder in both Klein's and Clark's theories.

How might the HDA cash out in diagnostic practice? Ideally, it should settle border disputes in psychiatric nosology, ensuring that the DSM identifies only genuine mental disorders and avoids path-ologizing normal emotional functioning. Wakefield's analytic strat-egy has two steps, the first descriptive, the second prescriptive.[12] He first tests whether the HDA captures consensual professional judgments about clear-cut, uncontroversial instances of disorder. If the HDA correctly classifies the reasonably easy cases of disorder, then we can apply it to the border region between disorder and nondisorder—the kind of controversial cases that motivated the search for a valid concept of disorder in the first place.

In a descriptive mode, the HDA clarifies the basis for consen-sual judgments about mental disorders. Mood-regulation mecha-nisms are clearly awry in melancholic depression; the theory-of-mind module enabling individuals to take the perspective of others is malfunctioning or absent in autistic disorder; and mechanisms of reasoning, affect, and perception are dysfunctional in paranoid schizophrenia. Dysfunctions in these evolved mechanisms produce suffering and other harms, thereby certifying these conditions as canonical cases of mental disorder.

However, if the HDA merely rendered explicit the underlying logic governing consensual diagnostic practice today, then its im-portance would be modest at best. It would clarify the status quo, but it would provide no guidance about how to solve the bound-ary problem in DSM-5. Yet the point of the HDA is not merely to provide conceptual clarification of today's diagnostic practice. It should also provide normative, prescriptive guidance to adjudicate controversial cases of proposed disorders. The HDA should enable us to eliminate false positives from the DSM—those conditions er-roneously classified as mental disorders—and it should clarify diag-nostic criteria of syndromes, ensuring that criteria identify only genuine disorders and exclude other conditions.

Consider conduct disorder. As many as 17 percent of adoles-cents in community studies have this condition, but the behavioral

DSM-IV criteria can be fulfilled without any evidence for dysfunction in underlying psychobiological mechanisms.[13] Children whose mechanisms of impulse control, empathy, and conscience are functioning just fine can qualify for the diagnosis, even if their deviant behavior is an adaptive response to an adverse environment. For example, a girl who has been sexually victimized by her stepfather may very well meet criteria by running away from home, by lying repeatedly to her parents, and by staying out past her curfew. Likewise, a boy may join a street gang to ensure his own safety, yet his gang-related antisocial behavior need not result from any internal dysfunction. Indeed, Tom Sawyer and Huckleberry Finn would have been surprised to learn that they suffer from conduct disorder.[14] Tom's and Huck's antisocial behavior was an expectable response to a harsh, adverse environment, not a consequence of mental dysfunction.

THE HDA AND EVOLUTIONARY PSYCHOLOGY

Wakefield's HDA comports well with evolutionary psychology.[15] Evolutionary psychologists hold that natural selection has shaped the cognitive mechanisms that govern behavior and constitute adaptive solutions to problems that confronted our hunter-gatherer ancestors during the Pleistocene era. Accordingly, one important aim for psychopathologists is to identify the dysfunctional adaptations that produce the symptoms of mental disorder.

It is important to realize that what evolutionary psychologists mean by adaptation differs from what clinicians and physiologists usually mean by the term. Clinicians often refer to behavior patterns as either adaptive or maladaptive, and their standard is the psychosocial adjustment of their patients. Physiologists use the term to denote short-term homeostatic adjustments such as those triggered by exposure to reduced oxygen at high altitudes.

By contrast, evolutionary psychologists favor the historical definition of adaptation. The philosopher of biology Elliott Sober defines it as follows: "To say that a trait is an 'adaptation' is to comment not on its current utility but on its history. To say that the mammalian heart is (now) an adaptation for pumping blood is to say that mammals have hearts because ancestrally, having a heart conferred a fitness advantage; the trait evolved because there was selection for having a heart, and hearts were selected because they pump blood. The heart makes noise, but the device is not an adaptation for making noise: The heart did not evolve because it makes noise. Rather, this property evolved as a spin-off; there was selection of noise makers but no selection for making noise."[16]

Thus a currently useful ("adaptive") phenotypic feature that was not a target of selection is not an adaptation. Conversely, a currently useless, or even harmful, feature is an adaptation if it conferred fitness benefits in ancestral environments. The historical, evolutionary definition of adaptation is equivalent to the concept of a "designed" or natural function. Wakefield endorses this definition: "Currently adaptive traits may or may not correspond to designed functions, which are those traits that were adaptive in the past and caused selective pressures that explain the existence or structure of mechanisms today."[17] The historical concept of adaptation provides an ultimate rather than a proximate explanation for a phenotypic feature.[18] An ultimate explanation answers a "why" question, whereas a proximate explanation answers a "how" question. An ultimate explanation for the heart, for example, explains why hearts evolved, whereas a proximate one explains how hearts operate today.

IDENTIFYING ADAPTATIONS AND DYSFUNCTIONS

The HDA requires us to identify adaptations whose dysfunctions provide the basis for distinguishing disorders from nondisorders. If disorder amounts to derangement in a natural function, then it appears essential that we parse the human phenotype into its adaptations. So how do can we identify adaptations and distinguish them from other, incidental features of the phenotype?

Reconstructing Evolutionary History

Evolutionary psychologists endorse the historical approach to adaptation. Unfortunately, reconstructing evolutionary history seems an especially daunting task given that neither cognition nor emotion leaves a direct fossil record. As the linguist Noam Chomsky remarked, "It is perfectly safe to attribute this development [of human cognitive capacities] to 'natural selection,' so long as we realize that there is no substance to this assertion, that it amounts to nothing more than a belief that there is some naturalistic explanation for these phenomena."[19] Despite Chomsky's nativism about language, he is pessimistic about our chances of deciphering the details about how our cognitive capacities evolved. Only Creationists deny that human cognition is a product of evolution. Yet affirming that our cognitive capacities evolved says nothing about how this happened and about which aspects of our cognitive phenotype qualify as adaptations that can go awry in psychopathology.

The geneticist Richard Lewontin is very skeptical about the scientific prospects of evolutionary psychology.[20] He points out that evolution by natural selection occurs when individuals within a species have a trait that confers a reproductive advantage over others within the same species that lack it. Merely because a trait, such as language capacity, is useful to an entire species once all members possess it does not mean that individuals who first developed it left more fertile offspring than those who did not. In fact, Lewontin remarked, the social deviance of early possessors of rudimentary language abilities might have resulted in homicide by their peers.

Language is clearly adaptive today. Yet we can never be sure whether it counts as an adaptation in the evolutionary historical sense. As Lewontin argued, "Plausible stories about what might be the reproductive consequences of aphasia are not sufficient. The issue, after all, is not whether linguistic ability might have been favored by natural selection (obviously it might have been), but whether, in fact, it was."

As Lewontin says, to confirm that a trait fosters fitness requires several steps. First, we must identify large subgroups within a species that vary in their possession of the trait. Second, we must track the reproductive histories of individuals in the subgroups. Given that a 1 percent difference in average reproductive capacity is very large in terms of an evolutionary time scale, we would need many subjects to test whether those with the trait outproduce those without it (for example, 100,000 per group). Third, even if those with the trait exhibit greater fertility than those without it (or more precisely, exhibit the propensity to produce fertile offspring that reproduce) we must still confirm that differential reproductive capacity is attributable to genetic differences between the groups, not to correlated environmental inputs.

Conducting such an analysis to parse the human cognitive phenotype into its constituent adaptations seems nearly impossible. Indeed, natural selection tends to reduce trait variability, yet measuring selection requires the presence of variant types whose reproductive rates must be calculated. It is very difficult to catch natural selection in the act of altering the average value of a trait in a species because by the time the trait approaches fixation, the process is over. Accordingly, Lewontin concludes that we must "give up the childish notion that everything that is interesting about nature can be understood. History, and evolution is a form of history, simply does not leave sufficient traces, especially when it is the forces that are at issue. Form and even behavior may leave fossil remains, but forces like natural selection do not. It might be interesting to know how cognition (whatever that is) arose and spread and changed, but we cannot know. Tough luck."

Adaptation as Universal, Complex, Functional Design

Rejecting Lewontin's pessimism, evolutionary psychologists believe that we have ways to identify adaptations other than by reconstructing the evolutionary history of human cognition. They believe that we can recognize the signature of selection in universal, complex, functional design.[21] Adaptations tend to be universal features within a species because natural selection winnows through phenotypes, reducing genetic variance, and often converging on a single design that efficiently solves a stable environmental problem. Moreover, complex, functional designs that solve these problems are very unlikely to have emerged solely by chance in the absence of the shaping force of natural selection. Meeting these criteria, the heart and eye qualify as adaptations. The faculty for language is yet another.

In their efforts to parse the human cognitive phenotype into its adaptations, evolutionary psychologists use two main methods. The reverse engineering method begins with a candidate adaptation and then requires reasoning about the ancestral environment to ascertain the problem that the adaptation evolved to solve. The other approach begins by reasoning about the ancestral environment to identify the persistent problems that our ancestors had to solve to survive and reproduce. Beginning with the problems, we can then hypothesize about cognitive adaptations that must have evolved to solve them. Hence, the first method requires us to infer the problem from the solution, whereas the second method requires us to infer the solution from the problem.

Identifying phenotypic features possessing complex, functional design is a more promising approach to confirming adaptations than trying to reconstruct the natural history of cognition. Yet it still has its own limitations. Because we have no metric for complexity, we must rely on intuition to identify whether something is sufficiently complex to qualify as a possible adaptation. Indeed, judgments of complexity are always relative, and whenever someone nominates a trait as complex, we can always ask, "Complex compared with what?" Furthermore, there is no obvious reason that natural selection should invariably result in complexity, however defined. Some adaptations may be simple features that efficiently solve survival problems.

Evolutionary psychologists often mention the eye, the heart, and other aspects of functional anatomy when providing examples of complex design. Yet convincing examples from cognitive psychology are harder to find, the language faculty notwithstanding. This presents a problem for evolutionary psychopathology in that the failure of these conjectured cognitive organs to function as designed provides the basis for Wakefield's HDA.

In fact, it turns out that even in anatomy, inferring design is by no means an easy task.[22] Anatomists encounter considerable problems when they attempt to elucidate complex systems, thanks to the diversity of goals potentially subserved by anatomical traits. For example, the fingers of the human hand seem to be an adaptation designed for manual manipulation because they conform to mechanical engineering standards of good design. Yet human anatomy itself inspired these standards of good design, not the other way around. Moreover, the fingers-as-adaptation-for-grasping explanation runs counter to work showing that these features of the vertebrate forelimb predate terrestrial life and thus cannot be adaptations for manipulation.

If biologists encounter difficulties identifying the original selected effect of a structure, psychologists have an even greater challenge. Not only do patterns of phenotypic interconnections arising from pleiotropy (a single gene having multiple effects) make it tough to parse the phenotype into isolated traits, but cognitive adaptations, unlike their anatomical counterparts, leave only indirect records (for example, tools), not direct fossil evidence.[23]

Yet another obstacle to the reverse engineering approach is that natural selection operates within constraints. As the Nobel laureate François Jacob emphasized, "Natural selection has no analogy with any aspect of human behavior. However, if one wanted to play with a comparison, one would have to say that natural selection does not work as an engineer works. It works like a tinkerer—a tinkerer who does not know exactly what he is going to produce but uses whatever he finds around him whether it be pieces of string, fragments of wood, or old cardboards; in short it works like a tinkerer who uses everything at his disposal to produce some kind of workable object."[24]

In contrast, engineers begin with a plan already in mind and work to design an optimal solution to the problem at hand. A trait that now has multiple functions that exert conflicting influences on design may wind up looking as if designed optimally for neither function.[25]

Adaptations, Exaptations, and Harmful Dysfunctions

The harmful dysfunction approach to psychopathology requires that we identify which features of human psychobiology qualify as adaptations in the evolutionary historical sense. Only harmful dysfunctions in these adaptations count as mental disorders.

However, not all currently useful features meet criteria as historical evolutionary adaptations. Some are spandrels, whereas others are exaptations.[26] Spandrels are originally neutral byproducts of other, naturally selected traits that have acquired current utility. For example, blushing reliably signals embarrassment in social settings today, but its current communicative function does not explain why blood is red.

Exaptations are features that evolved for one function and then acquired additional functions. The current utility of an exaptation does not explain its origin. For example, aerodynamic modeling experiments indicate that insect wings in at least some species apparently originally evolved because of their thermoregulatory function and only later became co-opted for flight.[27] Accordingly, the insect wing is an adaptation for thermoregulation but an exaptation for flight. Invoking the function of flight may explain why insect wings persist in successive lineages, but it does not explain their evolutionary origin.

The late biologist Stephen Jay Gould argued that most currently useful features of the human cognitive phenotype are exaptations, not adaptations. The mechanisms that mediate reading, writing, mathematics, music, and so forth evolved, he said, for reasons other than their current utility. Commenting on the mind, he quipped, "the list of exaptations is a mountain to the adaptive molehill."[28]

The psychologists Scott Lilienfeld and Lori Marino pointed out that if Gould is right, then the HDA is in trouble.[29] Indeed, if only harmful dysfunctions in adaptations count as disorders, then harmful dysfunctions in exaptations do not qualify. To the extent that derangements in historical adaptations alone count as disorders, the HDA will fail to capture most instances of apparent disorder.

However, the distinction between adaptations and exaptations is more arbitrary than it first appears to be. Depending on how broad or narrow we define a particular trait, and depending how far we go back in time, nearly everything qualifies as an exaptation.[30] Consider the evolution of middle-ear bones in human beings. These bones originated as gill arches in fish, then evolved into parts of the reptilian jaw, and eventually evolved into structures enabling hearing in human beings.[31] As two biologists quipped, "Breathing aids have become feeding aids, and finally hearing aids."[32] If we regard all three features as versions of the same trait, then middle-ear bones are mere exaptations for hearing because they originated for another function. If only original functions can underwrite ascription of disorder, a deaf person whose hearing loss arose from dysfunctional ear bones would not have a disorder.

In fact, as Wakefield points out, natural selection plays two roles even in exaptations.[33] First, natural selection often tweaks pre-existing structures that originated for one function, shaping them to perform the new, co-opted function as optimally as constraints allow. Second, even when the preexisting structure does not require further tinkering to assume its additional role, natural selection for the new function maintains it in the population. Feathers may have evolved because they fostered fitness in birds by supporting thermoregulation, and later became exapted by enabling flight. Stabilizing selection maintains feathers in birds today because they enable flight as well as thermoregulation. Hence the original selective pressure that fashioned the trait is not the only selective pressure that explains why the trait persists today. Feathers may have evolved for thermoregulation, but a bird that is unable to fly has a dysfunction. Whether the problem occurs in the original function or a current one, Wakefield says that the issue "becomes strictly a historical distinction with little theoretical interest."[34]

Broadening the scope of adaptation to include those traits currently maintained by selection is reasonable, but it erases the distinction between adaptation in the historical sense and current adaptiveness. If harmful dysfunction in an exaptation counts as disorder just as much as harmful dysfunction in a historical adaptation, why should we bother pondering how traits evolved in our distant hunter-gatherer past? Indeed, as Wakefield acknowledged,

"For now, detection of design failures relies mainly on intuitive judgments based on circumstantial evidence."[35] If determining the original, evolved functions of our psychobiology is both unnecessary and difficult to accomplish, why bother?

NONHISTORICAL CONCEPTUALIZATIONS OF ADAPTATION

Evolutionary psychologists and some philosophers, including Wakefield, identify the natural function of a trait with the selected effect that explains its presence today. They further argue that other perspectives on function are conceptually flawed.[36]

Their arguments, however, have become increasingly controversial in philosophy and areas of biology outside evolutionary research.[37] Indeed, defining the function of a trait in terms of its evolutionary history is by no means the only way that biologists conceptualize function. Other, nonhistorical views are common. For example, ecologists and functional morphologists define adaptation in terms of contribution to current fitness, not in terms of origin via natural selection.[38]

When studying populations in the wild, ecologists observe shifting mean values of many traits in response to selection. This makes it very difficult to distinguish the specific trait that is responding to selection from those that are merely exhibiting a correlated response. Ecologists are satisfied if natural selection has at least maintained a trait if it has the highest fitness among other options in the population of interest. Thus the biologists Hudson Reeve and Paul Sherman define an adaptation nonhistorically as "a phenotypic variant that results in the highest fitness among a specified set of variants in a given environment."[39]

A nonhistorical approach to adaptation permits behavioral ecologists to test adaptationist hypotheses experimentally. Rather than conducting longitudinal studies of differential fecundity as a function of phenotypic diversity, as Lewontin recommends, these scientists test whether alterations in presumptive phenotypic adaptations affect proxies of fertility. For example, the biologist Alexandra Basolo surgically manipulated sword length in male green swordtail fish and found that females exhibit more courting behavior with long-sworded males than with short-sworded males.[40] Although she did not track reproductive histories as a function of sword length, she nevertheless was able to document that this trait is an adaptation for attracting mates. Size does matter.

Like behavioral ecologists, functional morphologists favor a nonhistorical, viability conceptualization of adaptation.[41] For them, claims about adaptation concern which traits are essential for an organism to survive today; they are not conjectures about past selection. Without appealing to evolutionary history, they can explain the presence of a trait by showing, by experiment or otherwise, that an organism lacking the trait would not be able to survive and reproduce.

The amazing success of physiology has occurred largely in the absence of evolutionary theorizing about the origins of bodily features.[42] Ignoring evolutionary history, physiologists identify the function of a trait as the current causal role that it plays in the system of which it is a part.[43] Hence, the causal role of the heart in the circulatory system is pumping blood, not making noises useful in auscultation. The sounds made by the heart play no causal role in the circulatory system. Thus failure to pump is a dysfunction, whereas failing to make noises is not.

The current causal role approach to function and dysfunction is far more useful to psychopathologists than is the historical, evolutionary approach.[44] Although the central nervous system is vastly more complicated than the circulatory system, experimental research can disclose the causal effects of brain structures that mediate mental disorders. For example, researchers have learned that the function of the amygdala, a subcortical brain structure, is to register the emotional significance of stimuli. This is its causal, systemic contribution to the operation of the brain's emotional circuitry. In people with PTSD, this structure is overactive relative to other elements of this circuit that function to inhibit the amygdala.[45] If we replace the evolutionary definition of function with the nonhistorical, causal role definition, these findings would license a harmful dysfunction analysis of PTSD.

Understanding how psychobiological mechanisms of the mind currently work provides a foundation for psychopathology. We do not need to trace how these mechanisms evolved in our hunter-gatherer past. If we did, we'd be in trouble. We'd never get psychopathology off the ground. If harm arises from the failure of a psychological mechanism to perform its current causal role, then this alone should suffice.

To be sure, the science of psychopathology must ultimately be "based on" evolutionary biology in the same trivial sense that it must also be "based on" quantum mechanics. Fortunately, we do not need to ascertain the evolutionary history of our psychobiology as a necessary prelude to identifying harmful dysfunctions that call for treatment.

PROBLEMS WITH THE HARMFUL DYSFUNCTION ANALYSIS

According to Wakefield, the HDA is a conceptual hybrid comprising a factual dysfunction component and a value-laden harm component. By anchoring dysfunction in evolutionary history, Wakefield holds that at least part of our concept of disorder transcends norms, values, and the variable whims of cultural fashion. Hence, the presumably value-free dysfunction component puts psychopathology on a solid scientific foundation.

In reality, both components of the HDA involve factual and

normative elements. Consider the harm component. To say that someone suffers from the pain of depression is to make a factual assertion about the person. Our affirming the undesirability of depression, as Wakefield rightly emphasizes, incorporates values. Facts and values are intertwined in assertions about harm.

Although harms implicate values, this does not entail an anything-goes cultural relativism. Death, pain, impairment, inability to experience pleasure, and the loss of freedom are universal harms throughout the world.[46] No one values these harms unless there is some compensatory benefit. Even suicidal people opt for death only when they believe that there's no other exit from their pain. There is clear consensus about what constitutes harm.

Nevertheless, there can be ambiguity about the locus of harm for some disorders. Consider pedophilia. Pedophiles solely attracted to prepubescent children have a dysfunction in mechanisms of sexual attraction that precludes transmission of their genes. However, to qualify as a disorder under the HDA, this evolutionary dysfunction must result in harm for the person with the dysfunction. Yet pedophiles experience no distress about their deviation.[47] Young victims of pedophiles can certainly suffer emotional harm, but their victimizers do not. Any distress pedophiles experience concerns the prospect of arrest and imprisonment for actions stemming directly from their dysfunction. Because the harms of imprisonment directly result from an internal psychobiological dysfunction, pedophiles would qualify as disordered under the HDA, whereas ordinary criminals would not.[48]

However, the line of reasoning that certifies pedophilia as a mental disorder also certifies homosexuality as a mental disorder in societies that oppress, stigmatize, or criminalize gay people. The harms that befall them in homophobic societies directly result from "what is almost certainly an evolutionary dysfunction in their gender modularity systems," according to the evolutionary psychologists Leda Cosmides and John Tooby.[49] These hypothesized psychobiological systems determine the objects of sexual attraction. Unlike dissidents who suffer oppression for their political opinions, gay victims in homophobic societies suffer oppression as a direct consequence of what evolutionary psychologists call an evolutionary dysfunction. Ironically, Spitzer endorsed the HDA as rendering explicit the kinds of intuitions that motivated the exclusion of homosexuality from the DSM.[50] Yet the HDA would seemingly classify homosexuality as disordered in the many homophobic societies around the world.

The function component in harmful dysfunction implicates values as well as facts. To assert that a psychobiological mechanism is dysfunctional is to assert that things are not functioning as they *ought* to be, and *ought*-statements in biology are unavoidably evaluative, not merely descriptive.[51] Statements about dysfunction imply departures from a normative standard and therefore implicate values as well as facts. The mere fact that the standard of functioning arises from evolutionary speculation, not cultural or social norms, does not mean that it is nonevaluative. Because we take the values of survival and reproduction for granted, it is easy to overlook how these implicit values govern our judgments about adaptation and function. Functional ascription always presupposes a perspective.[52] In the case of the HDA, the perspective is the gene's eye view of value.

Moreover, if functional ascription were purely a factual matter, devoid of evaluative implications, then calling someone "dysfunctional" should have no pejorative implications. But this does not seem to be the case. Consider Cosmides and Tooby's claim that homosexuals, at least in a liberal society, have a dysfunction but no mental disorder. It is difficult to imagine many gay people cheerfully embracing the judgment that they are dysfunctional, albeit not disordered.

Norms infiltrate judgments of dysfunction in yet another way. The HDA requires us to have evidence that a harmful condition arose from dysfunction in an evolved psychobiological mechanism. Lacking this knowledge, we must rely on judgments of appropriateness and proportionality shaped by cultural norms. Our judgments about what counts as an unreasonable, excessive fear response to harmless insects, or about what counts as a prolonged depressive reaction following loss, rely on covert social norms.

DSM-IV prohibits clinicians from diagnosing an episode of major depression if it immediately follows the death of a loved one. Wakefield and his colleagues have argued that we should extend this grief exemption to other major stressors such as divorce and job loss.[53] Because they assume that depressive symptoms are understandable, expectable, and proportionate to the magnitude of the loss, the resultant suffering does not indicate that mechanisms of mood regulation have gone awry. Yet buried in these conclusions are unacknowledged social norms about how human beings *ought* to respond after loss.

Not everyone, however, agrees that diagnosing disorder is inappropriate in response to bereavement and other major losses. As the psychiatrist Sidney Zisook and colleagues argued, "No other life event (or precipitant) negates the diagnosis of depression when the full syndrome occurs. It is not clear why death of a loved one should cancel out the diagnosis of major depressive disorder, either."[54] The psychiatrist Peter Kramer seems to agree. Excluding episodes triggered by loss events amounts to "claiming that an episode of depression is *justified*, in a way that we would not call a bout of asthma justified even when the cause is clear."[55]

As these remarks imply, the HDA points to yet another ambiguity regarding when external stressors *prohibit* the assigning of a diagnosis and when external stressors *warrant* the assigning of a diagnosis. Wakefield allows that external stressors can cause a harmful internal dysfunction, thereby justifying a diagnosis, as in PTSD. So how can we distinguish between a normal psychobiological response to a stressor and a response that implies that the stressor has caused an internal dysfunction? At best, we can identify the precipitant and the resulting symptoms, but we often lack access to knowledge about the mediating psychobiological mechanisms. Without this knowledge, clinicians will rely on cultural norms about how they think most people respond to stressors and will draw their inferences about dysfunction accordingly. Once again, norms will infiltrate judgments about dysfunction.

Normative judgments about disproportionality can yield paradoxical conclusions. Consider someone who develops PTSD in response to a fender bender or after overhearing off-color jokes in the workplace.[56] Anyone who experienced PTSD in response to these relatively mild stressors must possess preexisting vulnerabilities that carry the causal burden of producing the symptoms. The stressor itself would recede into the causal background. Yet because the response is so disproportionate, these cases would seem to fit the HDA far better than do cases of PTSD caused by canonical traumatic stressors such as rape or combat. The most dubious cases of PTSD, precisely because the response is so disproportionate, would seem to qualify as disordered under the HDA, whereas PTSD resulting from horrific, life-threatening events would seem "justified" by the magnitude of the stressor.

Finally, another intention of the HDA is to reduce the number of false positives—people receiving a diagnosis who do not, in fact, have a disorder. Hence, the HDA should distinguish disorders from ordinary distress. If there were a gold standard for diagnosing disorder, such as a laboratory test to confirm or rule out the presence of a pathogen, the concept of false positive would have clear meaning. Unfortunately, we do not have such a test to distinguish cases of genuine major depressive disease from ordinary unhappiness.

Moreover, even if we did have such a test, rates of false positives and false negatives vary as a function of the base rate of the disease in the general population versus certain subgroups in the population.

For example, the screening test for HIV is extraordinarily accurate.[57] Among people who are infected with HIV, it correctly identifies 98 percent of them as HIV-positive. Among those not infected, it correctly identifies 99.8 percent as HIV-negative. However, because the base rate of HIV infection in the general population is so low relative to high-risk subgroups, a positive screen test on a randomly selected person will almost certainly be a false positive.

CLINICAL IMPLICATIONS OF THE HDA

Even if we assume that clinicians can identify harmful dysfunctions in the adaptations of the mind, what are the clinical implications? Wakefield emphasizes that judgments about the disorder versus nondisorder status of psychological suffering do not automatically determine treatment policy. Yet his reluctance to deny treatment to the nondisordered makes one wonder whether the HDA has any implications for clinical practice and insurance reimbursement after all. However, he and Horwitz have said, "One argument against medicalizing normal sadness is that it treats as pathological what is actually an inherent and valuable part of the human condition."[58] Sadness, like pain, directs our attention to circumstances that call for correction. But both function in the service of long-term hedonic needs. A failure to attend to the circumstances causing sadness or pain means that the person will suffer even greater pain in the future. The only advantage of experiencing sadness and pain today is to motivate us to change our behavior, reducing the likelihood of sadness and pain in the future. Even those who defend sadness on moral grounds, arguing that it deepens our humanity, presuppose *some* benefit arising from this deepening of our humanity.[59]

Further complicating matters, as the psychologist Derek Bolton observes, some recognized symptoms of mental disorder may not signify dysfunction per se, but may actually constitute maladaptive attempts to cope with dysfunctions arising elsewhere in the person's psychobiology.[60] For example, many patients with borderline personality disorder cut themselves during periods of extreme emotional distress. The physical pain may help the person escape from uncontrollable emotional pain. In these cases, the dysfunction may actually be in emotion-regulation mechanisms, not in the cutting itself. In fact, as the clinical psychologist Matthew Nock found in his ambulatory physiological monitoring study, self-cutting abruptly terminates unbearable, autonomic arousal.[61] Cutting triggers a massive activation of the parasympathetic nervous system, producing a profound soothing effect on the highly distressed self-cutter.

Locating the problem within the individual does suggest where we need to direct our intervention efforts. For example, as the psychiatrists Jacqueline Olds and Robert Schwartz emphasized, many people who seek medication for major depressive disorder suffer from social isolation and loneliness, not mental illness.[62] Given that human beings are social animals, it is doubtful whether medication or cognitive therapy to correct a conjectured internal dysfunction is what these people most need. Even if their isolation has caused an internal harmful dysfunction, it is unclear whether clinical interventions directly targeting symptoms are the most appropriate solutions.

REFORMULATING THE HARMFUL DYSFUNCTION ANALYSIS

Such criticisms notwithstanding, a reformulated version of the HDA can help us navigate the field of psychopathology. First, we should acknowledge that values and norms affect both imputation of function (and dysfunction) and judgments of harm. But that's okay. Unlike physical scientists, biologists and psychologists traffic in functions and dysfunctions and thus values and norms. Functional ascription presupposes a perspective, and, for the applied disciplines of psychiatry, clinical psychology, and social work, that perspective is one unabashedly committed to the alleviation of unnecessary emotional suffering. Values are integral to identifying dysfunctions and harms, but this does not undermine the factual basis of the enterprise, rendering it somehow hopelessly subjective and unscientific.

Second, psychopathologists should replace the evolutionary concept of function with the current causal role concept of function. Physiologists, psychologists, and cognitive neuroscientists care little for the evolutionary history of the psychobiological mechanisms mediating the mind. Their aim is to figure out how things work, not how they evolved, and clinical psychopathologists aim to find out how things get broken. To be sure, evolutionary speculation can yield heuristic benefits, but it is unnecessary to underwrite psychopathology.

Wakefield, of course, endorses research on how mechanisms of the mind operate today and how they go wrong. He also acknowledges the near inaccessibility of solid evidence about how these mechanisms evolved.[63] Yet he argues that the current causal role theory of function often violates our intuitions and hence fails to provide a suitable basis for discriminating function from dysfunction and disorder from nondisorder. For example, he says that it would compel us to conclude that the function of clouds in the water cycle is to produce rain, violating our intuitions about functions. However, no scientist is tempted to ascribe such functions to components of nonorganic systems anyway.[64] The important standard for evaluating different approaches to function is whether they help us understand the mechanisms of the mind and how they go wrong. Whether the approach can rebut hypothetical counterexamples that violate our intuitions is far less important.

Wakefield also believes that only an evolutionary approach to function can furnish standards of normality for identifying dysfunctions. Others disagree.[65] The philosopher of science Paul Wachbroit points out that models of normality in biology resemble idealized, model systems in the physical sciences.[66] Claims about normal functions and structures in biology appeal to a standard of normality akin to these model systems. Models of the central nervous system, the circulatory system, the immune system, and so forth are idealizations that represent integrated components making causal contributions to systems hierarchically organized in a human being. These models do not represent the statistical average of existing systems. Rather, they provide the conceptual template for the construction of more detailed, realistic models of these systems. For example, dentists possess an idealized model of human teeth enabling them recognize departures from this model, some of which have harmful consequences (for example, cavities). Model systems in biology do not appeal to the evolutionary history of their constituent components. Yet they provide a basis for identifying departures from the norm.

Assuming that these idealizations enable us to recognize when a heart, a tooth, or a brain structure differs from the model, how do we decide when a difference is a dysfunction? Indeed, there is considerable variability among people in the structure and function of the elements constituting emotional circuits in the brain, for example. When does a departure become a dysfunction?

Neuroimaging research by the clinical psychologist Jill Hooley and her colleagues exemplifies how to answer this question.[67] Hooley and others had shown that people with a history of major depression often suffer relapses when they live with hypercritical family members.[68] Hooley was keen to discover how the psychosocial variable of criticism gets under the skin of formerly depressed patients, rendering them vulnerable to relapse.

To answer this question, she had healthy control subjects and previously depressed women listen to audiotaped comments re-corded by their mothers. Mothers provided a neutral comment, a positive comment, and a critical comment about their daughters. Hooley audiotaped these remarks and played them back to subjects while they were in a brain scanner. In response to hearing criticism, relative to control subjects, the formerly depressed subjects exhib-ited greater activation of the amygdala and less activation of the dorsal lateral prefrontal cortex (DLPFC), a structure whose projec-tions to the amygdala attenuate emotional overreactivity. Hooley characterized the different pattern of activation in the formerly de-pressed group as abnormal.

However, the brain data alone show only a statistically sig-nificant difference between the groups. If we knew nothing about the audiotaped stimulus or nothing about the characteristics of the two groups, we would be unable to identify which pattern of ac-tivation was the abnormal one. Only knowledge about the meaning of the message and the different histories of depression in the two groups, coupled with knowledge about the brain circuitry, enabled Hooley to identify the pattern in the formerly depressed group as abnormal.

In sum, the HDA embodies one of two evolutionary approaches to psychopathology. Rather than identifying psychopathology as harmful dysfunctions in evolved psychobiological mechanisms, the second evolutionary approach interprets much of what we call psychopathology as serious mismatches between properly func-tioning mechanisms and contemporary environments drastically different from those in which these mechanisms evolved. Psycho-pathology as adaptation is the focus of the next chapter.

4

Evolutionary theorizing in the field of psychopathology extends beyond conceptualizing mental disorders as harmful dysfunctions in the evolved psychobiological mechanisms of the mind. A drastically different approach holds that mental disorders are *themselves* evolved adaptations rather than dysfunctions in adaptations. This perspective has clinical implications radically different from the first theory, exemplified by Wakefield's HDA. The HDA implies that clinicians must correct dysfunctions in evolved adaptations, thereby restoring mental health. In contrast, the second evolutionary approach implies that clinicians must tread lightly if mental disorders have adaptive significance. Treatment may interfere with the operation of adaptive coping mechanisms, only making matters worse.

THE EVOLUTIONARY PARADOX OF MENTAL ILLNESS

Mental disorders are very common. Yet they are also harmful and heritable. Why, then, hasn't natural selection eliminated them? Why haven't the genes that predispose people to develop schizophrenia, depression, and other psychiatric conditions disappeared from the gene pool?

One possible answer is that natural selection does not optimize outcomes, and so there is little reason to expect that human nature would be free of foibles, quirks, and mental disorders. Natural selection operates within constraints, tinkering with the material at hand, resulting in the most adaptive outcome among competing variants, or perhaps the least maladaptive. If you think about it, human beings are susceptible to developing all kinds of physical maladies, and selection hasn't eliminated the vulnerability genes for those, either.

Many common diseases, such as dementia, strike people later in life, long after their childbearing years are over, and would therefore be invisible to selection. Most mental disorders, however, emerge in childhood or early adulthood and often diminish fertility, mainly because they make it difficult to find a mate. They are common, heritable, and harmful, yet they have withstood natural selection. This is the central paradox of mental illness from an evolutionary perspective.[1]

Scientists have proposed several solutions to this riddle that vary in plausibility. Here I consider the arguments and the evidence for these proposals and make the case for the most convincing one.

Mental Disorders Are Harmful

The capacity for physical pain is an adaptation. Children born with congenital insensitivity to pain are at high risk for early death because the warning system that alerts them to danger does not function as it should.[2] Likewise, fever, coughing, and vomiting are themselves defenses against threats to health, not diseases in their own right.[3]

The capacity to experience sadness, fear, and anger, as well as joy, surely counts as an adaptation that provides vital feedback for navigating throughout the world.[4] Sadness, for example, signals failure of goal attainment, motivating people to alter either their goals or the means of achieving them.[5]

Nature does not care whether we are happy. It "cares" only that we survive long enough to transmit copies of our genes to offspring who, in turn, survive long enough to propagate them further. Anything that advances the interests of these genes in us and in our kin fosters inclusive fitness—the capacity to survive, reproduce, and transmit our genes—and anything that detracts from these interests is harmful by evolutionary standards. It is in this sense of harm that mental disorders pose an evolutionary puzzle. Moreover, we must not confuse fitness in this genetic, evolutionary sense with fitness in the sense of psychosocial adaptation to our environment. What is "good" for our genes need not be good for us.

Multiple lines of evidence confirm that mental disorders undermine fitness. Unlike disorders that emerge during the post-reproductive years and thus pose no puzzle, most psychiatric disorders begin in either early childhood or during the reproductive years.[6] Schizophrenia, alcoholism, and mood disorders greatly increase risk for suicide.[7] Approximately 10–15 percent of people with depression eventually kill themselves.[8] Strikingly, Americans are far more likely to die by suicide than by homicide.[9] Suicide is the eleventh most common cause of death, whereas homicide ranks fifteenth. Between 1 and 2 percent of all deaths each year in the United States are attributable to suicide, and up to 70 percent of those who kill themselves are suffering from a depressive illness.[10]

Mental disorders increase risk for other serious medical problems. Depression, for example, dysregulates the immune system, increases risk for coronary disease, and is associated with possibly adverse morphological changes in the brain.[11] Finally, people with serious mental disorders have lower fertility rates, as noted.[12] Given this evidence, the evolutionary harmfulness of mental disorders seems uncontroversial.

Mental Disorders Are Heritable

People do not inherit mental disorders; they inherit genes that code for proteins whose downstream consequences can result in mental disorders. Environmental input activates genes, initiating the process that produces these protein products. Except in rare instances, such as Huntington's disease, genes do not foreordain the emergence of disorder. Genetic determinism—the notion that a certain gene or genes invariably cause the emergence of disease irrespective of environment—is rarely true for neuropsychiatric conditions. Rather, the presence of versions of certain genes increases the probability that disease will develop.

People vary in their vulnerability to developing mental disorders. What's more, risk for psychiatric illness is more attributable to differences in people's genes than to differences in their environment. Mental disorders have multiple causes, including environmental inputs that activate genetic predispositions. For example, a person must consume alcohol in order to develop alcoholism, and an individual must be exposed to trauma to develop PTSD. Until someone begins drinking or encounters traumatic stressors, the vulnerability for alcohol dependence or PTSD remains dormant. Most people who drink or who experience serious stressors develop neither disorder, thereby implying that differences in genes account for differences in vulnerability.

The evidence for genetic influence on risk for mental illness is overwhelming.[13] Monozygotic (identical) twins are more likely to develop the same mental disorder than are dizygotic (fraternal) twins. This holds true for many conditions, including schizophrenia, bipolar disorder, autism, and panic disorder. The stronger the genetic relationship between two people, the more likely they are to develop the same disorder. Adopted or foster children reared in a family with a mentally ill parent are not at heightened risk for developing the mental disorder, whereas the biological offspring of the ill parent are. This implies that adverse rearing conditions, resulting from the ill parent, are insufficient to produce the disorder in the unrelated child.

At the same time, genes are not destiny. The Finnish psychiatrist Pekka Tienari found that the offspring of mothers with schizophrenia spectrum disorders who had grown up in healthy adoptive families were no more at risk for developing these disorders than were adoptees of mothers without them. However, the offspring of mothers with schizophrenia did fall ill far more often when they grew up in dysfunctional adoptive homes, whereas the offspring of healthy biological mothers did not.[14] Hence, dysfunctional families cannot create schizophrenia in children unless they possess genes that make them vulnerable to the illness. Moreover, a healthy rearing environment has a protective effect on children who do possess these genes.

Genetic differences among people occur because there are different versions, or alleles, of some genes. Whereas a monomorphic gene comes in only one version, a polymorphic gene comes in two or more versions. The vast majority of genes are monomorphic and hence identical for everyone. Monomorphic genes provide the genetic basis for the universal aspects of human nature such as the capacity to acquire language. Polymorphic genes provide the genetic basis for differences among people, including differential vulnerability to mental disorders.

Answers to the evolutionary paradox must lie with our polymorphic genes. Different alleles usually vary in their fitness, averaged across time and across environments. That is, those who possess a certain allele are more likely to leave more viable, fertile offspring than are those who lack the allele. Natural selection tends to reduce allelic variation for a specific gene by favoring the allele having the greatest fitness. Eventually this version goes to fixation, becoming the sole version of that gene in the population. If variant alleles do not vary in average fitness, then they will continue to co-exist in the population. If people with blue eyes are no more or less likely to have fertile offspring than are people with brown eyes, then alleles responsible for different eye colors will persist in the gene pool.

Polymorphic genes result from mutation. A mutant allele arises when a gene is "incorrectly" copied. The overwhelming majority of mutant alleles are harmful, reducing fitness. Mutations are random events, and just as randomly altering the code of a computer program rarely improves its function, so mutations seldom increase fitness, and usually reduce it. But every now and then a mutant allele does increase the fitness of those who carry it, and it will spread throughout the population, moving quickly toward fixation. Random mutation followed by selection produces evolutionary change.

That most genes are monomorphic is testament to the power of natural selection. Competition among allelic variants quickly results in a winner that dominates the gene pool. Less fit variants go quickly to extinction. Herein lies the core of the paradox: given the efficiency of natural selection at eliminating fitness-reducing alleles, why do susceptibility alleles for mental disorder persist in the gene pool? The puzzle is not why people are not optimally adapted but why genes for such dramatically maladaptive traits as mental disorders remain so common.

Natural selection, by favoring allelic variants that foster fitness more than others do, tends to diminish genetic variation in the population. That is why the heritability of adaptations—universal features of the human phenotype—tends to be zero. Heritability refers to the proportion of the variance in a phenotypic trait in a population that is attributable to genetic variance among members of that population. If every member of the population possesses the same allele for a certain gene, the heritability is 0 percent. Any variation in the trait would be attributable solely to environmental differences. For example, human beings possess two ears, implying that the relevant genes responsible for having two intact ears are monomorphic. When people are missing their ears, or parts of them, some environmental cause must be responsible for this variation, as the cases of Vincent van Gogh and Evander Holyfield illustrate. The terms *heritability* and *inherited* mean different things. Everyone inherits the genes that result in (nearly) everyone's having two ears. Yet because there is almost no difference among the genes resulting in two ears across people in the population, the heritability of having two ears is effectively zero.

Heritability is a population statistic; it concerns differences *among* people. It does not apply at the level of a single person. When psychologists estimate that the heritability of IQ is about 60 percent, they mean that 60 percent of the differences among people in their IQ scores result from differences among people in their genes. It does not mean that a certain person's IQ score is 60 percent caused by his or her genes and 40 percent caused by his or her environment. A person's IQ results from both genes and environment, and the effects of each are inseparable at the level of the person. Likewise, it would make no sense to ask whether the area of a rectangle is due more to its width than to its height. Its width and height contribute inseparably to its area.

Heritability varies as a function of the environment. If there are relatively few differences among people in their environments, phenotypic differences among them can only be attributable to differences in their genes. By definition, then, as environments become more standardized, heritability increases. For example, if we provided uniformly excellent education to children throughout America, remaining differences in their performance on standardized academic tests would be more attributable to genetic differences among the children than is the case today. If we were to diminish environmental variance, the heritability of their test performance would necessarily increase.

Mental Disorders Are Common

Relative to other genetic diseases, mental disorders are extremely common.[15] Consider these facts. In the United States, the odds that someone will develop juvenile-onset Parkinson's disease are less than one per 100,000 people. By contrast, out of every 100,000 people, 1,000 will develop schizophrenia and 800 will develop bipolar disorder. The risk of clinical depression is even greater, with estimates ranging from 5,000 to 17,000 individuals per 100,000.

About 2 percent of genetic diseases are Mendelian. Mendelian diseases occur when a person inherits two copies of an aberrant allele at a single locus. In these cases, the deviant allele is recessive such that a carrier who has one deviant allele and one normal one at that genetic locus will be phenotypically normal. The normal, dominant allele overrides the otherwise harmful influence of the aberrant recessive allele. However, if two individuals, each heterozygous at this genetic locus, have children, 25 percent of their offspring on average will unluckily inherit a copy of the aberrant allele from each parent. The person homozygous for both aberrant recessive alleles will express the disease phenotype.

A mutation-selection model can explain why rare, Mendelian diseases persist in the population. The relevant gene undergoes mutation at a certain low rate, and natural selection will eliminate these new alleles from the gene pool at a rate proportional to their cost to fitness. That is, the greater the reduction in the likelihood of producing fertile offspring, the greater the fitness cost associated with the allele and the faster it will disappear from the population. The most serious fitness costs occur when disease alleles prevent carriers from living long enough to reproduce. Selection eliminates these variants from the gene pool with ruthless efficiency. Disease alleles that exact less harmful consequences disappear at a slower rate. So if the mutation rate for the relevant gene stays one step ahead of selection, then the disease will persist in the population at a very low, stable frequency. Accordingly, Mendelian diseases pose no paradox for evolutionary theory.

Mental disorders, by contrast, are an entirely different matter. They are hundreds to thousands of times more common than are Mendelian diseases.[16] In the not-too-distant past, psychopathologists hypothesized that certain mental disorders might very well be characterized by a Mendelian pattern of transmission. Single-gene models are implausible, however, because the high prevalence of mental disorders is much greater than the prevalence of Mendelian diseases. Vulnerability to schizophrenia, bipolar disorder, and similar conditions likely arises from the contribution of many genes, not one single aberrant one. Still, why hasn't natural selection eliminated these multiple, aberrant alleles?

ARE MENTAL DISORDERS ADAPTATIONS?

One possibility is that susceptibility alleles for mental disorder had either neutral or even positive effects on fitness in ancestral environments. Some theorists have interpreted the signs and symptoms of psychiatric illness as adaptations (or exaggerations thereof) to the ancestral hunter-gatherer environment. To explain why something as currently maladaptive as schizophrenia or depression abides today, some theorists assume that these illnesses must have yielded adaptive benefits. As the psychiatrist Randolph Nesse and the biologist George Williams put it, "the genes that cause schizophrenia (and other severe mental disorders) must somehow confer an advantage that balances the severe costs."[17] The psychiatrists Anthony Stevens and John Price argued, "The reason why depression is adaptive, is precisely because it promotes adjustment to attachment loss and loss of rank, both at the same time."[18] That is, depression would presumably help people emotionally disengage from irrevocable losses (for example, of a loved one or a valued job). These theorists represent the second of two major evolutionary approaches to psychopathology.[19] Rather than construing psychopathology as dysfunction in an evolved adaptation, as Wakefield does, they regard at least some forms of psychopathology as adaptations themselves.

A related possibility is that mental disorders evolved as an adaptation to ancestral circumstances radically different from those of postindustrial society. An adaptation to the hunter-gatherer environment might constitute a mismatch with today's environment. Evolutionary theorists have adduced convincing examples of such medical mismatches.[20] Consider obesity. The energy needs of our hunter-gatherer ancestors were great, and the risk of starvation was always present. Hence, natural selection favored a taste for high-calorie foods that is still with us today. This adaptation, so vital in the past, is no longer so important in the postindustrial world where human energy needs have eased and food abounds. It is an adaptation whose consequences today are often harmful, as the obesity epidemic illustrates. Diabetes, high blood pressure, and other medical problems are the indirect effects of an adaptation's functioning precisely as designed.

Is our capacity for depression like this? Despite its manifestly harmful effects, did it once increase fitness in ancestral environments? Does it persist today as a vestige of our hunter-gatherer past? Or does it continue to promote fitness even today? Perhaps a major depressive episode fosters fitness by underscoring a person's need to stop pursuing unachievable goals. Consider a young person whose depression arises in a terrible marriage. The pain of depression would curtail unrealistic optimism about the odds of the marriage surviving, thereby signaling to the person the need to escape. A capacity to experience depression might have evolved because it yielded fitness benefits by directing people away from hopeless pursuits and toward those likely to pay off.

Theorists who speculate about the adaptive significance of depression and other mental disorders run the risk of falling prey to the Panglossian error.[21] According to the biologists Stephen Jay Gould and Richard Lewontin, the Panglossian theorist conceptualizes all anatomical, physiological, and behavioral capacities of the organism as adaptations to selection pressures operative throughout the course of evolution. Interpreting these features as optimal solutions to environmental problems, they strive to discover how (not if) a given feature has served an adaptive function and contributed to fitness. Panglossians conceptually parse organisms into component features (for example, capacities, structures), each having naturally selected functions that foster fitness and survival. The unavoidable trade-offs among responses to conflicting selection pressures provide the only limit on perfection of each component. Any apparent suboptimality (say, an agoraphobic patient's irrational avoidance of venturing into public spaces) can be explained by formulating an adaptive scenario that shows how the suboptimal feature contributes to optimal overall design, thereby fostering survival (in the case of the agoraphobic patient, avoiding predators or hostile hunter-gatherer groups).[22]

Although Gould and Lewontin emphasize that natural selection is certainly the most important evolutionary mechanism for explaining complex design, other mechanisms are also operative. Accordingly, they urge scientists to test other hypotheses in addition to adaptationist ones.

What might these hypotheses be? Some currently adaptive features may originate as neutral architectural by-products (that is, spandrels) of other, naturally selected features.[23] Noses usefully support eyeglasses, but this does not explain why human beings have noses. Other features that evolved for one reason may later acquire additional useful functions (exaptations).[24] However, even if certain features originate as spandrels or exaptations, natural selection might still explain their persistence in the population.

Some features may have either neutral or negative consequences yet persist because of their genetic linkage to adaptive traits. If genes predisposing a person to depression, phobia, schizophrenia, and similar disorders reside on the same chromosome in close proximity to genes controlling crucial adaptive functions, selection pressures will favor the persistence of the disorder despite its deleterious effects. That is, genetic linkage can result in selection *of* a mental disorder in the absence of selection *for* it.[25] Merely because natural selection has not eliminated risk genes for mental disorders does not mean that mental disorders themselves are adaptations.

Moreover, pleiotropy—multiple effects of a single gene—may explain the persistence of psychiatric symptoms without the symptoms themselves constituting adaptations. A new mutation is likely to have diverse effects throughout the lifetime of a carrier, and the probability that all effects will be beneficial is negligible. If the mutation confers fitness benefits early in life, it will tend to propagate through a lineage even if it has lethal consequences late in life. Genes predisposing people to bipolar disorders may also foster energy, creative thinking, and socially valued achievement.[26]

Finally, genes can become fixed within a species because of genetic drift even though they provide no fitness benefit.[27] Genetic drift refers to random fluctuation of different alleles in (usually) a small, isolated population when alternative forms are indistinguishable from one another in terms of their relative fitness effects.

If alternative forms of the gene are selectively neutral, one may predominate over the other forms.

Evolutionary psychologists have expressed exasperation with Gould and Lewontin's critique, claiming that the Panglossian theorist is little more than a caricature of the scientist who applies adaptationist reasoning carefully. As Steven Pinker put it, "Needless to say, there is no such madman. A sane person can believe that a complex organ is an adaptation, that is, a product of natural selection, while also believing that features of an organism that are *not* complex organs are a product of drift or a by-product of some other adaptation."[28]

Evolutionary psychologists object to Gould and Lewontin's dismissal of their approach as nothing more than cranking out untestable "Just-So" stories about how some phenotypic feature evolved as an ancestral adaptation.[29] The best work in the field has always generated testable hypotheses.[30]

For example, the evolutionary psychologist Leda Cosmides used an adaptationist framework to formulate and test predictions about how people reason in contexts concerning reciprocal cooperation.[31] In a series of laboratory experiments, she tested and refuted alternative nonadaptationist hypotheses. Her findings led her to conclude that people have an evolved heightened capacity—a cheater-detection module—to reason in these contexts. Hence, an evolutionary, adaptationist framework enabled her to discover new facts about cognition. At its best, this approach is a powerful heuristic about the mind. Formulating adaptationist hypotheses should be the beginning, not the end, of inquiry.

Does this mean that the Panglossian critique is nothing more than an attack on a straw man? No, it does not. To be sure, its dismissal of all extant evolutionary approaches to human behavior and cognition is far too sweeping, bordering on caricature. But there are many instances where theorists, including psychopathologists, have generated evolutionary explanations for some aspect of human behavior rather than using the evolutionary approach as a heuristic for discovery. The Panglossian error often crops up in psychopathology.

For example, phobia theorists have often assumed that people possess an evolved predisposition to develop fears of situations and animals that posed survival threats to our hunter-gatherer ancestors.[32] Because many people fear spiders, these theorists have assumed that spiders must have presented threats to our ancestors just as snakes or heights would have posed. Yet only 0.1 percent of the world's spider varieties are potentially harmful to human beings.[33] It is difficult to see why people would have developed a predator-defense system for defending against these creatures. Far more spiders die each year at the hands (or feet) of human beings than vice versa. In nearly all lethal encounters between a spider and a human being, the spider loses.[34]

IS DEPRESSION AN ADAPTATION?

Many people throughout the world suffer from depression, and many have suffered from it throughout history. It clearly exacts costs on those who struggle with it. People with major depression experience intense suffering, impaired immune function, social impairment, and sometimes die by their own hand. To be sure, pleiotropy might account for why some suboptimal traits might persist, but depression is not merely suboptimal; it can be fatal.

Yet natural selection has not eliminated susceptibility genes for depression. Is it, then, possible that depression itself is an adaptation, favored by natural selection? Indeed, the very fact that it has not been eliminated by selection seems to imply that it might have had hidden fitness benefits for our hunter-gatherer ancestors that outweigh its obvious costs. As the psychologist Alison Longley said, "we can say with confidence that depression is an adaptation—the result of eons of positive selection."[35]

Has the capacity to experience depression itself been favored by natural selection? Its manifest personal costs notwithstanding, depression itself may be an adaptation for coping with certain adverse circumstances. Evolutionary psychopathologists have formulated theories whose central claim is just that.

Postpartum Depression as an Adaptation

The anthropologist Edward Hagen has proposed an evolutionary theory of postpartum depression inspired by the concepts of inclusive fitness and parental investment in offspring. He argues that postpartum depression "shows evidence of having been designed by natural selection to solve three important problems of the puerperium, and is therefore not an illness, but an adaptation."[36] Evolved mechanisms foster the propagation of genes by motivating people to further their interests and those of their biological relatives. People must allocate their inevitably limited resources, time, and energy as optimally as possible. They can invest in somatic effort (activities essential for one's own survival, such as securing food) or in reproductive effort (producing children who survive to reproductive age). In terms of reproduction, they can distribute their effort between securing mates and rearing offspring. Hagen points out that if parental investment in offspring can occur only at the expense of investing in mating efforts or investing in oneself, then parents must decide how best to allocate their limited resources—to themselves, to searching for mates, or to caring for their children. The upshot is that investing resources in a new baby makes evolutionary sense only to the extent that doing so fosters one's net inclusive fitness. If the child is unlikely to survive to reproductive age, then spending effort, time, and resources may detract from the mother's inclusive fitness by draining resources from maintaining her own health and well-being and that of her other children. Parental investment would then predict that sickly newborns are more likely to be victims of infanticide than are robust ones. If the child's viability strongly depends on paternal investment, then gauging the degree of investment of the father can influence the mother's assessment of her own investment in the child.

Assuming that the psychological pain of postpartum depression is an evolved signal to the mother regarding a threat to her inclusive fitness, Hagen points out that certain facts about postpartum depression fit his evolutionary theory. Variables associated with diminished viability predict postpartum depression (difficult birth, prematurity, low birth weight), as do variables associated with diminished paternal investment (marital conflict). Caring for infants of dubious viability imposes fitness costs on the mother, and signs of reduced investment on the part of the father and other kin likewise signal additional costs to the mother. Depressed mood in response to these circumstances informs the mother that fitness costs are exceeding fitness benefits. Features of postpartum depression include loss of interest in the child, plus accompanying self-reproach. Full-blown depression, hypothesizes Hagen, represents a convincing cry for increased investment from spouse and other kin. The signs and symptoms of depression, including failure to care for oneself, let alone one's infant, indicate to others that the depressed mother is poised to defect from child rearing, thereby impairing the fitness of those sharing genes with the infant, including the father.

Postpartum depression is not a conscious strategy for extracting concessions and resources from others. Rather, evolution has shaped mechanisms to respond as if the mother were consciously making this decision. Postpartum depression, Hagen says, is akin to factory workers' going on strike. As he put it, when the depressed mother loses interest in her own welfare, she "is making a very credible threat of defecting from cooperative endeavors that others find reproductively beneficial."[37]

Hagen's account is typical of thoughtful adaptationist reasoning in psychopathology. That is, he does not use an evolutionary framework to predict novel facts about postpartum depression. Indeed, the clinical phenomenon is well known. Instead, he formulates an explanation of why it might persist despite its obvious emotional costs. Some critics might dismiss it as a "Just-So Story" designed to explain known facts rather than to predict new ones. Yet it is a testable theory. For example, the occurrence of postpartum depression, irrespective of independent measures of resource availability, would refute the theory. The actress Brooke Shields developed a severe postpartum depression despite abundant resources ensuring the well-being of her child. Her case runs counter to the theory that this syndrome is an adaptation.

Depression as an Adaptation for Social Navigation

According to Paul Watson and Paul Andrews's social navigation hypothesis, depression in general, not just the postpartum variety, remains as adaptive today as it was in the ancestral environment.[38] Emotional pain is a signal to the sufferer, alerting him or her to an urgent social problem posing a threat to fitness. The pain of depression motivates the person to devise solutions to the problem.

Depression, they believe, has motivational and cognitive functions. Depression motivates the sufferer to change his behavior lest fitness be imperiled, and it motivates family and friends to change their behavior in ways that alleviate fitness threats to the sufferer.

Depression places burdens on these social partners, and it may extract concessions from them that they might otherwise be disinclined to make. This implies that especially severe depressions will strike those experiencing conflicts with family members. Even the propensity to attempt suicide counts as an adaptation. As a form of evolutionary brinksmanship, it places the sufferer in mortal peril. But the seriousness of the attempt provides an unmistakably urgent signal to social partners that something must be done.

Watson and Andrews also argue that depression serves a cognitive function. It focuses the attention of the depressed person on the stressful situation, thereby fostering problem solving that corrects the challenging fitness threat. They interpret many symptoms as supporting this function. Loss of the capacity to experience pleasure (anhedonia), they believe, prevents the person from being distracted by positive incentives that might delay resolution of the problem.

Watson and Andrews likewise interpret diminished activity, social interaction, and psychomotor retardation as further evidence that depression functions to focus the person's attention on solving the social problem. Although depressed people perform poorly on many cognitive tasks, Watson and Andrews see these impairments as further evidence that depressives are deploying limited resources on matters far more important, namely, solving the fitness-threatening social problem. Moreover, they argue, depressed people have cognitive styles that foster fresh solutions. They cite studies on depressive realism that suggest that depressed people are "sadder but wiser" than nondepressed people, who have inflated self-concepts and exhibit overly optimistic, unrealistic appraisals of their environment.[39]

Depression, as noted, motivates social partners, who share a fitness interest in the sufferer's well-being, to come to the aid of the depressed person. This implies that the severity of depression should be greatest when a person is in conflict with intimate partners. Symptoms of depression are social signals to partners, warning them to change their behavior. The more serious the signal and potential cost to the signaling person, the greater the motivational impact on partners with fitness interest in the person.

Watson and Andrews elucidate the clinical implications of their theory. If depression is an adaptation for solving difficult, fitness-threatening social problems, then directly reducing symptoms may indirectly imperil fitness by short-circuiting the problem-solving process. Consider a woman married to an inattentive or perhaps abusive spouse. A doctor who diagnoses her with major depressive disorder and prescribes medication for her symptoms may be making a mistake, under Watson and Andrews's theory. In fact, they point out, DSM-IV-TR already prohibits the diagnosis of depression in a person who has just lost a loved one. Just as acute grief does not indicate disease requiring treatment, depression triggered by fitness-threatening stressors would be equally unwise to treat.

Antidepressant medication, they believe, may undermine patients' ability to navigate and influence their social environments and, in turn, reduce the chances that they will make changes necessary to increase the quality of their lives. As Watson and Andrews put it, "it may be best to let depression work its miserable yet potentially adaptive magic on the social network under protective supervision [of the therapist]."[40] Medication should not be prescribed unless the therapist is attuned to helping the patient discover and solve the social problems that incited the depression in the first place. Medication, they say, must "not be allowed to emasculate the ruminative and motivational functions of a potentially adaptive depression."[41]

Social Competition Theory of Depression

John Price and his colleagues proposed a social competition theory of depression.[42] They theorized that the capacity for depression evolved during the hunter-gatherer stage of human evolution when small bands of individuals, often related, lived in small groups. Status hierarchies emerging in these groups influenced access to food, mates, and other vital resources. Competition for these resources resulted in winners and losers. Losers encountered two undesirable options: loss of status within the group or outright expulsion from the group—the latter being a fatal consequence. The emergence of depression signaled to the loser the importance of conceding defeat to a powerful competitor, accepting the loss, and thus a lower place in the status hierarchy. Continuing to compete when one could not plausibly win made no sense. Depression, then, is an adaptation that ensures that losers in social competition accept their loss, thereby preventing their fatal ejection from the group. It reflects the operation of a mechanism for yielding in response to loss.

Social competition theorists have suggested that *clinical* depression may emerge only when the person has failed to surrender when losing in the social competition. To be sure, success in the struggle for higher status would have clear-cut fitness benefits in the form of a greater quantity and quality of resources. Yet persistence in an unwinnable battle might have fatal consequences, such as expulsion from the group. Given the alternative, accepting one's lower rank is the lesser of two evils.

INTERIM CRITIQUE AND CLINICAL IMPLICATIONS

Attempts to explain mental disorders as adaptations have met with mixed success. On the positive side, theorists have identified common triggers for depression as situations that would have threatened inclusive fitness in ancestral environments. Relationship breakup, conflicts with spouses and children, and occupational failure are social stressors that often precede depression today. But does this tell us anything that we didn't know before? In response, evolutionary theorists contend that the reason these stressors are especially likely to trigger depression is that such stressors would have imperiled fitness in the ancestral environment.

What's novel about evolutionary accounts is that they propose that depression evolved *because* it functioned to remove threats to fitness in ancestral populations. The psychic pain of depression motivates behavioral change that ultimately increases inclusive fitness, they say. Depression, then, does not signify a breakdown in function.

This hypothesis seems more plausible for depressed *mood* than for the syndrome of clinical depression. Changes in mood may provide feedback to people as they pursue their goals. Yet there is far more to clinical depression than sad mood. Clinically depressed people experience guilt, shame, anxiety, and anger in addition to sadness, and in especially severe depression, the person may complain of feeling emotionally dead rather than intensely sad. Moreover, anhedonia entails nonreactivity of mood to incentives. Anhedonic people fail to respond to stimuli that would otherwise elicit pleasure. The fatigue and passivity of depressed people impede their ability to get their lives back on track.

The claim that depressed people are sadder but wiser arose mainly from studies of college students whose scores on the Beck Depression Inventory were elevated but below levels suggestive of clinical depression.[43] This depressive-realism effect has often failed to replicate.[44] More important, suicidally depressed patients exhibit marked deficits in interpersonal problem solving, and these improve upon recovery from their illness.[45] These findings contradict the notion that depression somehow confers greater ability to solve social problems.

Some theorists have speculated about the possible adaptive significance of certain symptoms in terms of energy conservation. They regard reduced activity and social withdrawal as adaptive. But these symptoms do not replenish depressed people. In fact, precisely the opposite occurs. Loss of appetite, inability to sleep, and psychomotor agitation all contribute to feelings of exhaustion and leaden fatigue. Moreover, depressed people have chronically elevated activity in the hypothalamic-pituitary-adrenal (HPA) axis.[46] They are physiologically hyperaroused as their high levels of circulating stress hormones indicate.

Although resolution of the social problems that incited the episode can certainly aid recovery from depression, this is not always true. Individuals who suffer a depressive episode are also at increased risk of suffering another depression, and later episodes are increasingly less likely to be triggered by stressors.[47] Depression is often either chronic or recurrent, and seemingly decoupled from the kinds of threats to inclusive fitness that evolutionary theorists propose that depression is designed to solve. Depression has all the earmarks of an autonomous disease whereby mechanisms of mood regulation are outright dysfunctional.

And, of course, there is suicide risk. Suicide attempts may have the adventitious consequence of eliciting help from kin, but it is doubtful that suicidal tendencies evolved as an adaptation to recruit resources to foster one's fitness. The anguish of seemingly inescapable pain leads people to take their own lives, and many victims conceal their suicidal plans from members of their social network. Others have no social network from which to recruit resources, and so there is no one who might respond to suicidal cries for help. Suicidal behavior reflects a fatal breakdown in evolved mechanisms for regulating mood, not an evolved adaptation itself.

We can acknowledge that emotions and moods are evolved adaptations without conceding that clinical syndromes are as well. The capacity to experience sadness and other emotions is universal. Except in psychopaths, whose capacity to experience guilt is impaired or absent, the capacity to experience emotions is universal and a credible adaptation. Yet proneness to experience clinical depression varies greatly, and genetic differences at least as much as environmental differences account for this variability.

Regarding clinical implications, the psychiatrists Robert Gregory and Ripu Jindal ask, "If depression is adaptive, could its treatment be maladaptive?" They conjecture that "when severe depression is serving an adaptive purpose for the patient, improvement in depressive symptoms results in net harm."[48] These comments illustrate the divergence between inclusive fitness and personal well-being. What is "good" for the patient's genes may not be "good" for the patient, as most evolutionary psychologists fully recognize.[49] Most people suffering from severe depression are more concerned with recovering than with spreading their genes to the next generation. There is no necessary connection between what is good for our genes and what is good for us as persons. For example, because our genes are selfish does not mean that we must be.

Gregory and Jindal's remarks are reminiscent of the naturalistic fallacy—the belief that whatever is "natural" must be "good."[50] But cancer, heart disease, and other devastating illnesses are natural, and yet no one assumes that we should permit them to run their course, killing patients in the process. Nature does not prescribe what we should do. We cannot derive an "ought" from an "is."

But even though nature does not stipulate what we should do, clinical aims that run counter to our biology may be difficult to achieve and may yield tragic results, as the case of David Reimer illustrates.[51] Reimer's doctor botched his circumcision, seriously damaging his penis. Clinicians, convinced that the social environment overrides biology and molds gender identity, persuaded Reimer's parents to rear him as a girl. The psychologist John Money described Reimer's case as a success, adducing it as evidence that nurture trumps nature. In reality, Reimer grew up as an extremely unhappy tomboy who felt as if he were a boy trapped in a girl's body. When he learned the secret of his medical history, he decided to live as a male. He later married but committed suicide after his wife left him.

Most cases are not as dramatic as Reimer's. But clinicians confront costs and benefits when considering when and how to intervene. Medication may not always be the best option for people whose depression stems from loneliness and other adverse social circumstances.

EVOLUTIONARY GENETIC THEORIES

Debate about the possible adaptive significance of depression and other mental disorders has been focused mainly at the phenotypic level. Nevertheless, some accounts concern evolutionary genetic models. In a landmark article, the geneticist Matthew Keller and the evolutionary psychologist Geoffrey Miller provide trenchant critiques of the strengths and limitations of these models, and they make a compelling case for a polygenic mutation-selection balance theory that promises to resolve the central evolutionary paradox of mental disorders.[52] Their work provides the basis for the analysis that follows.

Ancestral Neutrality of Susceptibility Alleles?

One proposed resolution of the paradox holds that genetic variation at loci responsible for mental disorders was maintained in the population because the aberrant alleles were no more nor less fit than other variants throughout evolutionary time. That is, susceptibility alleles had neutral effects on fitness until relatively recently. But as Keller and Miller point out, random genetic drift—the process that governs the frequency of neutral variants in the population—almost always winds up resulting in one allele drifting toward fixation anyway, even though it has not been chosen by natural selection. Purely random events unrelated to fitness result in one of the neutral variants' becoming more common than others are. Certain alleles will appear through mutation and later disappear from the population, and the likelihood that a mutation will replenish these randomly lost alleles is vanishingly small, rather like lightning striking the same place twice.

Few scientists believe that neutral mutations can explain much phenotypic diversity. Although most polymorphic variation across DNA originated in neutral mutations, most DNA is phenotypically inert, and hence it cannot be the source of phenotypic variation. Moreover, as Keller and Miller point out, mathematical geneticists have shown that for phenotypically expressed neutral alleles to persist across time, their effects on fitness must consistently average to nearly zero across all environments generation after generation. Only if the average fitness of carriers of a certain allele lies between 99.997 and 100.003 percent of the fitness of those without the allele will the frequency of the first allele be determined chiefly by neutral genetic drift. Departure from this extremely narrow range means that the allele will be visible to natural selection and treated accordingly. Over the course of evolutionary time, selection will eliminate an allele whose fitness dropped even slightly below this range.

Moreover, the neutral hypothesis implies that prevalence rates for mental disorders should range anywhere from 0 to 100 percent because there are no fitness differences among the relevant alleles. Yet the prevalence of the most severe mental disorders clusters well below 5 percent of the population, with the exception of those that strike only the elderly (for example, dementia).

Keller and Miller also demonstrate that if natural selection has only recently been targeting a handful of previously neutral susceptibility alleles for elimination, then absurd conclusions follow. Plugging empirical prevalence data on schizophrenia into standard evolutionary equations, they found that 42 percent of the population of Finland would have been suffering from this illness in the year 1600!

Thus for the ancestral neutrality hypothesis to hold, susceptibility alleles that today have devastating consequences on fitness would have to have had consistently neutral (or beneficial) effects on fitness in ancestral environments. Such a Gene × Environment interaction is wholly implausible. Given the devastating social consequences of schizophrenia, depression, and similar illnesses today, it seems difficult to imagine that hunter-gatherer groups would have been especially tolerant of such deviance in ancestral environments.

Balancing Selection?

Another possibility is that balancing selection has maintained susceptibility alleles in the gene pool. This account holds that these alleles have had positive effects on fitness in some environments that have balanced out their negative effects in others.

This theory shares many of the defects of the neutral theory. The compensatory fitness benefits of susceptibility alleles must have been massive to counteract the otherwise markedly harmful effects of severe mental disorders in the ancestral environment. Indeed, it is hard to see how the social environment of our hunter-gatherer ancestors would have rewarded psychotic behavior, paralyzing depression, or uncontrollable mania. Claims that schizophrenic individuals, for example, would have been prized as visionary shamans whose auditory hallucinations were imbued with mystical significance by their nonpsychotic peers ignore the full range of debilitating symptoms that constitute this illness. In fact, people in preindustrial cultures throughout the world recognize seriously ill people in their midst, distinguishing them from shamans.[53] For balancing selection to resolve the paradox, susceptibility alleles would have to have had fitness benefits in about half of the environments throughout evolutionary time—a very implausible assumption given their manifestly damaging effects across diverse environments today.

Natural selection usually diminishes genetic variation in a population, thereby reducing the heritability index for a trait. Universal adaptations arise from genes that have gone to fixation in virtue of their positive benefits on fitness. If, for example, a propensity to learn to fear heights or snakes is a universal, fitness-enhancing aspect of human nature, there should be little heritable variation for these traits. Theories that postulate that certain disorders were adaptive in certain environments cannot explain why alleles mediating these adaptations did not spread throughout the population. These alleles should have long ago gone to fixation, being present in everyone today, and hence exhibit no genetic variation any longer.

Illustrating this point, Keller and Miller criticize recent theories that fail to resolve the central paradox. For example, the psychologist Shan Guisinger proposed that anorexia nervosa evolved as an adaptation for fleeing famine during starvation conditions in ancestral environments.[54] Guisinger fails to explain why alleles fostering fitness under ancestral starvation conditions did not swiftly proceed to fixation among groups exposed to these conditions. If Guisinger were correct, then the heritability of anorexia nervosa would be close to zero among the descendants of these groups today. Differences in vulnerability for anorexia nervosa, if it were an adaptation, would be almost entirely attributable to environmental variance, and this is clearly not true. An evolutionary account that explains universal adaptations cannot account for phenomena characterized by considerable genetic variation.

Although balancing selection provides an implausible explanation for the evolutionary persistence of major mental illnesses, it does provide a plausible account of personality disorders. As covered in Chapter 6, personality disorders likely constitute extreme versions of naturally varying personality traits. Psychologists have long known that extroversion, conscientiousness, agreeableness, neuroticism, and openness to experience are highly heritable and vary dramatically among people. Natural selection tends to reduce genetic variance, leaving the fittest version to dominate the gene pool. Why, then, has personality variation persisted?

Evolutionary personality theorists persuasively argue that there is no universal optimal value for extroversion, neuroticism, and other personality traits.[55] Depending upon variations in local environments, high values of these traits may be adaptive, whereas in other conditions, low values will be. For example, high levels of extroversion may result in mating success, yet they also expose extroverts to accidents and early death. High levels of neuroticism may result in a propensity to experience anxiety and sadness, thereby impairing mating success, yet in dangerous environments, they will foster prudent wariness and survival. The upshot is that natural selection will favor different values in different places and times.

Because selection maintains genetic and phenotypic diversity, combinations of extreme values on these traits will result in personality disorders. For example, low values on agreeableness and conscientiousness and high values on neuroticism and extroversion will yield a profile consistent with antisocial personality disorder. Hence, balancing selection maintains levels of genetic diversity in the population that will ensure the inevitable emergence of personality disorders.

Heterozygote Advantage?

A genetic polymorphism may persist in the population when the heterozygote at a certain genetic locus has greater fitness than either of the homozygotes does. Someone with the Aa genotype, then, has a fitness advantage over those with either the AA genotype or the aa genotype. This case is most famously exemplified by sickle-cell anemia.[56] At the beta-hemoglobin locus, AA homozygotes are vulnerable to malaria, whereas aa homozygotes are at risk of dying from sickle-cell anemia. Heterozygotes, in contrast, are buffered against both negative outcomes. The average fitness effects of both alleles are equal.

More than three decades of research, however, has uncovered only a half dozen other cases involving persistence of polymorphisms via heterozygote advantage at a single locus. A recent scan of the human genome revealed no instances of genes subject to balancing selection other than the handful previously known to exist.[57] Accordingly, as Keller and Miller emphasize, it is very unlikely that balancing selection can explain the persistence of alleles for psychopathology.

Antagonistic Pleiotropy?

Keller and Miller likewise consider and reject pleiotropy—the process whereby a single allele affects more than one aspect of the phenotype—as the answer to the central paradox. Pleiotropy is extremely common, and antagonistic pleiotropy occurs when one allele heightens the fitness of one trait while lowering the fitness of another. Hence, an allele might increase neuroticism but also increase creativity, or increase longevity but diminish fertility. Claims regarding the hidden benefits for creativity of alleles for bipolar disorder have made this a popular hypothesis, and one that tends to destigmatize (if not romanticize) mental illness.[58] The fact that many creative people have suffered from this disorder shows that even devastating conditions have positive, redeeming features. Yet the odds that the positive fitness benefits would precisely cancel out the negative ones are extremely unlikely.

Frequency-Dependent Selection?

Yet another account appeals to frequency-dependent selection. This means that when an allele becomes progressively rare in a population, its fitness increases. Once its fitness increases, it becomes more common up until a point when its fitness once again peaks and then begins to decline. One theory holds that alleles for psychopathy may persist because of this frequency-dependent selection.[59] Psychopaths ruthlessly deceive, cheat, and exploit others, and in postindustrial society they may enjoy increased fitness (for example, fathering many illegitimate children). Alleles for psychopathy would spread until more such individuals are present in the population. But when this occurs, more people will be vigilant and alert to these predators in their midst, and their greater likelihood of being imprisoned, murdered by avenging victims, and so forth would diminish the frequency of the relevant alleles. Once the syndrome is rare, the frequency-dependent selection pattern would enable it to oscillate upward in frequency once again. As Keller and Miller point out, this account may fit for psychopathy, but it is unlikely to provide a general explanation for the central paradox.

POLYGENIC MUTATION-SELECTION BALANCE THEORY

Keller and Miller make a convincing case for a polygenic mutation-selection balance theory as the most likely resolution of the central paradox. As they put it, "if a mental disorder appears maladaptive, maybe it really is maladaptive—and always has been."[60]

They point out that at least 55 percent of the approximately 25,000 protein-coding genes in the human genome are expressed in the brain. Mutations in these genes are likely to affect cognition, emotion, and behavior to varying degrees, as will mutations in regulatory genes that do not code for proteins. The sheer mutational target size of the brain means that many mutations, whether new or inherited, will contribute to psychological diversity, including proneness to mental disorders. There are many ways that things can go wrong, yet many of these ways may lead to phenotypically similar disorders. Cases of mental disorder, even within a diagnostic category, likely have heterogeneous genetic etiologies.

The failure to find a single gene or even several genes responsible for major mental illnesses ensures that susceptibility to these disorders arises from multiple aberrant alleles at loci. The vast number of contributing genes, each with small effects, means that natural selection will not keep pace with mutation rates across all the relevant loci. Some of these may have pleiotropic consequences that yield benefits, as the heightened creativity in individuals with bipolar disorder and in their biological relatives. Yet a polygenic mutation-selection balance model does not require that these beneficial effects somehow fully counteract the otherwise devastating effects on fitness produced by bipolar disorder. This model explains why heritable disorders that impair fitness nevertheless persist at relatively high rates in the population without having been targets of positive selection. It relieves theorists from having to assume that mental disorders are, or ever were, adaptations.

Does Society Create (Some) Mental Disorders?

5 The standard view of medicine holds that astute clinicians discover diseases in nature. Psychiatrists are no different from other doctors. They, too, discern forms of pathology arising from dysfunctions in our universal human nature. Psychiatric experts, relying on clinical observation and research, formulate the diagnostic criteria that best describe the syndromes they have identified. Mental disorders are diseases of the brain, on a par with diseases of the circulatory system or the immune system. As the National Alliance for the Mentally Ill put it, "Just as diabetes is a disorder of the pancreas, mental illnesses are brain disorders."[1] Mental disorders are timeless natural kinds, originating in aberrant biology. Success in chemistry entailed discovery of the elements that constitute the periodic table; success in medicine, including psychiatry, will result in the discovery, description, and explanation of the diseases that afflict humanity.

This biomedical model of discovery and description deemphasizes the historical, social, and cultural factors of disease. Yet these factors play an important role in explaining its incidence and spread. Consider the obesity epidemic that began about 1980 in the United States.[2] The proximal cause of obesity is an energy imbalance: more calories consumed than expended. Yet the distal social, cultural, and economic factors that affect how much we eat, what we eat, and how physically active we are drive the incidence rate.[3]

For example, one cause of obesity is the manufacture and marketing of highly palatable foods containing high amounts fat, sugar, and salt.[4] Examining the brains and genes of obese people may provide clues to vulnerability, but it does not explain why far more Americans are fat today than in 1980. We have not witnessed a massive increase in the number of fat genes in the population. The difference in the prevalence of obesity in 2000 versus 1980 is due to culturally influenced changes in behavior.

SOCIAL CAUSATION VERSUS SOCIAL CONSTRUCTION

Social factors cause the spread of obesity and infectious diseases such as AIDS. Yet social factors are not constitutive of these conditions. The biology of disease exists independent of these factors. Diseases exist prior to their discovery and description by medical scientists.

Some scholars argue, however, that diseases are socially constructed, not merely socially caused. For example, when scientists studying the mummy of Ramses II concluded that the king had died of tuberculosis, the French sociologist of science Bruno Latour rejected this conclusion. He asked, "How could he pass away due to a bacillus discovered by Robert Koch in 1882?" Indeed, Latour argued, saying that Ramses II died of tuberculosis is just as ridiculous as saying that he died of machine-gun fire. "Before Koch," Latour asserted, "the bacillus had no real existence."[5]

Surely, a person can die from an unnamed disease; the disease exists prior to its discovery and description. Latour conflates concept with referent, diagnosis with disease. The description of the disease is socially constructed, but the object of the description is not.

In contrast to infectious disease, social factors may figure in the very substance of at least some psychiatric disorders. Psychiatric disorders may be socially constructed in ways that infectious diseases are not. Cognitive and emotional symptoms are constitutive of psychiatric disorder, and cultural and social factors affect how we think and feel. Therefore, social factors may become part of the very fabric of psychiatric disorder whereas they cannot for infectious disease. Unlike other medical conditions, psychiatric disorders may not be stable, ahistorical entities whose essence is invariant irrespective of cultural variation.[6]

Social constructionist approaches vary in breadth. Some scholars endorse biomedical accounts for many, if not most, psychiatric disorders, reserving their social constructionist accounts for only a handful of the conditions in the DSM.[7] Others claim that culture profoundly shapes nearly all mental disorders.[8]

Social constructionist theses also vary with regard to how deeply culture penetrates a syndrome. Least controversially, theorists merely note that culture affects the expression, but not the experience, of an otherwise universal disorder. For example, idiomatic expressions for sadness vary across cultures, exemplified by American patients who complain about feeling "blue" or feeling "down." Likewise, culture affects the content of delusions but not their form. The FBI often figures in persecutory delusions among Americans suffering from paranoid schizophrenia, but not among Australian aborigines.

A stronger form of social constructionism holds that culture profoundly shapes the experience as well as the expression of symptoms. However, even if people were to experience depression, say, in different ways around the globe, we would still need to identify *something* in common across these diverse manifestations. We cannot contrast culturally distinct ways of experiencing depression without identifying a cross-cultural universal that unites these experiences as versions of the same disease entity. Culture must leave untouched an identifiable core that abides irrespective of social, cultural, and historical circumstances.[9]

The psychiatrist and anthropologist Arthur Kleinman reported that Chinese patients suffering from depression complain primarily of pain, fatigue, dizziness, and other somatic symptoms, whereas their psychologically minded counterparts in the West voice cognitive and emotional complaints.[10] Somatic presentations in China often result in a diagnosis of neurasthenia, a label that patients embrace while rejecting one of depression. Physical diseases are more socially acceptable than shameful mental ones. However, when Kleinman explicitly questioned the Chinese patients about mood symptoms, 87 percent qualified for a DSM-III diagnosis of major depressive disorder, and many experienced improvement after receiving antidepressant medication. Although Chinese patients favor a neurological etiology for their depression, they seldom complain about mood symptoms unless the doctor explicitly asks about them. Depression has a common core despite cultural variations in which symptoms patients emphasize.

This pattern is not confined to China. In fact, patients in many cultural settings, including in the United States, are more inclined to disclose physical symptoms than emotional ones. The more comfortable patients are with their doctors, the more likely they are to mention potentially stigmatizing emotional and psychological symptoms to them.[11]

Panic disorder exemplifies how culture can modify the expression of an apparent universal psychobiological dysfunction.[12] Sufferers experience repeated, sudden attacks of terror that erupt unexpectedly and do not seem triggered by any obvious external precipitant. According to David Clark's influential theory, panic occurs when people misinterpret certain bodily sensations as indicative of impending catastrophe.[13] This interpretation, in turn, heightens fear and exacerbates the bodily sensations, thereby seemingly confirming the interpretation. The mounting fear escalates into full-blown panic.

Panic disorder affects people throughout the world, but the content of the catastrophic misinterpretations varies as a function of culture. In America and Britain, for example, many patients respond fearfully to heart palpitations as harbingers of cardiac arrest, dizziness as signifying an impending faint, and depersonalization as indicative of an imminent psychotic breakdown. Yet these catastrophic appraisals of symptoms can vary, often informed by culture-specific meanings of symptoms. For example, according to Cambodian folk physiology, wind as well as blood travels throughout the circulatory system. Certain symptoms, such as neck stiffness, signify potentially fatal wind blockade in this culture.[14] Misinterpretation of these benign symptoms incites panic. Although the symptom (neck stiffness) and interpretation (fatal wind blockade) vary, the psychobiological mechanism driving the panic process in Cambodian patients appears no different from that in Western patients.

Finally, some theorists hold that culture completely penetrates psychiatric disorders, leaving nothing untouched. For example, hysteria refers to physical symptoms that supposedly have psychological, not organic, causes. Noting its protean character, Mikkel Borch-Jacobsen questions whether there is anything in common across hysteria's diverse manifestations. He asks, "What is there in common between the 'vapours' of eighteenth-century ladies, characterized by respiratory difficulties and a quasi lethargic immobility; Charcot's grande hystérie, with its attacks in four very distinct phases, its anesthesias and hemianesthesias, its contractures, its shrinking of the visual field; the 'hysterical fugues' of the end of the nineteenth century; the varied symptoms of the 'conversion hysteria' of Breuer and Freud's Viennese clients—coughs, facial neuralgias, phobias; the 'shell shock' of soldiers in the Great War, characterized mainly by aphonia and trembling; or again, the spectacular 'Multiple Personality Disorders' of late twentieth-century North America?"[15]

Borch-Jacobsen regards all these examples as distinct syndromes arising in cultural niches, not manifestations of some timeless, underlying disease called *hysteria*. Invoking Ian Hacking's concept of a *transient mental illness*, he argues that the diversity of syndromes appearing under the hysteria rubric exemplifies this phenomenon.[16] The syndromes are idioms of distress that flourish only as long as their sociocultural niche exists. Just as biological species emerge and vanish depending on local ecology, so do transient mental illnesses.

SOCIAL CONSTRUCTION OF DSM SYNDROMES

Social constructionist theses imply that things could be otherwise.[17] To say that something is a social construction is to deny its inevitability and to affirm its basis in contingent social circumstances. The subject matter in the natural sciences is not like this. Chemists believe that the elements in the periodic table could not have been otherwise. If human beings had never evolved to discover them, the elements would still abide in the universe. They are utterly independent of human life and culture. Chemists developed the concepts to describe the elements, but the elements preexisted their discovery and description.

The subject matter in the social sciences differs in important ways from that of the natural sciences. Consider economics and its central concept, money. Money is socially constructed. It does not exist apart from the web of social practices that bring it into being. If human culture were to disappear, money would vanish with it, whereas the chemical elements would not. The chemical elements and money are both "real" in that they have consequences in the world, and both are part of the subject matter of rigorous, objective science.

Matters become complicated when we come to medicine and psychiatry in particular. Certainly psychiatric disorders require the presence of people, and people require culture. There would be no paranoid schizophrenia if there were no people to hallucinate and form delusions. Is the ontology of paranoid schizophrenia more like that of money than of the elements of the periodic table? Does this disorder have an inevitability that purely social phenomena do not? Or is it as socially contingent as the market economy? These are not merely semantic issues. Indeed, answering these questions is directly relevant to determining the causes of mental disorders, their etiology and pathophysiology.

The plausibility of various social constructionist theses in psychopathology varies as a function of disorder. To hypothesize that a syndrome is socially constructed is to make the counterfactual assertion that if certain social conditions were not present, the syndrome would vanish. Supportive evidence for a social constructionist hypothesis usually emerges from failures to observe the syndrome across cultures, failures to identify it in historical sources, or both. In the following sections, I consider several syndromes that have inspired such accounts.

Bulimia Nervosa

The behavioral hallmarks of bulimia nervosa are the rapid consumption of large quantities of food followed by self-induced vomiting, laxative abuse, or excessive physical exercise designed to counteract the caloric consequences of the eating binge. Epidemiological and historical evidence indicates that bulimia nervosa is a culture-bound syndrome occurring only in contemporary Western societies or in societies strongly influenced by contemporary Western media.[18] Moreover, the scattered historical references to bulimia prior to the twentieth century involve cases that depart in key ways from the DSM-IV disorder. For example, clinicians have reported binge eating throughout history. However, until the early twentieth century, no cases appeared involving compensatory vomiting and fear of obesity. Even then, cases of bulimia were nearly nonexistent until the second half of the twentieth century. Only in the 1970s did the incidence rate dramatically increase.

Bulimia mainly affects young women and has at its core a dread of becoming fat accompanied by difficulty achieving the Western cultural ideal of thinness as beauty. Preoccupation with these ideals motivates strict dieting that produces intense hunger, which culminates in binge-eating episodes often involving "forbidden" foods, such as high-caloric sweets and carbohydrates. Disgust with one's loss of self-control and fear of gaining weight usually motivate self-induced vomiting designed to purge the extra calories. Prompt return to stringent dieting sets the stage for the next binge-purge cycle, thereby perpetuating the problem.

A cultural ideal of thinness as beauty is essential for the syndrome to emerge. Moreover, the syndrome is unlikely to take root in settings where the patient does not have access to abundant food and the privacy to consume it rapidly and then vomit without others noticing.

For example, among the semi-nomadic Arabs of Niger, mothers force-feed their girls to help them achieve the body ideal of obesity.[19] Women in this culture strive to be as fat as possible, thereby enhancing their sexual attractiveness. With obesity comes indolence, yet this presents no problem. Servants do all the work in this former slave culture, and a woman's inactivity advertises the success of her husband. Because scarcity of food has been far more common than its abundance, the vast majority of cultures throughout history have idealized the large female body. The body ideals of Niger have been the rule, not the exception. It's little wonder that bulimia and the thin body ideal emerge only when food becomes plentiful.

Cultural factors are necessary, but not sufficient, for the emergence of bulimia nervosa. Not every young woman bombarded with media depictions of thin models and celebrities develops the disorder. People possessing certain psychological or biological risk factors may be especially vulnerable to the fear of becoming fat that motivates the diet-binge-purge cycle. Once this cycle is established, adverse biological consequences can result, ranging from electrolyte disturbances to erosion of teeth enamel. Yet in other cultural contexts, these same risk factors may provide the foundation for an entirely different syndrome.

Dissociative Amnesia

According to the DSM-IV-TR, dissociative amnesia is "an inability to recall important personal information, usually of a traumatic or stressful nature, that is too extensive to be explained by normal forgetfulness."[20] Dissociative amnesia is essentially synonymous with the notion of repressed memory of trauma.

The notion that exposure to trauma may render a person incapable of recalling the event has roots in nineteenth-century psychiatry.[21] It featured prominently in Freud's early claims that patients diagnosed with hysteria suffered the effects of repressed memories of childhood sexual abuse.[22] About one hundred years later, it resurfaced in allegations of repressed and recovered memories of sexual abuse.[23]

Curious about the historicity of this alleged phenomenon, the psychiatrist Harrison Pope and his colleagues used Internet search engines to scan the world literatures of medicine, history, and fiction to locate reports of dissociative amnesia for trauma prior to the nineteenth century.[24] Their case definition required that a person experience and encode a psychologically traumatic event but then become incapable of recalling it for an extended period before being able to remember it once again. Moreover, the inability to recall the trauma could not be attributable to physical insult to the brain (for example, a blow to the head).

The earliest case they found was that of Dr. Manette, who had amnesia for much of his experience of imprisonment in the Bastille in *A Tale of Two Cities,* published by Charles Dickens in 1859. A brief poem written by Emily Dickinson in 1862 alluded to the possibility that someone might develop amnesia for painful experiences. The character Penn in Rudyard Kipling's 1896 novel *Captains Courageous* experienced amnesia for the traumatic loss of his family, and then later recovered the memory of the trauma.

After failing to locate a single case prior to the nineteenth century, Pope posted a challenge on thirty Internet websites, offering to pay $1,000 to anyone who could locate a qualifying case reported before 1800. He received more than one hundred replies, but none met all criteria. Pope and his colleagues concluded that "dissociative amnesia is not a natural neuropsychological phenomenon."[25] The alleged capacity to encode, repress for an extended period, and then recover a psychologically traumatic experience appears never to have been described anywhere in the world prior to the nineteenth century, leading Pope to conclude that it is a culture-bound idiom of distress.

I came closest to winning the prize, nearly qualifying with my case of Madame de Tourvel in Choderlos de Laclos's 1782 novel *Les Liaisons Dangereuses.*[26] After committing adultery, the pious, guilt-ridden heroine is shocked when her lover abandons her, and she joins a convent. She develops a high fever, slips into a delirium, then recovers after getting some sleep. When she awakens, she has repressed her traumatic memory of the adulterous love affair. She cannot remember why she is at the convent, despite struggling to recall what had happened. After about thirty minutes, she becomes emotionally devastated when she recovers her repressed memory. Unfortunately, the brevity of the period of repression disqualified my case from winning the prize.

The media publicity generated by the publication of Pope's study subsequently produced a winner.[27] The case appeared in a 1786 French opera. As Pope and his colleagues pointed out, this eighteenth-century fictional example does not invalidate their conclusion that dissociative amnesia is a culture-bound notion; it merely dates the onset of the idea a few years earlier than their original threshold of 1800.

Pope and his colleagues considered and rejected potential objections to their conclusion. They acknowledged that it is impossible to prove the null hypothesis that no one had ever observed traumatic dissociative amnesia before the nineteenth century. Yet they emphasized that observers surely would have written about such a striking phenomenon had it occurred. Indeed, given that it appears in many novels and films throughout the twentieth century, we might have expected that Shakespeare, the Greek dramatists, or the authors of ancient epics of India would have described it. Authors in antiquity described mania, depression, and epilepsy in ways immediately recognizable by us, even though people once understood the phenomena in radically different ways. If dissociative amnesia were a genuine psychobiological phenomenon, we would expect someone to have mentioned it.

Another hypothesis is that dissociative amnesia reflects a natural capacity of the brain, but that it has emerged only during the past two hundred years. However, the notion that the mind protects itself by banishing horrific memories from awareness until it is safe to recall them years later is supposedly an involuntary defensive process. If such a process did exist, it would be part of our de-fensive evolutionary equipment and thus observable throughout time.

The most likely hypothesis is that dissociative amnesia for trauma is a culture-bound idiom of distress emerging in nineteenth-century Western culture. Europeans in the nineteenth century de-veloped a concept of the dynamic unconscious mind within the culture of Romanticism, and Freud and others developed it further, incorporating it into their theories. The notion that buried memo-ries of trauma could cause psychopathology infiltrated the culture. Just as Victorian women once swooned as an expression of distress, people presenting with a claimed inability to remember alleged trauma had acquired yet another way to exhibit emotional turmoil.

The concept of repressed and recovered memories of trauma flies in the face of abundant clinical and scientific evidence.[28] Yet people can come to believe that they harbor buried memories of trauma and that recovering them can lead to healing. Even if the brain cannot repress memories of trauma, rendering them inacces-sible to awareness until the person can safely recall them later, it certainly possesses the capacity to form false memories, includ-ing memories of trauma.[29] Accordingly, forming false memories of trauma is certainly a natural capacity of the brain, just as is swoon-ing in response to emotional stress.

Multiple Personality Disorder

The notion that the mind protects itself by repressing or dissociat-ing memories of trauma figures dramatically in cases of multiple personality disorder (MPD) in the late twentieth century.[30] A per-son diagnosed with MPD acts as if different personalities ("alters") take possession of him or her. These personalities vary in how they think, act, and feel. Each has a different name, a different history, and a different set of memories. The alters may vary in age, sex, and ethnicity. The person's ordinary "host" personality often claims amnesia for the alter personalities. However, experimental research indicates that subjects with an MPD diagnosis do not experience inter-identity amnesia, at least in the laboratory.[31] That is, both neutral and emotional material encoded by one personality is accessible to another one.

Scattered reports of dual personalities appeared in the medical literature throughout the nineteenth and twentieth centuries. A review that appeared in 1944 uncovered only 76 cases in the previous 128 years.[32] MPD had all but vanished from the landscape of psychiatry. Yet after the appearance of the best-selling book *Sybil* and the made-for-TV movie about the case, an epidemic of MPD swept through North America, peaking in the early 1990s.[33] The book, translated into 17 languages, sold 11 million copies.[34]

Sybil provided the prototype for subsequent MPD patients. Unlike previous multiples, most of whom had only one or two additional personalities, Sybil had sixteen, and some of her personalities served as repositories for memories of childhood physical and sexual abuse too horrific for Sybil's host personality to acknowledge. The central idea was that MPD was an especially severe form of posttraumatic stress disorder. Assuming that the mind can protect itself by dissociating or repressing memories of horrific trauma, MPD theorists argued that childhood trauma fractures the mind of patients, creating alter personalities that harbor these memories that the patient must recall via hypnosis for healing to occur.

From near-nonexistence, MPD spread throughout North America, with the number of diagnosed cases soaring to 50,000. Interestingly, only a handful of therapists seemed sufficiently astute to diagnose the disorder among their patients, and these MPD mavens began conducting continuing education workshops to teach other mental health professionals how to diagnosis and treat MPD.

These specialists explained the spectacular increase in the disorder's prevalence to other clinicians, who they claimed were misdiagnosing MPD as schizophrenia and other syndromes. The appearance of MPD as a formal diagnosis in 1980 in DSM-III was also crucial, making the diagnosis and treatment of MPD reimbursable by insurance. The founding of the International Society for the Study of Multiple Personality and Dissociation in 1984 helped reaffirm the view that MPD resulted from dissociated memories of horrific childhood abuse and that recovery from the illness required patients to recover these buried memories via hypnosis, emotionally process them, and thereby integrate their fragmented personalities.

The epidemic of MPD ended abruptly. Several factors contributed to the near-disappearance of patients carrying the diagnosis. Psychologists knowledgeable about the malleability of memory emphasized that hypnosis, suggestive interviewing characterized by leading questions, was far more likely to create false memories than to recover true ones.[35]

MPD therapists inadvertently undermined the credibility of their own field when they began helping patients recall alleged memories of satanic ritual abuse.[36] The FBI failed to uncover any physical evidence of satanic cult crimes, such as murder, infant cannibalism, and sadistic sexual abuse.[37] As former MPD patients retracted their recovered memories of abuse and began bringing successful malpractice suits against their former therapists for having hypnotically "implanted" false memories of trauma, the epidemic of MPD ceased.[38] It became legally hazardous for clinicians to follow assessment and treatment guidelines that MPD specialists had been recommending only a few years earlier.

MPD appeared in DSM-IV under the less inflammatory title of Dissociative Identity Disorder. Specialists now discouraged the use of hypnotic memory-recovery methods. Hospitals closed their once profitable dissociative disorders programs, and the National Institute of Mental Health closed its intramural research program devoted to the field. Professional interest in MPD, as evinced by publications on the topic, peaked in the mid-1990s, before plummeting dramatically by the early twenty-first century.[39] Echoing the authors of an earlier day, critics argued that MPD was a socially constructed idiom of distress whereby dramatic media portrayals of the disorder accompanied by therapists' use of hypnosis and other techniques created the syndrome in highly suggestible, distressed patients.[40]

The clinicians who treated the MPD patient depicted in the film *The Three Faces of Eve* argued that MPD enthusiasts were over-diagnosing the disorder at the height of the epidemic.[41] They had encountered only one genuine case of MPD among the tens of thousands of patients they had seen since they had treated Eve.

But if MPD is a socially constructed idiom of distress, then what constitutes a "real" case of MPD? Under DSM's atheoretical system, agnostic about etiology, anyone who fulfills the diagnostic criteria has MPD. Using structured interviews based on DSM criteria, clinicians can diagnosis the disorder reliably.[42] That is, when two clinicians ask the patient the same questions about symptoms on two occasions, the responses the patient provides often result in the clinicians' independently determining that the patient meets criteria for MPD. Such inter-rater reliability with regard to diagnostic agreement tells us nothing about its etiology or its psychobiological reality. Experts in Salem, Massachusetts, in the 1690s could reliably agree about the presence of signs and symptoms of bewitchment.[43] But that does not confirm the validity of witchcraft etiology.

The MPD debate concerns the etiology of the syndrome, not whether people will complain of certain symptoms. Clearly, patients can satisfy criteria for the disorder. The issue is why. Does MPD result from dissociated memories of horrific childhood abuse, accessible only to alter personalities? Or is the syndrome a cultural artifact, an idiom of distress shaped by exposure to media models of MPD and the hypnotic procedures of therapists? Under a descriptive diagnostic system, such as DSM-IV, we cannot answer this question. A descriptive system disallows inferences about etiology and pathophysiology.

Recent scholarly detective work has uncovered startling facts about Sybil.[44] Studying documents concerning the case, Borch-Jacobsen and Peter Swales ascertained the identity of the woman called Sybil and traced her origins to a small town in the Midwest. These scholars discovered that Sybil's mother was neither psychotic nor abusive. Rather than being a victim of horrific childhood trauma, Sybil was an imaginative only child who enjoyed a comfortable, rather spoiled, childhood. She later moved to New York City to pursue her artistic ambitions, and dissatisfaction with her life led her to seek psychoanalytic treatment with Cornelia Wilbur. The case depicted in *The Three Faces of Eve* had recently gained widespread publicity, and Dr. Wilbur, using hypnosis and medications, co-created with Sybil's tacit cooperation the dramatic alters who recalled their histories of childhood trauma. The psychologist Robert Rieber discovered audiotapes of Wilbur's sessions with Sybil, which Wilbur had given him many years ago as possible material for research.[45] These tapes provide convincing evidence of therapeutic shaping and the co-creation of MPD in Sybil. Indeed, Sybil admitted in writing to Wilbur that she had manufactured her MPD symptoms.[46] Wilbur disregarded this admission.

Schizophrenia

Suspicion that a disorder has cultural roots arises when it appears only in certain periods in history. The historicity of a syndrome suggests, but does not confirm, its cultural origins, as the case of schizophrenia illustrates.

Characterized by delusions, auditory hallucinations, disorders in thought, and blunting of emotional expression, schizophrenia has a lifetime prevalence of 0.7 percent throughout the world.[47] Although environmental factors such as maternal infection, a winter birth, perinatal birth complications, migration, and cannabis use are associated with increased risk for schizophrenia, no one disputes its status as a neurodevelopmental (or neurodegenerative) brain disorder strongly influenced by genetic factors.[48]

The German psychiatrist Emil Kraepelin assumed that schizophrenia, or dementia praecox, as he called it, was a disease of the brain.[49] During the mid-twentieth-century heyday of psychoanalysis, many American psychiatrists disagreed with him. Rejecting an organic etiology, doctors inspired by Freud assumed that psychosocial origins, unresolved unconscious conflicts, and similar factors caused schizophrenia. The failure of psychoanalytic treatment, and the success of psychopharmacology, paved the way for today's biological theories of schizophrenia.[50] Today's theorists endorse a diathesis-stress framework that postulates aberrant biology activated by psychosocial stressors.[51] Schizophrenia seems an unlikely candidate for being a socially constructed disorder.

If schizophrenia is a brain disease appearing in diverse cultures throughout the world today, we might expect to see it throughout history. However, this does not appear to be the case. An extensive search of historical, medical, and fictional literature in Greek and Roman antiquity uncovered no descriptions of schizophrenia.[52] Other syndromes, including mania, epilepsy, melancholia, delirium, alcoholism, and social phobia, appear in ways immediately recognizable to the twenty-first-century reader. Yet the authors were unable to locate a single description of schizophrenia with its onset in late adolescence or early adulthood, its delusions, hallucinations, social withdrawal, and chronic and deteriorating course.

To be sure, bizarre behavior occurred in antiquity, exemplified by Suetonius's biographies of the Roman emperors, especially Caligula and Nero.[53] But these accounts feature psychopathy, sadism, and sexual deviation, not symptoms of psychosis. Nothing in Suetonius's work suggests anything like schizophrenia.

In fact, not only are descriptions of schizophrenia absent from the literature of antiquity, but few, if any, convincing descriptions exist prior to the nineteenth century.[54] Schizophrenia, it appears, may be a disease of recent vintage whose prevalence increased throughout the nineteenth-century Western world. During this time, schizophrenia remained rare in non-Western areas but increased in prevalence during the twentieth century in the developing world.

Moreover, the course of schizophrenia appears more benign today than during the late nineteenth and early twentieth centuries, as evinced by the increasing rarity of the severely impaired disorganized ("hebephrenic") subtype.[55] Catatonic schizophrenia has also been waning in the West in recent decades, yet it still occurs in the developing world. These changes cannot be wholly attributable to advances in treatment. The profound psychological and social deterioration common in Kraepelin's day began to become less common even before the advent of antipsychotic medication in the 1950s.

Another interesting hypothesis, formulated by the psychologist Mary Boyle, is that many of Kraepelin's dementia praecox patients may actually have been suffering from a viral condition called *encephalitis lethargica* that swept through Europe between 1916 and 1927.[56] Patients with this disease had symptoms remarkably similar to those of Kraepelin's severely deteriorating cases.

The evidence that schizophrenia is a neurodevelopmental disease occurring in people with a genetic vulnerability is overwhelming. Its relatively recent appearance during a period of rapid industrialization and urbanization, first in the West and later in the developing world, is nevertheless consistent with biological causation. A mutation in an infectious agent, or a change in the immunological response to existing infectious agents, provides a plausible explanation for the sudden emergence of schizophrenia at the beginning of the nineteenth century.[57] The emergence of milder strains of the infectious organism, increased host resistance, or both may explain why the more serious disabling variants of schizophrenia are on the wane and why the course of the disease has become increasingly benign. The more we learn about biological etiology and pathophysiology, the less likely we are to endorse a social constructionist interpretation of disorders of recent origin. A disorder need not be timeless or invariant to qualify as a natural kind. For example, AIDS is a recent disease, yet no one questions its status as a natural kind.

Posttraumatic Stress Disorder

Controversy has haunted PTSD ever since its appearance in DSM-III. Defenders of the diagnosis regard it as a natural kind, a "universal human response to trauma that may be influenced by cultural factors."[58] Skeptics regard it as an idiom of distress arising in the socially contentious wake of the Vietnam War.[59] Moreover, moral issues complicate research into trauma and its consequences, further fueling controversy, making dispassionate inquiry difficult. Unlike the other anxiety disorders, PTSD implies perpetrators and victims. As the anthropologist-physicians Didier Fassin and Richard Rechtman have observed, "Rather than a clinical reality, trauma today is a moral judgment" that serves "to identify legitimate victims."[60]

The case of PTSD underscores the distinction between social *causation* and social *construction*. Traumatologists embrace the former and reject the latter. For example, a woman who develops PTSD in response to rape exemplifies the social causation of disorder. Yet to characterize her PTSD as a socially constructed artifact is to imply doubt about the legitimacy of her reaction, thereby inviting the wrath of traumatologists likely to accuse the skeptic of harboring a hidden agenda to silence the voices of survivors.

PTSD researchers working in the tradition of biological psychiatry have drawn moral implications from their research. As Rachel Yehuda and Alexander McFarlane said, "biological findings have provided objective validation that PTSD is more than a politically or socially motivated conceptualization of human suffering." They added that biological data provide "concrete validation of human suffering and a legitimacy that does not depend on arbitrary social and political forces. Establishing that there is a biological basis for psychological trauma is an essential first step in allowing the permanent validation of human suffering."[61]

Ambiguity plagues such sentiments. It is unclear how any empirical finding can either prove or disprove claims about the motivation driving the formulation of the diagnosis. Moreover, biological research is not essential for people to recognize human suffering. Empathy for victims did not have to await the discoveries of biological psychiatry. It is also unclear whether biological "validation" refers to abnormalities that result from PTSD or to biological factors that heighten risk for the disorder among those exposed to trauma. In either case, Yehuda and McFarlane invoke biology to support a moral claim—something that seldom occurs elsewhere in psychopathology.

Eager to prove that PTSD is more than a politically motivated concept, traumatologists have trawled through history in search of it. They argue that syndromes in previous wars, such as shell shock in World War I and battle fatigue in World War II, were really PTSD under different names, and they have recognized its symptoms in fictional characters such as Hotspur in Shakespeare's *Henry IV,* Part I, and Achilles in Homer's *Iliad.*[62]

The medical anthropologist Allan Young has expressed the contrasting social constructionist interpretation of PTSD: "The disorder is not timeless, nor does it possess an intrinsic unity. Rather, it is glued together by the practices, technologies, and narratives with which it is diagnosed, studied, treated, and represented and by the various interests, institutions, and moral arguments that mobilized these efforts and resources." He added that "traumatic memory is a man-made object. It originates in the scientific and clinical discourses of the nineteenth century; before that time, there is unhappiness, despair, and disturbing recollections, but no traumatic memory, in the sense that we know it today."[63]

His reference to social factors driving the ratification of the diagnosis in 1980 fits the contentious story of how PTSD wound up in DSM-III. At least since the American Civil War, doctors have observed symptoms such as guilt, anxiety, and inability to concentrate among troubled combat veterans.[64] Yet doctors who treated traumatized soldiers in World Wars I and II believed that these stress reactions dissipated soon after the soldier left the battlefield, unless he was malingering or had preexisting vulnerability or psychopathology. The trauma of war alone, they thought, was insufficient to produce lasting psychological damage. Moreover, if a soldier survived the war psychologically unscathed, he was unlikely to suffer problems later in life.[65]

The aftermath of the Vietnam War dramatically changed these views. Psychiatric casualties were very rare during the war itself. The rate of breakdown in Vietnam was only 12 per 1,000 men, whereas it got as high as 101 per 1,000 during World War II.[66] Many of the problems that did occur were unrelated to combat; only 3.5 percent of all psychiatric casualties received a diagnosis of combat exhaustion.[67]

In dramatic contrast to the low rate of mental disorder during the war itself, many veterans began experiencing serious and persistent problems months and years after reentering civilian life. As David Marlowe put it, "Vietnam produced an extremely low proportion of proximate combat stress casualties and produced or is claimed to have produced massive numbers of postcombat casualties. Therefore, Vietnam breaks with the past normative pattern of combat and war zone stress casualty production."[68]

To explain this unprecedented pattern, antiwar psychiatrists, such as Robert Lifton and Chaim Shatan, argued that the Vietnam War produced a chronic stress disorder having a delayed onset.[69] The war, they thought, was an immoral, atrocity-producing experience for many of the men who fought it. It did not allow soldiers the opportunity to grieve for their fallen comrades, resulting in psychic numbing and symptoms of stress that emerged only after their return to civilian life. Moreover, instead of viewing troubled veterans as suffering from preexisting problems merely exacerbated by the war, they argued that the war itself could produce lasting psychological damage.

During the 1970s, Lifton, Shatan, and other clinicians joined forces with leaders of Vietnam veterans' organizations to lobby the American Psychiatric Association for the inclusion of a "Post-Vietnam Syndrome" diagnosis in the then-forthcoming DSM-III. They aimed to ensure that distressed veterans were eligible to receive treatment from the Veterans Administration (VA) and service-connected disability payments for their psychiatric problems. Congress provides the VA with a list of compensable disorders, and the absence in DSM-II of a syndrome characterized by delayed onset of symptoms triggered by warfare meant that troubled veterans were out of luck.[70] As Shatan said, Vietnam veterans "can expect little help from the VA without proof that their affliction is 'service-connected' and can be diagnosed according to the revised APA classification" (that is, DSM-II).[71] Furthermore, the VA paid only for those disorders that begin either during the individual's military service or within one year after he left the military. Advocates for the diagnosis realized that for the government to accept clinical and financial responsibility for troubled veterans, they had to make the case that the problems of veterans stemmed from the war, not from preexisting problems. As the psychiatrist Arthur Blank put it, "At this time, the predisposition theory is an instance of blaming the victim."[72]

DSM-III task force members were initially reluctant to include a Post-Vietnam Syndrome in the new manual. Some thought that combinations of established diagnoses covered the problems of veterans, hence rendering the new diagnosis unnecessary. Moreover, one aim of DSM-III was to develop an atheoretical, descriptive system free of etiologic assumptions. Yet etiology was integral to the concept of the Post-Vietnam Syndrome.

Lobbyists for the new diagnosis succeeded, but only after changing their strategy. Instead of claiming that the Vietnam War resulted in a new syndrome unique to this conflict, they joined forces with other mental health professionals who had been working with victims of natural disasters, rape, and the Nazi Holocaust. Any terrifying, life-threatening event occurring outside the perimeter of everyday life could produce a chronic syndrome akin to that suffered by traumatized Vietnam veterans. The psychiatrist Nancy Andreasen, an influential member of the DSM-III task force, concurred, noting that she had observed strikingly similar symptoms in her patients who had suffered from extreme burns. The upshot of these developments was the replacement of "Post-Vietnam Syndrome" with posttraumatic stress disorder. Rather than being a historically situated syndrome linked to the idiosyncratic characteristics of the Vietnam War, PTSD became a universal syndrome incited by traumatically stressful events. Once PTSD appeared in DSM-III in 1980, Congress listed it as a disorder compensable by the VA. Moreover, because DSM-III specified that PTSD could have a delayed onset, the requirement that it had to emerge no later than one year after the individual left the military was dropped.

The political story regarding the ratification of PTSD in DSM-III is consistent with the social constructionist interpretation, but it does not confirm it. Indeed, we could argue that PTSD is a universal response to trauma, but one that society is reluctant to acknowledge. The federal government was not eager to fund treatment programs for troubled veterans; nor was it eager to provide psychiatric disability compensation. Therefore, we could argue that a powerful political movement was essential to overcoming other political forces aiming to downplay the psychiatric damage of the Vietnam War. Likewise, no one disputes that AIDS is a natural kind, yet putting AIDS on the radar screen of funding agencies, science, and society required vigorous political work on the part of gay activists. Political and social involvement in the recognition of a disorder does not necessarily mean that the disorder itself is a product of social forces.

Moreover, defenders of the diagnosis point out that PTSD is detectable around the globe, including in non-Western countries. The psychiatrists Janet Osterman and Joop de Jong said that it is time for anthropologists and mental health professionals "to end the debate about the validity of the diagnosis of PTSD," noting that PTSD "appears to be a universal reaction to severe stressors that has transcultural diagnostic validity."[73] For example, one community questionnaire survey in Sierra Leone indicated that 99 percent of citizens had scores indicative of severe PTSD.[74]

Kenyan employees of the American embassy who had survived the Al-Qaeda bombing reported PTSD symptoms strikingly similar to those reported by employees who had survived the bombing of the federal building in Oklahoma City.[75] However, it is likely that the Kenyans were partly Westernized. Indeed, a study of trauma survivors in Burundi indicated that a measure of exposure to Western trauma discourse predicted severity of PTSD symptoms even after the researchers had controlled statistically for trauma severity.[76]

On the other hand, some researchers have diagnosed PTSD in Kalahari hunter-gatherers.[77] However, the authors of this study acknowledge their uncertainty as to whether the respondents fully understood the meaning of particular symptoms, such as psychic numbing. Another concern is that because researchers arrived in these cultures with translated versions of PTSD assessment instruments, it's possible that the very questions asked influenced how people responded. It is unclear whether traumatized respondents from these cultures are merely acquiescing to questions about PTSD symptoms. Perhaps they would have mentioned entirely different symptoms had interviewers conducted open-ended rather than structured interviews.

The social constructionist interpretation of PTSD gains more support from the historical literature than from current cross-cultural studies. Differences in psychiatric symptoms among trauma survivors across time are striking, thereby undercutting claims that PTSD has appeared largely unchanged throughout history.[78] Shell shock victims in World War I exhibited symptoms suggestive of neurological disease, including tremor, paralysis, inability to walk, and inability to speak. Traumatized combat veterans have rarely exhibited these problems since World War I. Troubled veterans of the Persian Gulf War complained of a bewildering array of medically unexplained symptoms seemingly suggestive of exposure to toxins.

To investigate these issues empirically, the historian Edgar Jones and his colleagues consulted British military medical files of 1,856 men assessed for service-connected disability pensions.[79] Doctors had evaluated veterans suffering from postcombat disorders annually until their condition either remitted or stabilized. In some cases, files contained annual notes on symptoms for up to ten years postdischarge. During these assessments, veterans described the full range of their psychological and somatic problems. Jones and his team developed a checklist of PTSD symptoms, noting which ones appeared in each veteran's file. They were especially interested in testing whether flashbacks—involuntary, vivid, seemingly unchanging memories of combat—appeared in the files.

The results indicated that flashbacks were extremely rare among British psychiatric casualties until the Persian Gulf War. Only 3 of the 640 World War I veterans reported phenomena suggestive of flashbacks (0.5 percent), and only 5 of 367 World War II veterans did so (1.4 percent). None of the 428 psychiatric casualties of the Victorian campaigns and the Boer War reported flashbacks. Thirty-six of the 400 Persian Gulf War veterans described flashbacks (9 percent).

Moreover, when in doubt, Jones and his colleagues classified a symptom as a flashback. For example, one World War I shell shock victim suffered from vertigo, tremors, headaches, weakness, irritability, depressed mood, poor sleep, dreams about the war, claustrophobia, and loss of interest in people, among other things. He also reported awakening from sleep, seeing people standing in his room, and experiencing fear. It is unclear whether visions of intruders in the bedroom should count as a flashback from a combat experience. These appear to have been apparent hypnopompic ("upon awakening") hallucinations resulting from the intrusion of dream mentation into emerging wakefulness rather than a flashback of the war itself.[80]

Of the eight veterans who had experienced apparent flashbacks, one World War I and two World War II veterans did not fulfill DSM-IV PTSD criteria, whereas the other five apparently did. Overall, however, core PTSD symptoms of intrusive memory and avoidance occurred "relatively infrequently in earlier forms of traumatic stress disorders," as Jones and his colleagues observed.[81] Somatic symptoms are far more common in the medical files of traumatized veterans from the nineteenth century through the early twentieth century. Jones concluded that the extreme rarity of apparent flashbacks and full-blown PTSD in World Wars I and II implies that PTSD is a "contemporary culture-bound syndrome."[82]

What are the implications of these data for our understanding of PTSD? Can we assume that a failure to express symptoms, such as flashbacks, means that soldiers did not experience them? Does culture constrain experience as well as expression? Conversely, does culture enable the experience of symptoms? Does this mean that traumatized soldiers in the past were incapable of experiencing certain PTSD symptoms?

It is impossible to prove the null hypothesis that traumatized soldiers in the past did not experience PTSD. The absence of evidence is not evidence of absence. Yet as Jones and his colleagues emphasized, veterans interviewed for disability pensions were highly motivated to mention all their symptoms, and we would expect them to mention striking phenomena, such as flashbacks, if they had been experiencing them.

In another study, Jones conducted statistical analyses of symptoms appearing in the British military medical records of psychiatric casualties from the Boer War through the Persian Gulf War.[83] Three partly overlapping clusters of symptoms emerged. The first, "debility" cluster comprises complaints of chronic fatigue, weakness, anxiety, and breathlessness. The second, "somatic" cluster has a cardiac focus. Symptoms include rapid heart rate, dizziness, anxiety, and breathlessness. The third, "neuropsychiatric" cluster includes anxiety, depression, fatigue, sleep difficulties, irritability, startle reactions, personality changes, and chronic pain.

The bulk of historical scholarship on trauma, mainly war, indicates that the profile of posttraumatic symptoms varies drastically throughout history. To regard all such symptoms as disguised versions of PTSD would run counter to the DSM descriptive approach to diagnosis. If headaches, "hysterical" paralysis, fatigue, heart palpitations, and other complaints all count as manifestations of "PTSD," then the diagnosis has become a grab bag of miscellaneous problems and nothing more than a conceptual placeholder for an individual's response to trauma. There is no one syndrome emerging in response to the incontestable trauma of combat.

In fact, it is interesting to compare the hallmark symptoms of Shatan's Post-Vietnam Syndrome with those of PTSD in DSM-IV-TR.[84] The syndrome has quietly evolved. Shatan listed six characteristics shared by most of the veterans with whom he had been working. First, they experienced intense guilt about having survived Vietnam while many of their fellow soldiers had not. They also experienced guilt about having maimed and killed in Vietnam. These feelings fostered an urge to atone and sometimes a desire for self-punishment, manifested in substance abuse, one-car accidents, and reckless quasi-suicidal behavior. Second, they felt betrayed and felt like scapegoats. Third, they experienced rage at society in general and especially at those who tried to manipulate them. Fourth, they experienced psychic numbing. Fifth, they felt alienated from other people. Sixth, they experienced an inability to love or trust others or to accept affection in return.

Guilt has disappeared as a symptom of PTSD, and irritability and anger have replaced the generalized rage at society and established authority. Psychic numbing and difficulty experiencing loving feelings for other people remain in today's PTSD criteria. However, many symptoms are missing from Shatan's list, including exaggerated startle, sleep disturbance, avoidance of reminders of the trauma, intrusive recollections, nightmares, and physiological reactions to reminders.

In sum, PTSD paradoxically appears to be a transcultural universal but not a transhistorical one, even in Western societies. However, there is an Achilles heel in research on PTSD that may undermine claims about the disorder's cross-cultural validity. In the vast majority of studies, researchers translate Western PTSD questionnaires and structured interviews into local languages. These systematic data-collection methods have the virtue of standardization, but they leave no room for expression of local idioms of distress. These methods presuppose that response to trauma, as embodied in the latest version of the DSM, is a universal psychobiological syndrome. Worse yet, standard assessment methods may evoke affirmative responses that have little to do with the phenomenology of the trauma survivor. For example, among survivors of the tsunami in Sri Lanka, respondents did not realize the meaning and intent of the assessments done by Westerners, mistakenly assuming that the "correct" answers would enable them to receive food, clothing, and other kinds of material aid.[85] Hence, reports of PTSD prevalence rates are meaningless abstractions that have little to do with the experience of people in this country. The upshot is that the apparent transcultural validity of PTSD may be an artifact of Western measurement methods.

NATURAL KINDS AND INTERACTIVE KINDS

Psychopathology comprises more than one kind of entity. Some syndromes are likely natural kinds discovered by observant clinicians across cultures and throughout history. Mania, melancholia, panic disorder, obsessive-compulsive disorder, and alcoholism are among these candidates. For these syndromes, culture penetrates only the surface, affecting the content of delusions or the kinds of catastrophic appraisals of bodily sensations integral to panic disorder. The core of these syndromes is largely indifferent to cultural influence.

For other syndromes, culture is partly constitutive. In the case of bulimia nervosa, mental representations of thinness as an ideal body shape, absorbed from the ambient culture, interact with psychobiological vulnerabilities, such as difficulty regulating one's emotions, to incite the cycle of dieting, binging, and purging. As Dominic Murphy has argued, cognitive representations of cultural variables are the route through which culture gets under the skin, influencing the psychobiology of people who develop syndromes such as bulimia.[86] Here the distinction between social causation and social construction becomes blurred.

Ian Hacking's concept of an *interactive kind* illuminates these issues.[87] Syndromes such as MPD and PTSD are interactive kinds, whereas quarks and chemical elements are *indifferent* kinds oblivious to being classified. A person diagnosed with a disorder qualifying as an interactive kind responds to receiving this label. In the case of MPD, suffering people learned to express their distress in the form of alters who recovered "memories" of trauma and acted in drastically different ways from the host personality.

Even if there is a psychobiological core to a syndrome, such as traumatic Pavlovian fear conditioning in PTSD, how patients respond to receipt of their diagnosis may affect how they react to their symptoms. This, in turn, may affect the course of illness. For example, if sufferers understand PTSD as a chronic, relapsing disorder from which they can never truly recover, they are likely to apply for disability compensation and give up hope of recovery. Likewise, sufferers who understand their depression as arising from a chemical imbalance are likely to respond to their distress differently than will those who regard it as a response to adverse interpersonal circumstances. This is not to say that patients with PTSD or depression are not suffering or that there is no central psychobiological core giving rise to symptoms. Rather, receipt of the diagnostic label affects beliefs that in turn influence behavior affecting the outcome of the illness.

Concerns about the medicalization of the effects of trauma, embodied in the PTSD diagnosis, arise from concerns about how the label will affect resilience.[88] People acquire beliefs about trauma from their culture, and these may affect whether a trauma victim rebounds following adversity or develops chronic PTSD.

Some of the debates regarding socially constructed disorders, such as MPD, are irresolvable within our current atheoretical descriptive DSM system. For example, interpreting MPD as a contemporary manifestation of hysteria involves an appeal to factors that transcend the signs and symptoms of the disorder. Unfortunately, calling MPD hysteria explains little; the hypothesis lacks psychobiological substance. It does, however, imply rejection of an etiology rooted in the notion of massive repression or dissociation of memories of horrific childhood abuse.

Whether symptoms are subject to influence by consequences, either positive or negative, may be the key distinction between hysteria and the physical conditions that it mimics. Consider Jean Charcot's patients who suffered from genuine seizures versus those who exhibited pseudo-seizures. If we were to offer patients in each group a million dollars if they exhibited no further seizures for one month, the patients with then-untreatable epilepsy would not earn a penny, whereas those with pseudo-seizures would become millionaires. We need not appeal to metaphysical notions such as free will to capture the distinction between voluntary and involuntary behavior.[89] The key issue is whether the behavior in question is subject to consequential influence. Genuine seizures occur irrespective of their consequences, whereas pseudo-seizures do not. Socially constructed disorders or symptoms are more likely to be subject to consequential governance than are disorders counting as natural kinds.

Is It in Our Genes?

The APA is currently preparing DSM-5 and aims to publish the volume in May 2013. The clinical investigators working on this project face major questions. Has science progressed sufficiently so that psychiatry can finally define mental disorders in terms of etiology and pathophysiology and not solely by signs and symptoms? Is the field ready to join the rest of medicine by abandoning the atheoretical descriptive system that has held sway since DSM-III? In particular, can exciting advances in molecular genetics and neuroscience provide a foundation for a more scientifically sound, and perhaps etiologically informed, approach to psychiatric diagnosis?

MOLECULAR GENETICS AND GENOMICS

We know that mental disorders run in families. Family, twin, and adoption studies show that risk for schizophrenia is about ten times higher among the siblings and offspring of people with the disorder than it is among the general population.[1] Concordance rates for MZ ("identical") twins are about 50 percent, whereas those for DZ ("fraternal") twins are about 17 percent. In other words, if one twin has schizophrenia, his or her identical twin has a 50 percent chance of also developing the disease. The heritability for risk of schizophrenia is about 80 percent, meaning that approximately

80 percent of the variance in risk among people is attributable to differences in their genes rather than to differences in their environments.[2]

Heritability estimates for other disorders vary, but all show that variation in genes is associated with variation in susceptibility to illness. Estimates for anxiety disorders range from 30 to 40 percent, whereas those for bipolar disorder and autism are 65 and 90 percent, respectively.[3]

No psychopathologist doubts that genes influence risk for mental disorder. However, identifying the genetic culprits and their aberrant alleles is far more difficult than merely confirming that genes influence risk. Many factors complicate discovery of the genetic basis of mental disorders.[4] First, the relation between gene and disease is nearly always probabilistic, not deterministic. With few exceptions (for example, Huntington's disease), genes heighten risk for disease; they do not foreordain it.

Second, most scientists believe that risk for psychiatric disorders is polygenic. That is, many genes, most having small to modest effect, likely contribute to disease phenotypes. Schizophrenia, for example, almost certainly does not result from a single, pathogenic gene.[5]

Third, genes seldom have a single effect on the phenotype. Most genes have multiple effects, a process called *pleiotropy*. The downstream functions of proteins coded by genes are diverse. It is not as if we have a gene "for" and only for a psychiatric disorder.[6]

Fourth, genes interact, often in complex ways. The presence of certain alleles at various genetic loci may either increase or decrease the impact of a disease allele at another locus, a phenomenon called *epistasis*.

Fifth, Gene × Environment interactions may influence whether alleles conferring vulnerability result in the emergence of a disorder. Certain environmental inputs may be essential to activate a pathogenic gene. For example, people at genetic risk for alcoholism will never develop the disorder if they avoid drinking alcohol. Genes do not somehow propel people to the tavern.

Interestingly, the concept of Gene × Environment interaction means two entirely different things in the fields of quantitative behavior genetics and developmental biology, causing much conflict and confusion about nature versus nurture in psychology.[7] In behavior genetics, the phrase denotes a statistical interaction emerging in populations. In many population-level studies, analyses of variance indicate effects of differences in environments and differences in genes, but no statistically significant effect of the interaction between genes and environment. Hence, behavior geneticists conclude that we can characterize differences among people by treating environment and genes as additive, independent sources of phenotypic variation, ignoring any interaction between the two.

Developmental biologists regard dismissal of Gene × Environment interaction as preposterous. These scientists aim to elucidate the environmental and genetic causes of individual development. For them, development *always* involves an interaction between a genotype and an environment.

Realization that both camps mean entirely different things when they discuss Gene × Environment interaction would have prevented many acrimonious battles over nature versus nurture. Behavior geneticists aim to discover the causes of differences *among* people in the population, whereas developmental biologists aim to discover the causes of development *within* individuals.

Sixth, genetic heterogeneity may greatly complicate identification of risk alleles. Not only may multiple genetic loci contribute to risk, but multiple aberrant allelic variants may exist at a single genetic locus, each influencing risk for the same disorder. That is, genetic heterogeneity may result in phenotypic homogeneity at the level of psychiatric phenomenology. Indeed, allelic heterogeneity—

many mutant, aberrant alleles at the same genetic locus—usually characterizes complex diseases.[8] For example, mutations of nearly 100 genes all result in deafness, and nearly all of these alleles are recent and rare. Even more striking, more than 1,000 different mutant alleles at each of only two genetic loci confer risk for breast cancer. Thus not only do multiple mutant alleles confer risk at a specific genetic locus, but different genes also confer risk in different people.[9]

Seventh, ambiguities in the phenotype itself may complicate discovery of genes for risk. For example, the definition of major depressive disorder is very broad and is surely genetically heterogeneous as well as phenomenologically diverse. Genes may not honor mental disorders as defined in the current DSM.[10]

In sum, all these factors greatly complicate our attempt to identify genes "for" psychiatric disorders. They do not doom the enterprise to futility, but they do ensure that DSM-5 will not define mental disorders genetically.

Genetic Linkage Studies

We know that genes influence risk for mental disorder. That much is clear. Yet identifying the specific risk alleles is another matter entirely. Linkage analysis is the traditional method for identifying genes associated with a disorder. It involves identifying a polymorphic DNA marker with a known chromosomal location. Suitable markers may constitute either a sequence of DNA that varies among people or a single nucleotide polymorphism (SNP, pronounced "snip"). Genetic linkage is determined when the marker occurs more frequently among members of a family pedigree who have the disorder than among those who do not. If the marker and the disorder "travel" together through a pedigree, showing up in the same individuals, then a disease gene must reside near the DNA marker on the same chromosome as physically proximal neighbors. Usually, the more family members who carry the same version of the DNA marker and who have the disorder, the closer the disease gene is to the marker.[11]

Unfortunately, the scientific yield of these linkage studies has been modest. Identifying the chromosomal neighborhood of a disease gene is not the same thing as identifying the gene itself, let alone the allelic variants that cause vulnerability to the disorder. Moreover, scientists have encountered problems identifying genes for most complex diseases, presumably because linkage analysis is insufficiently powerful to detect genes having small to modest effects on risk for disease.[12]

Genome-Wide Association Studies

Genomics is a new branch of biology concerning the entire genome of an organism, and the mapping of the human genome has launched human genomics. Medical researchers working in this field conduct genome-wide association studies (GWAS) designed to identify the allelic variant (or variants) of specific genes that heighten risk for disorder. In the typical study, scientists ascertain the genotype of subjects with a certain psychiatric disorder and control subjects matched to the patients on demographic variables, such as sex and ethnicity. These studies involve hundreds of subjects and require testing the strength of association (effect size) between variants of a specific gene and the presence of the disorder.

There are three explanations for an association between a genetic variant and a disease phenotype.[13] First, the allele has a causal influence on disease expression. Second, the allele merely correlates with disease expression because it resides on the same chromosome near the allele that actually does exert causal influence on disease expression. Third, the association is spurious, a statistical fluke—

a false positive. Given that the human genome contains at least 20,000 genes, and given that the extremely low probability that any one gene confers risk for the disorder under study, the odds are high that spurious associations will emerge. Indeed, one genetic epidemiologist argued that most published findings are "false" (spurious), chiefly for this reason.[14] Many findings in the molecular genetics of psychopathology may reflect pure chance, not true associations.

Researchers have provisionally identified candidates implicated in certain mental disorders, including schizophrenia.[15] Yet matters remain complex even for the two most promising possibilities: the gene for dysbindin (DTNBP1) and the disrupted-in-schizophrenia gene (DISC1).[16] The dysbindin gene appears implicated in dopamine function, whereas the DISC1 gene regulates new neurons in the adult brain. The dysbindin gene is very large, and it includes at least 363 SNPs. Studies designed to identify allelic variants associated with schizophrenia have yielded confusing results. No one variant has been consistently associated with the disorder, and sometimes a variant is associated with increased risk in one study and decreased risk in another. A recent study involving 1,870 cases of schizophrenia and schizoaffective disorder and 2,002 control subjects failed to confirm a significant association between disorder and 14 candidate genes.[17] Researchers had previously reported significant associations between each of these genes and schizophrenia in studies with relatively small samples. Failure to replicate these early promising findings in such a large study is especially disappointing.

Indeed, throughout medicine, the pattern has been that early studies report larger effect sizes for the association of a candidate gene and a disease than do later studies.[18] Often the effect disappears in subsequent studies. Sometimes studies reporting nonreplication have too few subjects, and hence insufficient statistical power to detect genuine associations between a candidate gene and a disease. Moreover, genes conferring only a small degree of vulnerability will be harder to detect than will those exerting a large effect on risk. In addition, there may be hundreds of disease-causing mutant alleles at more than one genetic locus, as in breast cancer. Finally, although a genuine association may exist, it may be much stronger in certain subpopulations than in others. Taken together, these facts underscore the complexity of psychiatric genomics.

Can Endophenotypes Help?

Difficulties replicating allelic associations for complex diseases, including psychiatric disorders, have motivated efforts to ascertain associations between specific alleles and endophenotypes rather than disorders per se. An endophenotype is a process that mediates the relation between gene and phenotype and is less visible than the signs and symptoms of the disorder. Prior research and theory suggest possible endophenotypes for mental illness.

Irving Gottesman and Todd Gould suggest that endophenotypes should be heritable, should correlate with the psychiatric disorder, should be more common in healthy relatives of the patient than in the general population, and should be evident even when the patient's symptoms subside.[19] An endophenotype should be reliably measurable, and ideally should qualify as a psychobiologically plausible mechanism implicated in pathophysiology.

Hence, psychobiological correlates of psychiatric disorders are often good candidates for endophenotypes suitable for genetic analysis. Endophenotypes have included performance on cognitive tasks (to determine attentional impairment), personality measures, neuroanatomical abnormalities, metabolic variables, and electrophysiological measures.[20] Candidate endophenotypes are diverse, ranging from "hard" biological ones to "soft" psychological ones.

The causal distance between gene and endophenotype is shorter than the distance between gene and the disorder phenotype. Accordingly, scientists have hoped that it might be easier to elucidate the genetic basis of endophenotypes correlated with psychiatric disorders than to elucidate the genetic basis of the disorders themselves. This hope rests on the assumption that associations between certain genes and endophenotypes are stronger than associations between these genes and the psychiatric disorders themselves. That is, the fewer the pathways that produce an endophenotype, the easier it should be to ascertain its genetic underpinnings. Moreover, the reliability of endophenotypes is likely to be greater than the reliability of psychiatric diagnoses, further increasing the chance of discerning the relevant genetic architecture.

Researchers have conducted linkage and association studies of endophenotypes, each correlated with a syndrome or risk for a syndrome. In an exemplary study, Ahmad Hariri and his colleagues obtained DNA samples from the saliva of psychiatrically healthy subjects as a means of ascertaining each subject's genotype for the serotonin transporter gene.[21] This polymorphic gene has two common variants: a short allele and a long allele. An earlier study by Avshalom Caspi and his colleagues had indicated that individuals either homozygous or heterozygous for the short allele are at heightened risk for developing depression following exposure to stressful life events, whereas those homozygous for the long allele are relatively resilient.[22] Hariri and his team had two groups of subjects. One group consisted of fourteen subjects with two long alleles, and the second group consisted of fourteen subjects with at least one short allele. They had subjects view photographs of faces displaying emotional expressions, then assessed their brain activation via fMRI (functional Magnetic Resonance Imaging). The group carrying at least one short allele exhibited a larger amygdala response to faces depicting fear than did the group whose members were homozygous for the long allele. The effect size was very large; allelic status accounted for about 40 percent of the variance in amygdalar response to fearful faces. The amygdala mediates the registration of emotion-provoking stimuli. This study exemplifies the new subfield of imaging genetics.

Unfortunately, the effect size shrank dramatically when these researchers replicated their experiment, despite their having used far more subjects than in their original study.[23] Indeed, in the second experiment, they tested ninety-two subjects, and they included the data from nineteen subjects from the first study. These studies illustrate how estimates of effect size are often much larger in earlier studies than in later ones. Findings that capture the imagination of the field and the media are those characterized by large effects. Subsequent replications are unlikely to yield such amazing results, especially if chance inflated the size of the original effect.

Reviewing research on a diversity of candidate endophenotypes for various disorders, Jonathan Flint and Marcus Munafò found that the effect sizes for the association between candidate alleles and endophenotypes are no larger than the effect sizes for the association between candidate alleles and the psychiatric disorders themselves.[24] The genetic architecture of endophenotypes appears just as complex as the disorders themselves. However, even if the genetic complexity of endophenotypes matches that of the resultant diseases, this does not undermine the usefulness of studying endophenotypes.[25] Functional and structural aspects of the brain mediate the path from genes to behavior, and investigating their relation to genetic variants can illuminate the pathway from genome to clinical disorder.

Hariri's work was inspired by Caspi and his colleagues' landmark study showing that people who were homozygous for the short version of the serotonin transporter gene were at heightened risk for depression, but only if they encountered major life stressors. This study was remarkably influential, partly because it provided the hitherto elusive evidence of a Gene × Environment interaction that psychopathologists had long sought. The genotype predicted depression only in the context of life stressors.

The excitement generated by Caspi's findings inspired many attempted replications. However, the authors of two independent meta-analyses concluded that the original Gene × Environment interaction has not stood the test of time and repeated attempted replications.[26] Most studies show that exposure to major stressors increases risk for depression. This effect is the same, though, whether or not the subject carries copies of the short version of the serotonin transporter gene. Repeated failures to replicate the original finding raise the possibility that the original result might have been attributable to chance. At the very least, failures to replicate underscore the complexity of the pathway from genotype to depressive phenotype.

Yet an even more recent meta-analysis in this rapidly changing field indicated that the original Caspi finding *does* replicate when investigators use rigorous, objective methods for assessing stressful events.[27] The finding does not replicate in studies in which researchers used assessment methods of questionable reliability, such as self-report checklists of stressors.

Is the Assumptive Framework Incorrect?

The assumptive framework guiding much research has been that common diseases, such as schizophrenia, result from combinations of common alleles, each having a small effect, interacting with environmental variables. Because any single gene exerts only a small effect, locating risk genes is akin to finding a needle in a haystack. Hence, discovering a candidate gene, let alone replicating the original finding, is especially challenging. Discussing schizophrenia genetics, Jon McClellan, Ezra Susser, and Mary-Claire King question this framework.[28] As an alternative, they propose that schizophrenia may constitute a genetically heterogeneous disease caused by many rare, but highly penetrant, alleles. They suggest that mutant alleles may be specific to certain families or even to an individual patient. The implications of this hypothesis are sobering. If different aberrant alleles generate risk for schizophrenia in different families, then large-scale association studies are unlikely to bear much fruit. Moreover, pooling data from families with many affected individuals is unlikely to yield a strong genetic signal if schizophrenia arises from different mutant alleles across different families. Ordinarily, increasing sample size improves our ability to detect the signal amid the noise. Yet in this case, the noise increases with the signal, canceling out the advantage usually gained by increasing the number of subjects.

Multiple lines of evidence support this thesis. First, although schizophrenia runs in families, most people with the illness do not have immediate relatives with the disease. Yet in other families, many members develop schizophrenia. This pattern implies that some families carry highly penetrant alleles arising from relatively recent mutations, and that different aberrant alleles lead to schizophrenia in different families.

Second, older fathers are more likely to have schizophrenic offspring than are younger fathers. The odds of offspring developing schizophrenia are 2.8 times greater among children whose fathers were forty-five years or older at the time of their birth than among children whose fathers were aged twenty to twenty-four.[29] Older paternal age is associated with increased rate of mutations in sperm cells, and these mutant alleles may confer risk for schizophrenia.[30]

Third, people with schizophrenia have fewer offspring than do healthy people.[31] If alleles predisposing individuals to schizophrenia were ancient and common, then natural selection would have diminished their frequency in the population. By contrast, if aberrant alleles arise from recent mutations and thus are rare, this would explain why schizophrenia persists despite its diminished fertility.

Fourth, this hypothesis can also explain the absence of historical descriptions of schizophrenia before the past few hundred years, as discussed in Chapter 5. Mutant alleles of relatively recent origin cause schizophrenia.[32]

Finally, recent research confirms the association between rare, genetic abnormalities and schizophrenia.[33] In one study, researchers conducted a genome scan capable of detecting rare copy number variations (CNVs) associated with schizophrenia.[34] CNVs refer to loss or gain of large chunks of DNA. For example, if a section of DNA containing a gene on a chromosome is duplicated, then the carrier has three, not two, copies of the gene. Conversely, if the section is missing, then the carrier has only one copy of the gene. Although people can inherit CNVs, many of these errors appear *de novo* in the carrier. Although such scans cannot reliably detect rare single nucleotide mutations, they can detect rare CNVs. The research team identified a CNV on chromosome 1 and two CNVs on chromosome 15. The odds ratios for association with schizophrenia (or related psychosis, such as schizoaffective disorder) were 14.83, 2.73, and 11.54, respectively. When they confined the study group to schizophrenia, defined narrowly, the odds ratios diminished, thereby implying that the phenotype associated with these CNVs is broader than pure schizophrenia and is associated with psychosis more generally. In any event, these odds ratios are much larger than those scientists have traditionally found when they have studied single SNPs. The results are consistent with the hypothesis that rare, highly penetrant genetic abnormalities may bear a significant burden of the genetic risk for schizophrenia spectrum disorders.

Diagnostic and Clinical Implications

What are the diagnostic implications of molecular genetic research on psychiatric disorders? Can genomic findings revamp our phenotypes, altering diagnostic criteria in DSM-5? Some psychopathologists think so. Some have noted that psychiatric molecular geneticists are using twenty-first-century methods to ascertain the genetic basis of syndromes whose definitions have remained essentially unchanged since the nineteenth century.[35] Some are impatient with hoary diagnostic boundaries, such as that between schizophrenia and bipolar disorder, long associated with Emil Kraepelin.[36] Other researchers argue that discovery of genes that increase susceptibility to both schizophrenia and bipolar disorder signal the end of the Kraepelinian dichotomy.[37] They argue that genomics shows that we should abandon the distinction between these two diseases.

Some data indicate that schizophrenia and bipolar disorder share genetic underpinnings and thus do not appear to be distinct diseases.[38] For example, the disorders often do not breed true within family pedigrees. Relatives of individuals with schizophrenia are at elevated risk for bipolar disorder as well as for schizophrenia and schizophrenia spectrum disorders, and relatives of individuals with bipolar disorder are at risk for schizophrenia as well as for bipolar disorder.[39] A twin study uncovered genes that conferred susceptibility to both disorders as well as genes conferring risk for bipolar disorder but not for schizophrenia, and vice versa.[40]

Genome-wide studies have identified certain chromosomal regions linked to schizophrenia that are linked to bipolar disorder as well.[41] Research has shown that allelic variants of the DISC1 gene are associated with susceptibility to bipolar disorder and schizoaffective disorder as well as to schizophrenia.[42] Genome-wide association studies have identified several candidate genes having allelic variants that correlate with risk for schizophrenia and with risk for bipolar disorder.[43]

What are we to make of these findings? Should molecular genetics trump phenomenology, course, and response to treatment in providing the basis for nosology? Should we ignore data at other levels of analysis and collapse these two syndromes into one disorder?

For many reasons, we should not abandon the Kraepelinian dichotomy, at least not yet. First, the effect sizes for genes identified in association studies are not only very small but seldom replicate anyway.[44]

Second, numerous distinct diseases have overlapping genetic risk factors.[45] Genes that heighten risk for essential hypertension also increase the risk for both myocardial infarction and hemorrhagic stroke. Variants of the oncogene BRCA1 increase not only risk for breast cancer but also risk for prostate cancer and stomach cancer, among others. Yet common risk alleles have not led doctors to conclude that breast cancer and prostate cancer are "really" the same disease.

Third, risk alleles exist at a level of analysis different from the disorders themselves. A carrier of these alleles is at risk for disorder, but the multifactorial causal processes that produce clinical schizophrenia require environmental inputs as well. Common genes do not mean an identity of cause. Risk for all (or nearly all) psychiatric disorders is multifactorial. In addition to environmental influences on risk, multiple genes contribute to liability to disorder. Moreover, each gene has only small to modest effect on risk. Most genes have pleiotropic effects; that is, although each gene codes for a specific protein, the subsequent function of these proteins is diverse. The upshot is that most genes have multiple downstream phenotypic consequences. It is not as if schizophrenia, for example, is traceable to a single aberrant allele. Therefore, it seems premature to define schizophrenia and bipolar disorder at the molecular genetic level of analysis. At the very least, psychiatry needs to replicate its molecular findings before we can define mental disorders genotypically. Perhaps in some future DSM we will be able to do so, but not anytime soon.

Even if genomics does not revolutionize how we define mental disorders, might it affect how we treat them? The hope is that knowledge about aberrant alleles might someday enable medical scientists either to "correct" the problem at the genomic level or to use genomic information to guide selection of therapies. However, even in those rare cases in which scientists have determined that a single gene causes a disease, treatments may not be immediately forthcoming. Researchers have identified the gene responsible for Huntington's disease, but this knowledge has yet to yield a cure. On the other hand, interventions need not occur at the locus of the disease gene (or genes) itself. It might be easier to intervene downstream. It may also be possible to intervene at the epigenetic level.[46]

Phenotypic homogeneity accompanied by genetic heterogeneity does raise the possibility of subtyping patients according to their genotype. Such subtyping might have important clinical implications. Clinicians might conduct diagnostic interviews prior to obtaining a saliva sample from patients. DNA is readily extractable from these samples, and companies can quickly provide answers to questions about the genome of patients. Just as other physicians routinely send blood samples to the lab to determine whether a patient's respiratory symptoms have a bacterial or a viral cause, psychiatrists could send saliva samples to the lab to determine whether a bipolar patient's illness has one genetic cause versus another. Diagnosis would require genotypic as well as phenotypic (signs and symptoms) information.

At least in some cases, genetic information may help guide

treatment choice.[47] Using data from a very large effectiveness study on the treatment of major depressive disorder, researchers identified a group of patients who experienced emergent suicidal ideation after having started treatment with the SSRI citalopram. Two single nucleotide polymorphisms near the gene coding for cyclic adenosine monophosphate response element binding (CREB) protein were associated with the emergence of suicidal ideation in male patients. This finding, if replicated, might provide guidance to doctors prescribing this antidepressant. After genotyping depressed male patients, doctors could prescribe medications other than citalopram for those patients with this genotype.

In sum, molecular genetic findings alone are too preliminary to justify collapsing the Kraepelinian dichotomy, let alone overhauling the DSM. At best, molecular genetics can help refine the phenotype, characterized in terms of either categorical subtypes or dimensions. Yet these data require integration with other sources of consilient evidence before we can engineer fundamental changes in the nosological system. Perhaps clinical researchers might collect diverse phenotypic data without confining themselves to the DSM. Different ways of carving up the phenotype may yield more replicable, robust data.

CAN NEUROSCIENCE IMPROVE PSYCHIATRIC DIAGNOSIS?

Psychiatrists keen to advertise their discipline as a progressive biomedical enterprise stress that mental disorders have a "neurobiological basis."[48] Given that the brain mediates all behavior, normal as well as abnormal, this claim is true. But if the assertion implies that we have discovered the etiology and pathophysiology of mental disorders, then it is clearly false. Although many psychopathologists are impatient with a system that defines mental disorders purely by their signs and symptoms, we are not yet in a position to place the DSM on an etiological foundation.

Psychopathologists have tried to identify biological markers that correlate with various DSM syndromes. Yet as the psychiatrist Dennis Charney and his colleagues observed, psychiatry has "failed to identify a single neurobiological phenotypic marker or gene that is useful in making a diagnosis of a major psychiatric disorder or for predicting response to psychopharmacologic treatment."[49] The presence of a sign or symptom rarely indicates the presence of a specific disease, whereas its absence rarely signals the absence of the disease. Yet matters are especially complicated in psychiatry when supposed biological markers display variable associations with the disorder.

Consider the case of putative HPA axis dysfunction in PTSD. Contrary to the prediction that PTSD reflects an extreme version of the normal response to stress, research revealed that patients with PTSD tended to have lower levels of the stress hormone cortisol than did healthy control subjects.[50] This finding encouraged the view that PTSD was a genuine biological disease whose marker was low cortisol. However, there was tremendous overlap in the distribution of cortisol values between patients and control subjects, and none of the patients had values that would worry an endocrinologist.[51] A handful of PTSD cases in the low-normal range, and a handful of control subjects in the high-normal range, resulted in an average difference between the groups. It was not as if all the PTSD patients were clustered at the very low end of the cortisol distribution, each patient characterized by this hormonal abnormality. A mean difference between groups cannot provide the basis for a biological marker when the overlap between the groups is so large.

Most scientists expressing optimism about the neuroscience

informing diagnosis acknowledge that we cannot yet define and conceptualize mental disorders in terms of abnormalities in the structure and function of the brain. Nevertheless, they observe, there are ways in which neuroscience might enrich our understanding of pathophysiology, paving the way for a more etiologically informed nosology in the future.

The psychiatrist Steven Hyman holds that "neurobiological information can, along with clinical observations and family and genetic studies, help to shape a reconsideration of the DSM system."[52] In particular, Hyman urges that we reconfigure the DSM-5 to enable it to accommodate new findings from neuroscience and genetics as they emerge rather than waiting another decade or so for DSM-6. More usefully, he suggests that researchers focus on elucidating neurobiological circuits that cut across traditional diagnostic boundaries rather than confining inquiry to validating specific categorical entities. The emphasis on dimensional approaches to psychopathology, he says, will likely pay diagnostic dividends in the future, even if those payoffs do not immediately transform the DSM-5.

Dominic Murphy, a philosopher of science deeply immersed in the details of psychopathology, points out that eliminating theory from the DSM "cuts psychiatry off from any hope of finding out how things really are."[53] He advocates aiming for a nosology based on causal explanations of mental disorders while acknowledging how daunting this task will be. Murphy holds that psychiatry is applied cognitive neuroscience, and wherever possible, our nosology should incorporate causal knowledge about how breakdowns in the mind/brain occur.

At first glance, we seem to be at an impasse. We have had a series of relatively atheoretical descriptive systems since DSM-III that organize the domain of psychopathology in terms of surface similarity of signs and symptoms, not in terms of their causes. Yet few psychopathologists would claim that we now possess sufficient knowledge about etiology and pathophysiology to establish our nosology on a causal foundation. The best solution is to have a system that fosters the research that will illuminate the causal basis of mental disorders. Although atheoretical in itself, the DSM descriptive system has certainly stimulated considerable research that ultimately will provide the answers to questions about causality. Moreover, these answers will almost certainly come in piecemeal fashion. Future DSMs will contain a mix of disorders, some characterized causally and some characterized descriptively. Knowledge about causation is unlikely to proceed at the same rate across the domain of psychopathology.

Psychopathologists, however, must take care not to reproduce the problems of a purely descriptive system when they make conjectures about underlying causal structure. Arguments for a diagnostic system based on etiology and pathophysiology can sometimes send clinical researchers looking in the wrong direction.

Consider clinicians' proposal for the concept of obsessive-compulsive spectrum disorders.[54] According to this concept, several seemingly unrelated syndromes fall along a continuum anchored by compulsive characteristics associated with avoidance of harm and behavior designed to reduce anxiety, and by impulsive characteristics associated with pleasure-seeking and immediate gratification at the other end. Risk aversion anchors one end of the spectrum and risk taking anchors the other. The compulsive end includes obsessive-compulsive disorder (OCD), body dysmorphic disorder, hypochondriasis, and tic disorders (for example, Tourette's syndrome). The impulsive end includes syndromes such as trichotillomania, exhibitionism, and pathological gambling. Other conditions that researchers include within the spectrum are eating disorders, autism, and compulsive shopping. What supposedly ties these incredibly diverse syndromes together is that each involves repetitive thoughts and behavior. More recently, advocates of obsessive-compulsive spectrum disorders have argued that endophenotypic features, such as shared abnormalities in brain circuits, mediate expression of disorders along this spectrum.[55]

Apart from the fact that neurobiological, genetic, and other evidence adduced for the concept of an OCD spectrum ranges from weak to unreplicable, advocates for the concept direct their etiological focus at the wrong level of analysis.[56] As Eric Storch, Jon Abramowitz, and Wayne Goodman emphasize, we must examine the psychological function of the repetitive behavior.[57] OCD patients engage in repetitive checking and washing to reduce the distress associated with obsessions and to prevent feared outcomes. Washing and checking rituals reduce distress in the short term but prevent patients from learning that their distressing obsessions will diminish even if they refrain from performing these compulsive rituals.

Focusing on the mere *form* of the behavior—its repetitive character—at the expense of its *function*—the motivation for performing it—misleadingly implies etiological commonalities when none exist. For example, postulating unconfirmed neurobiological abnormalities shared by obsessive-compulsive washers and heroin addicts merely because one group repetitively washes and the other repetitively injects drugs provides no basis for nosological refinement. The motive for compulsive washing is distress reduction, not pleasure. The motivation for heroin use, at least initially, is pleasure and only later acquires the additional motive of avoidance of withdrawal symptoms. Theory-based diagnoses require psychological motivation, exemplified by the functional analyses that sharply distinguish OCD and addictions, exhibitionism, and other "impulsive" problems. One is governed by avoidance motivation, the other by pleasure-seeking.

Ironically, the spectrum concept requires us to pluck repetitive behavior out of its context and ignore its motivational basis, thereby making it abstract. Neuroscience can sometimes seduce us into looking in the wrong places for a theoretically rich understanding of etiology. We cannot make sense of OCD by focusing on neurobiology alone. We must examine the cognitive and motivational bases driving the symptoms of the disorder.

This caveat about OCD holds for other conditions as well. When it comes to functional imaging of the brain, the provocative context is at least as important as the neural response. Jill Hooley found that formerly depressed patients and never-depressed control subjects exhibited different neural responses to maternal criticism.[58] Her knowledge of brain circuitry and the role of criticism in relapse led her to describe this difference as an abnormality (dysfunction) in the brains of the formerly depressed subjects. Hence, the *relation* between a standard context and variability of neural response was informative, whereas the brain scans themselves would not have been.

The opposite may also occur. Consider a hypothetical case whereby healthy subjects encounter a threatening stimulus and patients with snake phobia encounter a harmless snake. The neural signal of fear will likely be identical in the two groups. Nothing in the functioning of the brain, characterized at the neural level, will distinguish the patients from the control subjects. The relation between the provocative context and the neural response again provides the basis for inference about dysfunction, but the dysfunction emerges at a higher level of description than the neural response. Cognitive mechanisms that mediate the interpretation of threat are not working properly. Patients respond to harmless threats as if they were dangerous. These mechanisms are instantiated in the brain but are not reducible to descriptions at the neural level. In fact, experimental cognitive psychopathologists have identified biases in attention, interpretation, and memory in patients with mood and anxiety disorders.[59] At the very least, such biases are constitutive of these disorders and may figure in their etiology as well.

EMERGING TRENDS

Research on the genetics of psychopathology is developing at a very fast pace, and conclusions appearing in this chapter may soon be overturned as new findings emerge. Several trends warrant special emphasis.

Research teams from around the world have formed consortia, enabling them to pool data from thousands of patients and healthy control subjects, greatly increasing the likelihood that they will discover genetic risk factors for mental disorders. The International Schizophrenia Consortium has discovered that thousands of common alleles, each having very small effects, contribute to risk for bipolar disorder as well as for schizophrenia, but not for several other nonpsychiatric diseases.[60] This group also discovered that people with schizophrenia have a high burden of CNVs, each rare, but of large effect.[61] Hence, both common genes of minuscule effect and rare genes and CNVs of large effect may contribute to risk for schizophrenia and related disorders.

The Cross-Disorder Phenotype Group of the Psychiatric GWAS Consortium is explicitly investigating the range of conditions whose risk is increased by certain allelic variants.[62] Instead of beginning solely with a phenotype (for example, DSM schizophrenia) and then examining its genetic correlates, this group is taking a certain gene of theoretical interest and examining its phenotypic profile. Findings from these consortia will help shape the structure of diagnostic systems in the future.

Attempts to identify vulnerability alleles associated with psychiatric disorders amount to testing for a straightforward main effect of the genetic variant, as in GWAS research. This approach can identify versions of genes that contribute to risk for psychopathology that no one had ever imagined played any role. Yet another approach, one requiring far fewer subjects, is to use multiple converging lines of evidence to identify candidate genes whose variants should theoretically increase risk, especially in certain environments.[63] Indeed, this Gene × Environment approach is exemplified by Caspi's findings on heightened risk for depression in response to stressors in people with two short versions of the serotonin transporter gene.

Interestingly, people with "vulnerable" genotypes may actually do better than those with "resilient" genotypes when environments are favorable rather than harsh. Although the results are not always statistically significant, carriers of the two short alleles tend to have fewer psychological problems than do carriers of two long alleles when both groups experience nonabusive environments. That is, rather than having a vulnerable genotype per se, they may have one that is highly sensitive to the environment for better or for worse.[64] At least some vulnerability genes seem better viewed as plasticity genes. The developmental researchers Bruce Ellis and Thomas Boyce liken children with these genotypes to orchids that decline rapidly under adverse conditions but blossom into flowers of stunning beauty under conditions of nurture and support, whereas children with resilient genotypes are like dandelions that manage to survive no matter what the conditions.[65] If genes predisposing a person to psychopathology in adverse environments foster plasticity and flourishing in favorable environments, then it is easy to see why they would remain in the gene pool throughout the course of human evolution.

Findings on Gene × Environment interaction prompt questions about how the environment manages to alter the impact of genes. There may be as many as 25,000 genes in the human genome, and about half of them are expressible in the brain.[66] Yet a gene is expressed only when its DNA is transcribed into RNA and translated into protein. Otherwise, it remains inactive. Genes remain dormant until proteins called transcription factors bind to their DNA, thereby activating the expression of the gene. Socio-environmental factors activate processes in the central nervous system that influence the activity of hormones and neurotransmitters throughout the periphery of the body, resulting in the interaction of signaling molecules with receptors on cells that activate transcription factors.[67] Via these pathways, the environment regulates the expression of genes, either turning them on or turning them off.

Certain processes affect how accessible a gene's DNA is to transcription factors. For example, if a chemical methyl group binds to the promoter region of a gene, it blocks the enzymes that transcribe DNA, thereby silencing the gene.[68] Because DNA methylation alters the expression of a gene without changing the actual nucleotide sequence of its DNA, it counts as an *epigenetic* process, meaning "in addition to the genes."

Scientists have been investigating epigenetic processes in rats, and these findings have importance for how stress gets under the skin in human beings.[69] For example, rat pups whose mothers licked and groomed them at high rates are much more resistant to later stressors than are pups whose mothers licked and groomed them infrequently. Rats who received abundant licking and grooming rarely exhibit methylation of the promoter region of the glucocorticoid receptor gene. Therefore, this gene is easily expressed, leading to low levels of stress hormones in response to aversive stimuli. In contrast, rats that experience low levels of licking and grooming by mothers exhibit methylation of this gene, making them highly reactive to stressors.

Psychopathologists have begun to investigate how early experience induces epigenetic processes that make it either easier or harder for genes to be expressed.[70] For example, postmortem analyses of the brains of suicide victims who either had or did not have histories of abuse during childhood revealed evidence of epigenetic regulation of glucocorticoid receptor expression. Unlike suicide victims and control subjects who did not die by suicide, those suicide victims with abuse histories exhibited evidence of methylation of the promoter region for this gene.[71] How the environment initiates epigenetic processes that either facilitate or impede environmental regulation of gene expression is destined to become a major research topic in psychopathology for years to come.

7

Ever since DSM-III, our diagnostic manuals have embodied a descriptive, neo-Kraepelinian approach to conceptualizing psychopathology. This approach regards each disorder as a discrete, categorical entity defined by its signs and symptoms.[1] Disorders differ by kind, not by degree. The assumption is that schizophrenia, panic disorder, anorexia nervosa, and other mental illnesses are qualitatively distinct conditions just as are breast cancer, AIDS, and bacterial pneumonia. A further assumption is that descriptive characterization of discrete mental disorders would foster research that would validate the diagnostic categories.[2] Validation would entail discovery of each syndrome's distinctive etiology, pathophysiology, biological markers, and results on psychological tests. This information, in turn, would foster specific treatments for specific disorders. Indeed, the key purpose of diagnosis is to ensure that the patient receives the correct treatment.

In many ways, our categorical system has been a success. Explicit inclusion and exclusion criteria for diagnosing mental disorders have provided a lingua franca for researchers of diverse theoretical orientations to study the causes and treatments of the same conditions. The categorical approach is an efficient means of communicating information about a patient. When clinicians learn that a patient has borderline personality disorder, they envision the prototypical patient who engages in parasuicidal self-cutting, has an unstable self-image, has a history of stormy interpersonal relationships, and experiences great difficulty regulating emotions, especially rage. Knowing the categorical diagnosis enables clinicians to predict many features of the patient.

The categorical approach has fostered a tremendous amount of research. In epidemiology, for example, discrete syndromes are easy to count, enabling researchers to determine how common mental disorders are in the general population. Pharmaceutical companies may favor discrete diagnoses for which they can develop drugs and receive FDA approval. The FDA, however, does not demand that medications target a categorical disease entity as a requirement for approval. Painkillers and diuretics, for example, target symptoms, not discrete diseases.[3]

Finally, evidence-based practice guidelines presuppose categorical diagnoses.[4] These guidelines inform practitioners about which treatments work best for bipolar disorder, panic disorder, and other conditions. Because third-party insurers typically allow a certain number of treatment sessions depending on the patient's diagnosis, a categorical system simplifies the reimbursement process.

PROBLEMS WITH CATEGORICAL DIAGNOSES

The virtues of the categorical system notwithstanding, its limitations have become increasingly apparent. One problem concerns widespread comorbidity or co-occurrence of multiple disorders in the same person. Most people in epidemiological as well as in clinical samples who qualify for one disorder also qualify for other disorders.[5] Extensive psychiatric comorbidity undermines the expectation that diagnosis amounts to determining the one, true disorder from which the patient suffers, ruling out similar conditions.

Comorbidity presents less of a conceptual problem in the rest of medicine than it does in psychiatry. A person with breast cancer can certainly develop a respiratory infection and diabetes, and no one questions whether the patient suffers from three distinct diseases. Yet when someone receives diagnoses of generalized anxiety disorder (GAD), social phobia, and major depressive disorder, we wonder whether the person truly suffers from three distinct disorders or whether each "disease" is a variant manifestation of the same fundamental emotional disturbance. The symptomatic resemblance among these conditions makes us wonder whether we have imposed artificial boundaries on the phenomena, creating discrete categories where none exists in nature.

Many symptoms in medicine, such as fever, fatigue, and cough, are nonspecific to any particular disease. Yet even direct symptom overlap does not present an insurmountable barrier to accurate diagnosis. Consider a patient who suffers from a persistent cough. Does it signify a viral respiratory infection, emphysema, or bacterial pneumonia? Laboratory tests can easily distinguish among these options, enabling correct diagnosis and treatment. In psychiatry, there is no such court of appeal. To be sure, other sources of evidence can help tip the balance one way or another, such as age of onset and course of illness. Yet none possesses the authority of laboratory tests in general medicine.

Providing some guidance for grappling with apparent comorbidity, the DSM instructs clinicians to diagnose only one disorder when the second one is "due to" the first one. For example, a patient may experience unexpected panic attacks accompanied by fear and avoidance of places where panic might strike again. The patient may also express intense fear and avoidance of windowless rooms, elevators, and other enclosed places. Does the patient suffer from two distinct entities, panic disorder with agoraphobia and claustrophobia, or merely from panic disorder with agoraphobia? Clinicians will diagnose only panic disorder with agoraphobia if they believe that the patient's fear of enclosed spaces is a manifestation of this disorder. By contrast, if panic erupts only in enclosed spaces, then claustrophobia is the diagnosis. Clinicians will then ask whether the patient has experienced panic attacks in settings other than enclosed spaces, and whether any of the attacks were unexpected. If so, then only panic disorder with agoraphobia is diagnosable. Yet this fundamental distinction rests entirely on the patient's subjective appraisal of how surprising the attacks were. No biological test can distinguish a spontaneous attack from an expected one.

Another problem concerns diagnostic instability. Kraepelin, for example, distinguished between schizophrenia and manic-depressive psychosis by their differential course of illness. Patients with the former disease had a deteriorating course, whereas those with the latter had periods of recovery and relapse. Using course of illness to determine diagnosis presupposes that one disorder does not morph into another. Yet this is precisely what happens with many DSM disorders. For example, patients with eating disorders may qualify for a diagnosis of anorexia nervosa at one point in their lives, later "recover" from this illness, and then develop bulimia nervosa or another form of pathological eating.[6] What should we make of this pattern? Has the patient really suffered from two distinct disorders in succession? Or has the patient been suffering from a single disease that manifests itself in a diversity of abnormal eating patterns?

Yet another problem with the categorical system concerns the residual diagnosis of "not otherwise specified" (NOS). The DSM provides an NOS category for each diagnostic group, such as eating disorder not otherwise specified (EDNOS), to cover patients whose clinically severe symptoms do not qualify for any other specific diagnosis. To secure access to treatment for the patient, the clinician will assign an NOS diagnosis. An adequate categorical system should include enough discrete diagnoses to cover nearly all patients who seek treatment for severe, impairing symptoms. Accordingly, clinicians should rarely need to assign an NOS diagnosis. This residual diagnosis exists to cover those rare patients who do not qualify for any single diagnosis.

Sometimes this supposedly residual category represents the largest proportion of patients. In the eating disorders field, EDNOS is by far the most frequently assigned diagnosis. For example, in one study, 5 percent of patients received a diagnosis of anorexia nervosa, 35 percent received a diagnosis of bulimia nervosa, and 60 percent received a diagnosis of EDNOS. Working within a categorical approach, some clinicians argue that the DSM-5 committee should replace EDNOS with a diagnosis of "mixed eating disorder" because of similarities between EDNOS patients and those with anorexia and bulimia nervosa.[7] Renaming EDNOS, however, does not solve the problem; it merely restates it.

Another possibility is dividing EDNOS into several new syndromes, such as purging disorder, binge eating disorder, and night eating syndrome.[8] Splitting a large category into several smaller ones may partly solve the NOS problem, but it may aggravate other ones. Indeed, seemingly excessive splitting is the chief reason for the proliferation of "new" disorders in successive editions of the DSM. Moreover, splitting will likely generate more spurious comorbidity. The more finely divided diagnostic categories become, the more likely patients will qualify for several neighboring diagnoses of dubious validity.

An additional problem with the categorical system is the tremendous variety that can occur among patients who qualify for the same disorder. Consider the case of conduct disorder. To meet criteria for the disorder, a child must have some combination of three symptoms from a list of fifteen. It is entirely possible, then, for an eleven-year-old girl who shoplifts, violates her parents' curfew by staying out late with friends, and is truant from school to receive the same diagnosis as a seventeen-year-old boy who has forced a girl to have sex with him, has committed arson, and tortures animals.[9] It seems unlikely that these children have the same disorder.

The categorical system compels diagnosticians to make binary decisions: either a person has or does not have a specific disorder. Yet individuals on either side of a diagnostic threshold can resemble each other more than two patients who qualify for the diagnosis. In the case of major depression, a person must have at least four symptoms of the nine listed to qualify for the disorder, including either sad mood or anhedonia (loss of pleasure). Accordingly, a person who reports sadness, fatigue, guilt, and insomnia has the same illness as someone who reports sadness, guilt, anhedonia, and appetite loss, exhibits psychomotor retardation, and plans to commit suicide. Yet a third person who reports sadness, insomnia, and fatigue resembles the first person far more than the second person does, even though only the first two receive a diagnosis of major depression. The diagnostic threshold of requiring at least four symptoms implies that patients with four (or more) symptoms are qualitatively different from those with only three symptoms. Yet if depressive symptoms fall on a smooth dimensional continuum with differences among people being a matter of degree, not of kind, then the imposition of a diagnostic threshold distorts the phenomenon of depression, creating a category where none exists in nature.

Yet a group of distinguished experts has made a convincing case for recognizing melancholic depression as a discrete entity distinguishable from major depression whether construed dimensionally or categorically.[10] People suffering from melancholia experience profound loss of pleasure, psychomotor retardation (slowed thinking, movement, and speech), agitated restlessness, appetite loss, loss of interest in sex, early morning awakening, and impaired concentration. They are at high risk for suicide, exhibit elevated levels of the stress hormone cortisol, and seldom respond to placebos or psychotherapies. They often benefit from electroconvulsive therapy and tricyclic antidepressants, but not selective serotonin reuptake inhibitors. The arguments of these experts illustrate how DSM-5 might incorporate dimensional diagnoses of nonmelancholic depression while retaining melancholia as a discrete category of disease.

DIMENSIONAL OPTIONS

Critics of categorical diagnoses argue that psychopathology varies continuously along multiple dimensions of mood, cognition, behavior, personality, and temperament with no natural breakpoint demarcating illness from health. Some suggest that the time is ripe to overhaul the DSM, placing it on a dimensional foundation. Others are less radical, urging instead that we retain most categorical diagnoses but supplement them with dimensional measures of psychopathology. Yet another possibility would be to characterize some disorders categorically and others dimensionally.

The DSM-5 committee members are now considering dimensional options for the new manual.[11] One scenario involves reconceptualizing all forms of psychopathology in terms of dimensions, discarding categorical diagnoses altogether. This is very unlikely to occur.

Another option involves the use of dimensional research to clarify the relation among categorical diagnoses, motivating their rearrangement in DSM-5. These studies have involved correlational and factor analyses revelatory of patterns of symptom overlap and comorbidity that run counter to the current conceptualization of mood and anxiety disorders. For example, certain anxiety disorders are more closely related to some mood disorders than they are to other anxiety disorders. In fact, drawing on this work, the psychologist David Watson has made the case for an overarching category of emotional disorders comprising three subclasses.[12] The bipolar subclass would include bipolar I disorder, bipolar II disorder, and cyclothymia. The distress disorders would comprise dysthymia, major depressive disorder, generalized anxiety disorder, and PTSD. The fear disorders would comprise panic disorder, agoraphobia, specific phobia, and social phobia.

The statistical sophistication of these studies is undeniable. Yet the payoff from rearranging syndromes seems modest. The original purpose of grouping phenotypically similar syndromes (for example, GAD and social phobia) was merely to ease differential diagnosis by alerting clinicians to conditions resembling the one, true diagnosis that fit the patient. Yet rampant comorbidity among these syndromes indicates that few patients qualify for only one disorder anyway.

More important, empirical similarities may imply similar or shared causes. Consider GAD and major depression, two syndromes that often co-occur. Their co-occurrence may reflect common etiology. In fact, twin studies indicate that the same genes increase risk for GAD as increase risk for major depression.[13] Differences between the syndromes arise from different environmental events. A common diathesis seems to put people at risk for developing either illness. At the genetic level, they appear identical. Should we then conclude that both are phenotypic variants of the same underlying disease process?

We must be cautious about what we can conclude about the causal basis of empirical similarity among the distress disorders, for example. Most studies rely solely on symptoms reported on questionnaires or during structured interviews. Behavioral or biological data seldom play a role in these studies. Indeed, a purely self-reported symptom approach would yield misleading results in other areas of medicine. Factor analyses of self-reported symptoms would likely group viral respiratory tract infections, bacterial pneumonia, emphysema, and lung cancer as variations of the same "underlying" respiratory disorder when, in fact, these similar symptoms signify diverse diseases with different etiologies. Similar subjective symptom reports need not signify common etiology and pathophysiology.

Another concern of these dimensional analyses is that the resulting rearrangement depends on the disorders studied.[14] Researchers usually omit syndromes having relatively low prevalence rates (for example, OCD), leaving us to wonder where these syndromes belong in a reconfigured system.

Let's suppose that several factors underlie the diversity of symptoms reported by patients meeting criteria for anxiety and mood disorders. What are we to conclude from this fact? Of course, these findings don't tell us where to look. They only imply that whatever lies at the root of a symptomatic cluster must explain why some symptoms hang together.

Can this approach tell us anything more than that some symptoms go together, whereas other symptoms do not? Knowing someone's factor score on dimensions of negative affectivity and positive affectivity may be interesting, but these data points exist at a higher, abstract level of analysis. Treating patients requires interventions at the most useful level of analysis, neither too coarsegrained nor too fine-grained. CBT therapists target specific distorted thoughts, catastrophic appraisals, and other cognitive biases, and they treat specific fears and avoidance behaviors. Doing exposure therapy is not a matter of treating fear and avoidance in the abstract; it is a matter of treating fear of high places, traveling in the subway, flying in airplanes, and so forth. The hierarchical structure of mood and anxiety disorders may be accurate, but its clinical relevance remains obscure.

Supplementing Categories with Dimensional Measures

Contributors to a DSM-5 volume on dimensional approaches to psychopathology argued that we should not replace the categorical system entirely. Rather, we should supplement it with dimensional diagnostic measures. For example, drawing on multiple data sets, John Helzer and his colleagues convincingly argued that alcohol problems lie on a single dimension of severity that spans normal drinking and the categories of alcohol abuse and dependence.[15] They recommended a straightforward method for integrating dimensional analysis into categorical diagnosis. For each symptom of the categories alcohol abuse and alcohol dependence, the assessor assigns one of three numbers (0, 1, or 2) to signify either its severity (for example, withdrawal) or its frequency (none, some, a lot). Although we could compute a single dimensional value by summing the scores for each symptom, Helzer and his colleagues recommended certain statistical analyses for deriving a formula for combining scores for different symptoms. For example, some symptoms may be more strongly correlated with categorical diagnoses of alcohol dependence than other symptoms (say, tolerance of alcohol versus others' complaining about one's alcohol use), and therefore should be weighted more heavily in the formula that yields a dimensional score. In addition, there is no assumption that the dimensional score lies on an interval rather than on an ordinal scale. That is, a person whose score is 32 is not necessarily twice as alcoholic as someone whose score is 16. The distance between a 0 and a 1 need not be equivalent to the distance between a 1 and a 2.

Factor analytic studies show that a single severity factor accounts for symptoms of substance abuse and dependence.[16] Alcohol abuse and alcohol dependence are not two discrete disorders. Rather, symptoms fall along a continuum of severity with no natural breakpoint separating abuse from dependence.

Remarkably, the single-factor, dimensional model holds for every substance except nicotine. A single severity continuum characterizes the abuse and dependence of cocaine, amphetamines, opiates, cannabis, and sedatives. Helzer recommends that a dimensional score indicating severity supplement the discrete categories of substance abuse and dependence.

Adding a dimensional score to a categorical diagnosis might be easy to do for other syndromes as well. Clinical researchers have long used dimensional measures to reflect severity of illness and response to treatment. Rather than having a single, generic severity measure as for the substance abuse and dependence disorders, the DSM committee may elect to recommend well-tested dimensional measures for each categorical diagnosis or cluster of diagnoses (for example, the Beck Depression Inventory for mood disorders).

Dimensionalizing within a Diagnostic Group

The diagnostic group of eating disorders is another area ripe for dimensional retooling. The variables of concern with body shape and size, restricted eating, binging, purging, and compensatory activities designed to counteract fat (for example, extreme exercise, laxative abuse) capture most of the variation among people with eating disorders. Because people with eating disorders vary across these dimensions, one possibility would be to acknowledge these transdiagnostic features, diagnose a generic eating disorder, and then provide scores on continuous measures on each of these dimensions.[17]

Dimensionalizing these problems solves many diagnostic puzzles. The fact that patients "lose" one disorder and "acquire" another is easily interpretable within a dimensional system, and the EDNOS problem vanishes as well. On the other hand, some taxometric studies indicate that bulimia nervosa exists as a category, qualitatively distinct from other eating disorders and from normality, whereas anorexia nervosa appears to reside on a continuum with normal eating.[18] Nature may be messy; some people with eating disorders may suffer from discrete categorical disorders, whereas others have problems because they are deviant on several eating-related dimensions (for example, dietary restraint and body-image disturbance).

Dimensionalizing Personality Disorders

The problems with the categorical system are most apparent for personality disorders.[19] These conditions share Axis II with mental retardation, implying that disorders of personality are stable, chronic, and impairing conditions. The authors of DSM-III placed personality disorders on Axis II to highlight serious conditions potentially overshadowed by the florid, acute syndromes on Axis I (for example, bipolar disorder and panic disorder).

The distinction between the supposedly acute, episodic Axis I syndromes and the supposedly chronic Axis II personality disorders is hard to sustain, however. Schizophrenia, acute exacerbations notwithstanding, is usually as chronic as antisocial personality disorder, yet it resides on Axis I, whereas antisocial personality disorder resides on Axis II. Moreover, one longitudinal study revealed that 39.2 percent of patients with borderline personality disorder no longer met criteria for the disorder at the two-year follow-up assessment, and 88 percent had remitted after ten years.[20] These findings dramatically contradict the assumption that personality disorders are stable, chronic conditions that seldom remit.

It is unclear, however, whether therapy has much to do with the favorable prognosis of patients with this disorder. A follow-up study of Canadian borderline patients indicated that the majority of patients lost the diagnosis as they became middle-aged.[21] However, patients who had received few psychotherapy sessions were as likely to have a favorable outcome as those who had undergone intensive therapy for many years.

Another major study indicated a favorable prognosis for patients with borderline, obsessive-compulsive, avoidant, or schizotypal personality disorder.[22] Even after only two years had elapsed, more than half of these patients had remitted.[23] Defining remission as two consecutive months with no more than two symptoms present, the research team found that the proportion of remission ranged from 50 percent for avoidant personality disorder to 61 percent for schizotypal personality disorder. However, most patients still had residual problems, often impairment in social relationships. For example, many borderline patients continued to exhibit emotional instability and inappropriate intense anger, whereas their frantic efforts to avoid abandonment and repetitive self-injury disappeared.[24] These findings imply that personality disorders comprise relatively stable extreme personality traits plus aberrant behavioral problems designed to cope with the consequences of these traits. Aberrant personality traits are more chronic than are personality disorders themselves. Patients with borderline personality disorder may cut or burn themselves to counteract intolerably distressing episodes of emotional upheaval. Interestingly, when favorable changes in personality did occur, changes in maladaptive behavior followed later. Yet the reverse did not occur: reductions in self-harming behavior, for example, did not predict improvements in personality traits.

Other research further blurs the distinction between Axis I and Axis II syndromes. Avoidant personality disorder is indistinguishable from severe social phobia, borderline personality disorder may constitute a severe form of mood disorder, and schizotypal personality disorder appears to be part of a schizophrenia spectrum rather than an independent personality disorder.[25] In fact, one option for DSM-5 would be to place all personality disorders on Axis I and reserve Axis II for characterizing the patient dimensionally in terms of personality traits.[26]

Another problem is that patients diagnosed with a personality disorder seldom qualify for only one. In one study, the average patient met criteria for between two and three diagnoses.[27] It seems implausible that each of these co-occurring syndromes has its own distinctive antecedents, etiology, pathophysiology, and course.[28]

Although patients often meet criteria for several personality disorders, the opposite problem also occurs. Among patients with a personality diagnosis, between 21 and 49 percent receive the diagnosis of personality disorder not otherwise specified (PDNOS).[29] In structured interview studies, PDNOS is the third most common diagnosis, and in unstructured interview studies, it is the most common diagnosis. In other words, patients with seriously disturbed personalities often fail to fit into any of the standard DSM diagnostic categories.

Conversely, among patients who do qualify for a certain personality disorder diagnosis, heterogeneity abounds. Because diagnosis requires only that a patient have a subset of symptoms from a longer list, patients sharing the same diagnostic label can differ markedly. For example, for a person to qualify for obsessive-compulsive personality disorder, he or she must satisfy at least four of eight criteria. Accordingly, one patient can meet criteria by having the first four symptoms, whereas another patient could qualify by having the final four symptoms. Both patients would receive the same diagnosis without sharing a single symptom.[30]

Finally, unlike many syndromes first appearing in DSM-III, the personality disorders have not prompted significant amounts of research, at least until very recently. In fact, only three of the ten personality disorders have inspired much research at all, and only borderline personality disorder enjoys a robust and growing scientific base.[31] Antisocial and schizotypal personality disorders have a reasonable scientific data base, albeit one enjoying only modest growth in terms of publications. The scientific evidence pertaining to narcissistic, paranoid, dependent, avoidant, histrionic, obsessive-compulsive, and passive-aggressive personality disorders is nearly nonexistent despite their appearance in the DSM in 1980.

There are several possible reasons that seven of the ten personality disorders have inspired so little research. People with obsessive-compulsive, paranoid, or passive-aggressive disorder may not consider themselves in need of treatment. They may attribute their interpersonal problems to other people, failing to recognize their own contribution to their difficulties. Narcissistic personality disorder has been mainly of interest to psychoanalytic therapists, who generally do not pursue research. If clinical researchers rarely encounter patients with certain conditions, we should not be too surprised that the corresponding research base is small.

The problems with the categorical approach motivate arguments for recasting personality disorders in terms of personality dimensions.[32] The psychometric literature on personality is vast, rigorous, and sophisticated, and specialists have argued that we need to integrate the fields of normal and abnormal personality by reconceptualizing personality psychopathology in terms of deviance on fundamental dimensions of personality.

Such a change presupposes that psychologists have correctly identified the fundamental dimensions of personality. For years, this issue has been a topic of hot debate. A dwindling group of dissidents notwithstanding, most experts now believe that psychology has identified these dimensions.[33] Different methods usually uncover the same set of dimensions. For example, most psychologists have asked subjects to complete questionnaires about themselves, prompting the objection that subjects may not be in the best position to describe themselves. However, when the questionnaire is completed by an informant who knows the subject well, the results usually correspond to those emerging when the subject completes the questionnaire about himself or herself.

The Five Factor Model (FFM) has emerged as the favored approach.[34] It consists of five personality dimensions: Extraversion (versus introversion), Agreeableness (versus antagonism), Conscientiousness (versus impulsivity), Neuroticism (versus emotional stability), and Openness to Experience (versus dislike of novel experiences and ideas). Each of these five dimensions consists of six facets, and the score for each dimension is the sum of the scores for the six facets. To take just one example, Neuroticism consists of Anxiety, Angry Hostility, Depression, Self-Consciousness, Impulsiveness, and Vulnerability.

Psychologists have converged on the "Big Five" model of personality after having conducted extensive factor analytic research. Remarkably, the same five dimensions emerged from data collected in fifty cultures around the globe.[35] Moreover, in this study, subjects provided personality ratings of a person familiar to them. Yet the same five dimensions captured the variation of these observer ratings just as they do when subjects provide self-ratings of their own personality.

Twin data from North America, Europe, and Asia indicate an invariant genetic substrate underlying personality variation.[36] This genetic structure provides the basis for the apparent universality of the Big Five personality dimensions across cultures.

At first glance, assessing each patient on thirty facets of personality to arrive at scores on five dimensions seems like a daunting, time-consuming task. Some experts believe that clinicians may find dimensional assessment too cumbersome for routine practice.[37] Addressing these concerns, Thomas Widiger and his colleagues have sketched an efficient way of providing an assessment.[38] They recommend that each patient first complete a questionnaire yielding scores for the five dimensions and the thirty facets. After inspecting the patient's profile of scores, the clinician focuses his interview on only those aspects of personality exhibiting elevations on the questionnaire. Finally, the clinician assesses the degree of distress and functional impairment associated with problematic facets of personality functioning. If need be, Widiger maintains, clinicians could also match the profile of scores to the prototype for a categorical personality disorder. Of course, the main point of dimensional assessment is not merely to recover a categorical diagnosis or to reproduce the current system.[39] If the current categorical system is flawed, it should not be the gold standard for measuring the adequacy of an alternative approach.

Is an approach to normal personality sufficient to cover the deviant features of personality disorders? In other words, can we accurately represent personality psychopathology by a profile of scores on five dimensions of functioning? The data are mixed. Andrew Skodol and his colleagues found that patients with borderline, schizotypal, obsessive-compulsive, or avoidant personality disorder scored high on Neuroticism, low on Agreeableness, and low on Conscientiousness.[40] In a finding inconsistent with the hypothesis that different personality disorders would have different profiles of extreme scores on the Big Five dimensions, the same extreme configuration of scores characterized all four disorders. The Big Five did not distinguish among the different personality disorders, although it did distinguish personality disorders from normality.

By contrast, a meta-analysis yielded favorable results.[41] Overall, personality disorders tend to be associated with elevated Neuroticism and low Agreeableness. Yet each of the ten personality disorders had its own distinctive profile. Subjects with antisocial personality disorders had very low levels of Agreeableness and Conscientiousness but average levels of Neuroticism, Extraversion, and Openness to Experience. Those with avoidant personality disorder had high levels of Neuroticism and low levels of Extraversion but average levels of the other traits. Subjects with borderline personality disorder had high levels of Neuroticism and low levels of Agreeableness but average levels of the other traits. None of the personality disorders had either high or low levels of Openness to Experience, implying that dimensional characterization of personality pathology requires only four of the Big Five personality traits.

Extreme values on the Big Five personality traits are insufficient for characterizing psychopathology. At best, questionnaires that tap these traits assess the temperamental basis for problematic behavior. Questionnaires tapping normal personality variation seldom assess for highly deviant behaviors (for example, wrist slashing or paranoid ideation) that prove especially maladaptive for people with personality disorders. Indeed, the emerging conceptualization of personality psychopathology is a hybrid: it consists of relatively stable temperamental dispositions and episodic behavioral problems. Hence, clinicians need to assess maladaptive behavior as well as personality variation to obtain a reasonably comprehensive picture of disordered personality.

SOME LINGERING CONCERNS ABOUT THE BIG FIVE

The Big Five approach dominates personality psychology today, and it may provide the best basis for recasting personality disorders dimensionally. Yet scholars continue to voice significant concerns about the Big Five. Some worry that the lexical approach to personality that confines key concepts to single trait adjectives may fail to do justice to the richness and complexity of human personality, let alone human motivation.[42]

A related concern is that language, usually that of self-report questionnaires, provides the basis for personality description. Anxiety is one facet of neuroticism, yet the meaning of this term often depends greatly on the source of evidence for its application.[43] For example, self-report and physiological indexes of the trait often don't correspond. The Big Five terms denote highly abstract concepts devoid of contextual reference.[44] Neuroticism includes the facets of angry hostility and self-consciousness. Both share variance, yet knowing that someone is high on neuroticism doesn't reveal whether that person is hostile and angry or shy and self-conscious. It is little wonder that scientists have been unable to identify any reliable biological correlates for such a broad, sweeping term as "neuroticism," its high heritability notwithstanding.[45] For example, a GWAS study involving 2,054 subjects and assessing 452,574 SNPs failed to uncover *any* genes that could account for more than 1 percent of the variance in neuroticism.[46] The authors concluded that the 40 percent heritability figure for neuroticism likely arises from many genes, each having a minuscule effect on differences among people on this trait.

Other researchers question the explanatory import of neuroticism.[47] Measures of neuroticism predict diverse negative outcomes, including life stress, depression, unexplained medical symptoms, and substance abuse. Because neuroticism reflects a person's average level of emotional distress over time, the association between neuroticism and negative outcomes borders on the tautological. Thus neuroticism cannot provide an explanation for any of these outcomes. People who complain about feeling anxious, depressed, and angry at one point in time are those mostly likely to express similar complaints in the future. To avoid circularity, theorists must discover the psychobiological substrate of neuroticism. To say that neuroticism is a shorthand marker predicting distress tells us nothing about the nature of neuroticism. Personality traits severed from theory are devoid of explanatory import.

Finally, the Big Five constructs are latent variables postulated to account for individual differences among people. To be sure, these traits must somehow have their source in the psychobiology of human beings, but none is a mechanism accounting for intra-individual development, cognition, emotion, or behavior. Likewise, a measure of general intelligence, or psychometric g, taps a source of individual differences among people; it does not correspond to a cognitive module within a person's brain.[48] The upshot is that personality dimensions are not directly revelatory of the cognitive, emotional, and biological mechanisms that drive behavior.[49]

ARE MENTAL DISORDERS NATURAL KINDS?

The neo-Kraepelinian revolution inaugurated by DSM-III was a necessary provisional step for liberating psychopathology from its psychoanalytic past. The descriptive approach to diagnosis involving explicit inclusion and exclusion criteria was essential to increasing the reliability of diagnosis, thereby enabling research into causes and treatments for mental disorders. Unburdening the diagnostic process of empirically unsubstantiated theoretical assumptions was vital to this progress.

The authors of DSM-III championed what they called an "operational" approach to mental disorders suitable as a lingua franca acceptable to mental health professionals of diverse theoretical and therapeutic orientations. In reality, the rhetoric of operationism was mere window-dressing that provided a rationale for a provisional system that would increase diagnostic reliability and enable research into the causes of mental disorders and their treatment.

Having explicit inclusion and exclusion criteria does not entail a theoretical commitment to operational definitions. Indeed few, if any, psychopathologists would have endorsed genuine operational definitions of mental disorders.

Operationism defines concepts by their method of measurement.[50] In other words, a disorder defined operationally is nothing but its signs and symptoms. This doctrine is undesirable and unworkable in psychopathology. It directly contradicts the aim of devising a classification system that carves nature at its joints, whether the joints reflect categories or dimensions. Operational concepts are stipulative; they are whatever we say they are. Equating a concept with its method of measurement eliminates the possibility of error in measurement and renders incoherent the claim that the revisions to the DSM constitute improvement.[51]

Moreover, it prohibits two different procedures from measuring the same entity or process. Consider two inventories for measuring depression. If they provided highly correlated data, we would conclude that both tap a common source, process, or entity. This conclusion, however, requires appeal to causal, theoretical assumptions that transcend these observations. Indeed, measures of lightning and thunder are highly correlated, but each taps an entirely different phenomenon.[52] That is, some unobservable source gives rise to the correlated measurements. An underlying reality generates the phenomena we observe. The mechanisms that mediate symptoms in medicine are the pathophysiology of the disorder. Yet the austere doctrine of operationism forbids such inferences to pathophysiology because it confines the concept solely to the measurement of its signs and symptoms.

Revising DSM presupposes philosophical realism—the doctrine that there exists a mind-independent world and that it is the business of science to describe it correctly and to explain how it works. The success of any nosological system rises or falls on how well it corresponds to reality. Failure to get it right—or at least approximately so—diminishes our ability to diagnose and treat patients effectively. Diagnostic criteria are, however, fallible indicators of an underlying entity that produces its observable signs and symptoms. As Hilary Putnam once remarked, realism is the only philosophical doctrine that does not make the success of science a miracle.[53]

Realism about mental disorders seemingly implies that they may qualify as natural kinds. According to the traditional account, a hidden essence defines a natural kind, making it the type of thing that it is. The inherent causal powers of its underlying microstructure explain the observable manifestations of a natural kind. Natural kinds abound in physical science. The periodic table of elements tabulates the natural kinds of chemistry, each defined by an essential microstructure possessing causal powers that explain the behavior of the element. Gold, for example, has the atomic number 79. A substance counts as gold if and only if it has 79 protons. Any successful chemistry would eventually discover the same elements now listed in the periodic table. Predating the development of chemistry, the elements were out there awaiting discovery by scientists.

Whether psychiatric disorders count as natural kinds in the traditional sense is questionable. Some philosophers believe that emergent natural phenomena above the levels of physics and chemistry lack essences and do not qualify as natural kinds as do the elements of the periodic table.[54]

Consider the concept of *species* in biology. According to the late biologist Ernst Mayr, in pre-Darwinian times, scientists held that each species of plant and animal had a fixed, immutable, timeless essence that made it the sort of thing it was. However, the Darwinian revolution changed all that. It replaced this essentialist thinking about species with populational thinking.[55] The idea that a fixed, immutable essence defined a species was incompatible with the view of evolution occurring in populations of interbreeding organisms. Immutable essences cannot evolve.

Although recent historical scholarship has debunked the legend that nearly all biological thinkers before Darwin were essentialists, it remains true that biologists today do not hold simple essentialist views.[56] In any event, we do not have to posit immutable essences to elucidate the causal powers, the mechanisms that produce the signs and symptoms of mental disorder. Biologists have been elucidating the causal structure of the natural world without having to postulate that species or other concepts possess essences.

In fact, as Dominic Murphy has observed, there are several types of natural kinds in play today in the philosophy of biology.[57] One version, articulated by Richard Boyd, holds that a natural kind constitutes a cluster of properties that tend to hang together despite perturbations in the environment.[58] That is, the covariation of its properties is stable or homeostatic. Hence, homeostatic cluster theory is realist without being traditionally essentialist.

Expressing another, broadly similar view, Rachel Cooper holds that "members of a natural kind all possess similar determining properties, where the determining properties of an entity are those properties that determine its other properties."[59] Accordingly, members of a natural kind behave similarly under similar circumstances. In terms of psychopathology, similar dysfunctions give rise to similar symptoms. These causal properties need not be identical, as the notion of essence implies. Cooper's approach means that mental disorders count as nonessentialist natural kinds in that instances of a disorder have similar determining properties that support abductive inferences and that figure in explanations.

Some mental disorders may be interactive kinds, but even these have an endophenotypic core. The distinction between pathogenic and pathoplastic features is relevant here. Certain psychobiological dysfunctions may count as natural kinds indifferent to cultural penetration, and these are the pathogenic features. Culture can shape the expression of these conditions, and these varying features are pathoplastic. Schizophrenia, for example, may fail to qualify as a natural kind in that it covers several related but psychobiologically different subtypes.

Cooper holds that whether mental disorders are natural kinds is important.[60] She writes, "If mental disorders are natural kinds then this implies that the domain of mental disorders has a natural structure that it should be possible to discover via empirical research." She adds that "only natural kinds can support counterfactuals and function in explanations." Moreover, "if mental disorders are natural kinds then there will be laws, explanations, and sound inductive inferences in psychiatry—in short psychiatry will be a genuine science." On the other hand, economics involves socially constructed kinds and has its laws, and yet it is one of the most rigorous and quantitative of the social sciences. Moreover, whereas laws are essential to physics and chemistry, they seldom figure in explanations in either psychology or biology; mechanisms do.[61] Nevertheless, the key point is that understanding the causes and mechanisms of psychopathology commits us to ontological realism, but it does not require postulation of timeless, immutable essences "underlying" the signs and symptoms of mental illness. We can have natural kinds, either categorical or dimensional, without needing to aspire to a psychopathological version of the periodic table.

DO DISORDERS DIFFER IN KIND OR BY DEGREE?

We might have thought that the Darwinian revolution would have settled debates about the meaning of *species*. This has not happened.[62] In fact, there are more than two dozen different definitions of what counts as a species in biology today.[63] No single view commands the allegiance of all biologists. For example, one version defines the concept in terms of evolutionary lineage, whereas another defines it in terms of physiological and morphological characteristics.

What are we to make of this conceptual anarchy? The philosopher of science John Dupré believes that no single, univocal concept of species will work in biology because of the diversity of its scientific aims.[64] There may be no single, correct way of categorizing the biological world suitable for all purposes. Although geneticists, evolutionists, ecologists, and physiologists all seek to describe and explain the features of the living world, their questions are so different and their aims so diverse that it seems unlikely that a single concept of species will fit their diverse aims.

If biologists cannot agree on the foundational taxonomic concept in their field, is there any hope for psychopathologists to achieve this aim in their domain? Is it unrealistic to aim for a single system that works for practicing clinicians, neuroscientists, psychiatric geneticists, and third-party payers? Are their purposes simply too diverse? The undeniable progress of biology indicates that the field has progressed just fine without everyone agreeing on how to define the concept of *species*. The example of biology suggests that the absence of a universally accepted taxonomy does not always impede progress. Psychopathologists, clinicians, and other stakeholders likewise may not necessarily agree on a final concept of mental disorder. However, Dupré has argued for biology that, given a specific domain or question, there will be one best way of fixing the taxonomy. Each system may pick out different features of the domain to organize the field. There may not be one single, correct system for characterizing psychopathology because the questions asked by the stakeholders may require different kinds of answers. Nosological systems have purposes, and the purpose of a molecular geneticist may differ from that of a psychotherapist. Within the field of psychopathology, phenomena emerge at different levels of analysis, and questions and purposes posed at one level may require a conceptual taxonomy that differs from those appropriate for other questions and purposes. Each system picks out different aspects of the same underlying reality. Just as the wave and particle theories of light are both correct, so may be different systems for organizing mental disorders.

Debates regarding whether DSM-5 should represent mental disorders as categories or dimensions often turn on issues of clinical utility.[65] Some believe that it is a matter of taste, preference, or convention whether we conceptualize psychopathology categorically or dimensionally. If there is no way to determine which approach is the true one, then we might as well let clinical utility be our guide. Others entertain the possibility that we might be able to determine whether psychopathology is categorical versus dimensional, but that pragmatic considerations should still be the final arbiter. A false picture of clinical reality may be more useful in daily clinical practice than a true one.

The late Paul Meehl vigorously opposed the notion that solutions to taxonomic questions are merely a matter of preference, not a matter of fact. Whether a disorder is taxonic or nontaxonic is a discoverable fact, not a matter of taste, pragmatic utility, or methodological preference. Some DSM diagnoses may reflect latent taxa, or categories, to which patients may belong. Other patients may belong to no taxon but be "simply deviates in a hyperspace of biological, psychological, and social dimensions, arousing clinical concern because their deviant pattern causes trouble," as Meehl said.[66] The goal is to determine which is which.

To answer these questions, Meehl developed a set of statistical procedures, called taxometrics, to determine whether symptomatic indicators reflect a latent category ("taxon") or a latent dimension.[67] Taxometrics entails examining how indicators of psychopathology covary, enabling researchers to ascertain whether these patterns are more consistent with a latent category or with a latent dimension.

Taxa may be either natural categories (for example, chemical elements, biological species) or social categories (say, Communist, or Boston Red Sox fan) or other artifacts (spoons, knives, forks). Taxometrics can determine whether the data arise from a latent category versus a dimension, but the method is agnostic about the origins of the taxon. As Meehl emphasized, the statistical results never speak for themselves, and the kinds of input variables and relevant theory are essential to interpreting the meaning of any taxon.

Consider the case of dissociative disorders. Using data from a self-report measure of dissociative experiences, Niels Waller, Frank Putnam, and Eve Carlson discovered a dissociative taxon. They found that dissociation is not merely a continuum reflecting the tendency to become absorbed in daydreaming or to be forgetful.[68] Only one-third of their patients diagnosed with a dissociative disorder were members of the taxon, and only eight questionnaire items were good indicators of this pathological taxon. Among patients diagnosed with dissociative disorders, a subset differs qualitatively from the rest.

Waller and colleagues determined that a subset of these patients differed qualitatively from all the others, despite the entire group's having received a diagnosis of dissociative disorder. However, the taxometric method is agnostic about etiology. Waller's findings are compatible with the social-cognitive theory that MPD is a culturally shaped idiom of distress, just as they are with a theory that massive childhood trauma causes dissociative disorders. The taxometric method can determine whether disorders differ by kind or by degree, but it tells us nothing about etiology and pathophysiology. That is why Meehl always recommended that a well-corroborated theory about the disorder inform selection of input variables to the analyses. The statistics never speak for themselves.

Although Meehl and his associates have been developing taxometric methods for the past several decades, the approach has only recently begun to have an impact in psychopathology. Only a handful of clinical psychologists have been forging ahead, trying to ascertain the latent structure of mental disorders. Psychiatrists have almost never used taxometrics to answer taxonomic questions despite the great promise of the approach to answer, perhaps definitively, these questions. The mathematics is unfamiliar to most psychopathologists, and the method requires large numbers of patients (300–500 or more). Moreover, input variables have usually involved self-report data from questionnaires. Behavioral and biological data have seldom figured in these studies even though discovering taxa with such input could provide important clues to etiology and pathophysiology. The upshot is that taxometrics may provide ultimate answers to hitherto intractable taxonomic questions. If the approach comes too late for DSM-5, then it will surely play a larger role in subsequent revisions of the DSM. Finally, taxometrics does not provide a direct solution to the boundary problem. The method does not distinguish mental disorders from mental distress. Rather, it promises to distinguish among mental disorders.

8

The boundary between mental distress and mental illness will never be neat and clean. What counts as a mental disorder depends on shifting cultural, political, and economic values as well as on scientific facts about how our psychology and biology can go wrong, producing suffering and functional impairment in everyday life. We'll never have a clear-cut list of criteria that will enable us to identify all instances of mental disorder and exclude everything else.

This conclusion should not be so surprising. As Wittgenstein observed, examples of most useful concepts bear only a family resemblance to one another.[1] Most have some overlapping attributes without sharing an essence present in every case. However, the more attributes a given case has, the better an example it is of the concept. Take the idea of *game*. It covers many activities—poker, solitaire, bowling, baseball, and boxing—and yet there is no single defining property shared by every activity that makes it a game. Because baseball possesses more attributes than solitaire, it is considered more game-like.

In the manner of Wittgenstein, the psychologists Scott Lilienfeld and Lori Marino persuasively argued that mental conditions vary in the degree to which they are disorder-like.[2] A set of loosely correlated features tends to characterize mental disorders without any single feature being necessary and sufficient to make a condition a mental disorder. The more attributes present in a given case, the more disorder-like it tends to be.

Consider an easy example, such as schizophrenia. This disorder originates in brain pathology, involves involuntary symptoms (hallucinations), and produces intense emotional suffering, increased risk of early mortality (heightened suicide risk), diminished fertility, social and occupational impairment, disturbances in cognitive functioning (reasoning, language), delusions, and high heritability. Ambiguous cases will possess few of these attributes. For example, adjustment disorder involves marked distress or impairment in social or occupational functioning in response to a stressor, such as job loss. Not only is it difficult to distinguish this condition from normal reactions to life's misfortunes, but adjustment disorder lacks attributes associated with undeniable mental disorders (for example, cognitive abnormalities, diminished fertility, brain pathology).

The psychiatrist Paul McHugh contends that the wide diversity of mental health conditions tend to fall into four clusters.[3] One cluster includes diseases that produce disturbances in perception, cognition, and emotion. Psychological symptoms arise involuntarily from structural and functional pathology of the brain. Alzheimer's disease, bipolar disorder, and schizophrenia are all included in this group. The cluster is characterized by what patients "have."

The second cluster includes problems that arise when patients fall at extreme points on psychological dimensions of traits such as introversion and neuroticism. Their problems occur because of who they "are" rather than what they "have." Their temperament renders them vulnerable to the challenges of everyday life. Whether extremes on these dimensions signify disorder depends on the person's circumstances. Marked shyness, for example, is not always social phobia.

The third cluster includes behavioral patterns that have immediate positive consequences but delayed negative consequences. People with drug dependence fall into this category; their problems concern what they are "doing," not what they have or who they are. To be sure, repetitive substance abuse can produce changes in the brain that make it difficult for people to refrain from using a particular substance. But unlike people with schizophrenia, addicts do not have problems that originate in brain pathology, nor do any resultant brain changes render their behavior immune from its consequences, as the model of addiction as a chronic, relapsing brain disease implies.[4] Addicts experience great difficulty abstaining from drugs, but that doesn't mean that their behavior is entirely beyond their control or that they can't benefit from treatments that reward abstinence. Indeed, perhaps the most effective intervention for cocaine addiction is behavior therapy whereby addicts earn rewards for producing drug-free urine screens.[5] By contrast, truly involuntary symptoms, such as auditory hallucinations in schizophrenia or memory impairments in Alzheimer's disease, won't disappear regardless of how much we reward patients for not having them.

Finally, the fourth cluster includes problems that arise as a result of something that patients have "encountered." These problems, exemplified by PTSD, are more like injuries than infectious diseases.

McHugh realizes that patients often fall into more than one cluster. A quiet person who becomes anxious very easily and thus scores high on the dimensions of introversion and neuroticism (cluster two) may be especially prone to developing PTSD following exposure to a traumatic event (cluster four). Nevertheless, McHugh's four clusters illustrate the range of qualitatively distinct problems that fall within the domain of mental health professionals.

Yet the range of conditions treatable by nonpsychiatric physicians is at least as large as is their means of identifying them. Doctors define malignant tumors by their histopathology, infections by their causative microorganisms, mitral stenosis by its morbid anatomy, Down's syndrome by chromosomal aberration, migraine headache by self-reported symptoms, and fractures by x-ray.[6]

Moreover, nonpsychiatric medicine has its own shifting boundary between health and sickness, as the physician and historian of medicine Jeremy Greene has documented.[7] During the second half of the twentieth century, medicine began to classify healthy people as needing treatment on the basis of their numerical deviations on measures of blood sugar, blood pressure, and cholesterol. These people did not feel sick or complain of any symptoms, but elevations on these measures were statistically associated with increased risk for serious medical problems such as stroke. The Framingham Study, a major effort of the National Heart Institute and the American Heart Association, popularized the concept of the *risk factor,* expanding the domain of the treatable to include those who *might* get ill.

The public came to accept this change when pharmaceutical companies introduced new medications with few side effects that could lower values on laboratory tests. Doctors, patients, and drug companies increasingly began to regard moderately elevated blood pressure as a treatable disease in its own right, not merely a risk factor that increased the odds of someone's having a stroke or a heart attack one day. Ironically, the more we can treat people, the more sick, or "pre-sick," people there seem to be. For example, expert panels consisting of doctors specializing in coronary heart disease have recently lowered the thresholds for what counts as elevated blood pressure, cholesterol, and fasting glucose. More than 97 percent of American adults now qualify for medical surveillance and pharmacotherapy to reduce levels of at least one of these risk factors.[8]

WHY DOES IT MATTER?

Scientists discover the facts about how things go wrong with the psychology and biology of human beings. But science alone does not determine where we draw the line between mental distress and mental disorder. Multiple stakeholders have a voice in the matter. Some hope to contract the scope of treatable mental disorder, whereas others hope to expand it.

Insurance companies that pay for treatment are keen to confine their financial responsibility to genuine medical conditions. They understandably question whether they should reimburse clinicians for helping people cope with the problems of everyday life. For different reasons, critics of overmedicalization worry about broadening the scope of mental disorder. They fear that it will have unintended negative consequences ranging from diminishing resilience and autonomy to increasing stigma.

In contrast, the pharmaceutical industry is in the business of opening up new markets for its products, and thus aims to expand the scope of treatable mental disorders. It is far less expensive to market old drugs for new conditions than it is to develop new drugs for old disorders. It is easier to market SSRIs for very shy people than it is to discover new drugs with few side effects for severe social phobia. Likewise, clinicians understandably favor a system that reimburses them for treating a broad range of conditions from ordinary distress to severe mental illness.

In the end, attempts to reduce health care spending in America may limit the problems eligible for reimbursable treatment. One stringent option would be to confine reimbursable treatment to severe, "biologically based" mental disorders. This suggestion would merely shift the controversy to which disorders count as "based" on biology. Another developing trend is the refusal of insurance companies to pay for treatment of people receiving certain NOS diagnoses (for example, anxiety disorder NOS). This option, too, presents problems because many patients with an NOS diagnosis suffer considerably even if they fail to meet full criteria for a standard disorder (for example, panic disorder). Moreover, it provides a strong incentive for clinicians to assign a diagnosis that comes closest to capturing the patient's problems and that will ensure reimbursement even if it is not the correct diagnosis.

Efforts to reduce health care spending by reducing the range of disorders eligible for reimbursable treatment would seriously exacerbate the problem of unmet need. There is, however, a way to reduce spending and still provide needed services. If insurance companies paid only for the delivery of evidence-based treatments for mental disorders, then this would speed recovery of patients, thereby reducing costs. Unfortunately, even today there's no guarantee that a patient with a certain disorder will receive state-of-the-art treatment. For example, people seeking treatment for panic disorder, bulimia nervosa, or obsessive-compulsive disorder often fail to receive appropriate cognitive-behavior therapy for their problems despite abundant scientific evidence that these treatments work for most patients with these conditions. When patients do not receive optimal, evidence-based treatment, health care costs are bound to soar.[9]

Ideally, science can tell us what has gone wrong with a person and which treatments will work best to fix it. But it cannot tell us whether we ought to treat a certain condition. Sometimes side effects, expenses, and other costs of treatment exceed the potential benefits. Hence the mental health professions will forever grapple with values as well as with facts in their efforts to reduce human suffering.

1. An Epidemic of Madness?

1. R. C. Kessler, P. Berglund, O. Demler, R. Jin, K. R. Merikangas, and E. E. Walters, "Lifetime Prevalence and Age-of-Onset Distributions of *DSM-IV* Disorders in the National Comorbidity Survey Replication," *Archives of General Psychiatry,* 62 (2005): 593–602; R. C. Kessler, W. T. Chiu, O. Demler, and E. E. Walters, "Prevalence, Severity, and Comorbidity of 12-Month *DSM-IV* Disorders in the National Comorbidity Survey Replication," *Archives of General Psychiatry,* 62 (2005): 617–627.

2. K. Demyttenaere, R. Bruffaerts, J. Posada-Villa, I. Gasquet, V. Kovess, J. P. Lepine, M. C. Angermeyer, et al., "Prevalence, Severity, and Unmet Need for Treatment of Mental Disorders in the World Health Organization World Mental Health Surveys," *Journal of the American Medical Association,* 291 (2004): 2581–2590.

3. Kessler et al., "Lifetime Prevalence."

4. P. S. Wang, P. Berglund, M. Olfson, H. A. Pincus, K. B. Wells, and R. C. Kessler, "Failure and Delay in Initial Treatment Contact after First Onset of Mental Disorders in the National Comorbidity Survey Replication," *Archives of General Psychiatry,* 62 (2005): 603–613.

5. P. S. Wang, M. Lane, M. Olfson, H. A. Pincus, K. B. Wells, and R. C. Kessler, "Twelve-Month Use of Mental Health Services in the United States: Results from the National Comorbidity Survey Replication," *Archives of General Psychiatry,* 62 (2005): 629–640; quote p. 634.

6. Ibid.

7. Quoted in R. Moynihan and A. Cassels, *Selling Sickness: How the*

World's Biggest Pharmaceutical Companies Are Turning Us All into Patients (New York: Nation Books, 2005), 31.

8. Wang et al., "Twelve-Month Use."

9. T. R. Insel and W. S. Fenton, "Psychiatric Epidemiology: It's Not Just about Counting Anymore," *Archives of General Psychiatry,* 62 (2005): 591.

10. American Psychiatric Association (APA), *Diagnostic and Statistical Manual of Mental Disorders,* 4th ed., text revision [DSM-IV-TR.] (Washington: American Psychiatric Publishing, Inc., 2000). The fourth edition (DSM-IV) appeared in 1994. A revision of this edition appeared in 2000 (DSM-IV-TR). TR stands for "text revision" to signify that changes occurred in the text accompanying each disorder that summarized the latest scientific findings. There were very few changes in the diagnostic criteria themselves.

11. M. K. Nock, I. Hwang, N. A. Sampson, and R. C. Kessler, "Mental Disorders, Comorbidity and Suicidal Behavior: Results from the National Comorbidity Survey Replication," *Molecular Psychiatry,* 15 (2010): 868–876.

12. G. L. Klerman and M. M. Weissman, "Increasing Rates of Depression," *Journal of the American Medical Association,* 261 (1989): 2229–2235.

13. Ibid.

14. M. M. Weissman, M. L. Bruce, P. J. Leaf, L. P. Florio, and C. Holzer III, "Affective Disorders," in L. N. Robins and D. A. Regier, eds., *Psychiatric Disorders in America: The Epidemiologic Catchment Area Study* (New York: Free Press, 1991), 53–80.

15. Kessler et al., "Lifetime Prevalence."

16. R. D. Putnam, "Bowling Alone: America's Declining Social Capital," *Journal of Democracy,* 6 (1995): 65–78.

17. E. Diener and M. E. P. Seligman, "Very Happy People," *Psychological Science,* 13 (2002): 81–84.

18. Klerman and Weissman, "Increasing Rates of Depression."

19. J. M. Twenge, "The Age of Anxiety? Birth Cohort Change in Anxiety and Neuroticism," *Journal of Personality and Social Psychology,* 79 (2000): 1007–1021; J. A. Taylor, "A Personality Scale of Manifest Anxiety," *Journal of Abnormal and Social Psychology,* 48 (1953): 285–290.

20. J. M. Twenge, *Generation Me: Why Today's Young Americans Are More Confident, Assertive, Entitled—and More Miserable Than Ever Before* (New York: Free Press, 2006), 104–136.

21. S. A. Benton, J. M. Robertson, W.-C. Tseng, F. B. Newton, and S. L. Benton, "Changes in Counseling Center Client Problems Across 13 Years," *Professional Psychology: Research and Practice,* 34 (2003): 66–72.

22. R. Kadison and T. F. DiGeronimo, *College of the Overwhelmed: The Campus Mental Health Crisis and What to Do about It* (San Francisco: Jossey-Bass, 2004), 1. They cite the 2001 survey on p. 153.

23. R. Kadison, "Getting an Edge—Use of Stimulants and Antidepressants in College," *New England Journal of Medicine,* 353 (2005): 1089–1091.

24. C. Blanco, M. Okuda, C. Wright, D. S. Hasin, B. F. Grant, S. M. Liu, and M. Olfson, "Mental Health of College Students and Their Non-College-Attending Peers," *Archives of General Psychiatry,* 65 (2008): 1429–1437.

25. B. Carey, "Most Will Be Mentally Ill at Some Point, Study Says," *New York Times,* June 7, 2005, www.nytimes.com/2005/06/07/health/07mental.html (accessed June 7, 2005).

26. APA, *DSM-IV-TR,* 282.

27. Carey, "Most Will Be Mentally Ill."

28. H. D. Thoreau, *Walden; or, Life in the Woods* (New York: Signet Classic, 1960), 10.

29. R. Pear, "House Approves Bill on Mental Health Parity," *New York Times,* March 6, 2008, www.nytimes.com/2008/03/06/washington/06health.html?_r=1 (accessed March 6, 2008).

30. D. A. Regier, C. T. Kaelber, D. S. Rae, M. E. Farmer, B. Knauper, R. C. Kessler, and G. S. Norquist, "Limitations of Diagnostic Criteria and Assessment Instruments for Mental Disorders: Implications for Research and Policy," *Archives of General Psychiatry,* 55 (1998): 110.

31. W. E. Narrow, D. S. Rae, L. N. Robins, and D. A. Regier, "Revised Prevalence Estimates of Mental Disorders in the United States: Using a Clinical Significance Criterion to Reconcile 2 Surveys' Estimates," *Archives of General Psychiatry,* 59 (2002): 115–123.

32. Ibid., 121.

33. Ibid., 115.

34. R. L. Spitzer, "Diagnosis and Need for Treatment Are Not the Same," *Archives of General Psychiatry,* 55 (1998): 120.

35. R. C. Kessler, K. R. Merikangas, P. Berglund, W. W. Eaton, D. S. Koretz, and E. E. Walters, "Mild Disorders Should Not Be Eliminated from the *DSM-V,*" *Archives of General Psychiatry,* 60 (2003): 1117–1122.

36. The reanalysis appeared in ibid.; the main publication of the original NCS appeared in R. C. Kessler, K. A. McGonagle, S. Zhao, C. B. Nelson, M. Hughes, S. Eshleman, H. U. Wittchen, and K. S. Kendler, "Lifetime and 12-Month Prevalence of *DSM-III-R* Psychiatric Disorders in the United States: Results from the National Comorbidity Survey," *Archives of General Psychiatry,* 51 (1994): 8–19.

37. S. M. Monroe and K. L. Harkness, "Life Stress, the 'Kindling' Hypothesis, and the Recurrence of Depression: Considerations from a Life Stress Perspective," *Psychological Review,* 112 (2005): 417–445.

38. Regier et al., "Limitations of Diagnostic Criteria," 114.

39. J. C. Wakefield and R. L. Spitzer, "Lowered Estimates—But of What?" *Archives of General Psychiatry,* 59 (2002): 129–130.

40. P. R. McHugh, "Striving for Coherence: Psychiatry's Efforts Over Classification," *Journal of the American Medical Association,* 293 (2005): 2526–2528.

41. American Psychiatric Association (APA), *Diagnostic and Statistical Manual of Mental Disorders,* 3rd ed. [DSM-III.] (Washington: American Psychiatric Publishing, Inc., 1980).

42. American Psychiatric Association (APA), *Diagnostic and Statistical Manual of Mental Disorders,* 2nd ed. [DSM-II.] (Washington: American Psychiatric Publishing, Inc., 1968).

43. E. Shorter, *A History of Psychiatry: From the Era of the Asylum to the Age of Prozac* (New York: Wiley, 1997), 190–229.

44. D. Cooper, *Psychiatry and Anti-Psychiatry* (New York: Ballantine, 1967); R. D. Laing, *The Politics of Experience* (New York: Ballantine, 1967), 167.

45. T. S. Szasz, "The Myth of Mental Illness," *American Psychologist,* 15 (1960): 113–118.

46. R. K. McClure and J. A. Lieberman, "Neurodevelopmental and Neurodegenerative Hypotheses of Schizophrenia: A Review and Critique," *Current Opinion in Psychiatry,* 16, suppl. 2 (2003): S15–S28.

47. T. J. Scheff, *Being Mentally Ill: A Sociological Theory*, 3rd ed. (Hawthorne, NY: Aldine, 1999).

48. D. L. Rosenhan, "On Being Sane in Insane Places," *Science*, 179 (1973): 250–258; quotation from p. 257.

49. R. E. Kendell, J. E. Cooper, A. J. Gourlay, J. R. M. Copeland, L. Sharpe, and B. J. Gurland, "Diagnostic Criteria of American and British Psychiatrists," *Archives of General Psychiatry*, 25 (1971): 123–130.

50. H. Kutchins and S. A. Kirk, *Making Us Crazy: DSM: The Psychiatric Bible and the Creation of Mental Disorders* (New York: Free Press, 1997), 55–99.

51. R. W. Hanson and V. J. Adesso, "A Multiple Behavioral Approach to Male Homosexual Behavior: A Case Study," *Journal of Behavior Therapy and Experimental Psychiatry*, 3 (1972): 323–325.

52. G. C. Davison, "Homosexuality: The Ethical Challenge," *Journal of Consulting and Clinical Psychology*, 44 (1976): 157–162. The organization changed its name to the Association for Behavioral and Cognitive Therapies (ABCT) in 2005 to recognize the melding of behavior therapy and cognitive therapy.

53. Kutchins and Kirk, *Making Us Crazy*, 273.

54. G. Schilling, "Underworld Character Kicked Out of Planetary Family," *Science*, 313 (2006): 1214–1215.

55. J. P. Feighner, E. Robins, S. B. Guze, R. A. Woodruff, Jr., G. Winokur, and R. Munoz, "Diagnostic Criteria for Use in Psychiatric Research," *Archives of General Psychiatry*, 26 (1972): 57–63; R. L. Spitzer, J. Endicott, and E. Robins, "Clinical Criteria for Psychiatric Diagnosis and *DSM-III*," *American Journal of Psychiatry*, 132 (1975): 1187–1192; R. L. Spitzer, J. Endicott, and E. Robins, "Research Diagnostic Criteria: Rationale and Reliability," *Archives of General Psychiatry*, 35 (1978): 773–782; E. Robins and S. B. Guze, "Establishment of Diagnostic Validity in Psychiatric Illness: Its Application to Schizophrenia," *American Journal of Psychiatry*, 126 (1970): 983–987.

56. R. L. Spitzer, J. B. W. Williams, and A. E. Skodol, "*DSM-III*: The Major Achievements and an Overview," *American Journal of Psychiatry*, 137 (1980): 151–164.

57. S. A. Kirk and H. Kutchins, *The Selling of DSM* (New York: Aldine de Gruyter, 1992).

58. APA, *DSM-IV-TR*, xxxi.

59. American Psychiatric Association (APA), *Diagnostic and Statistical Manual of Mental Disorders,* 3rd ed., rev. [DSM-III-R.] (Washington: American Psychiatric Publishing, Inc., 1987); American Psychiatric Association (APA), *Diagnostic and Statistical Manual of Mental Disorders,* 4th ed. [DSM-IV.] (Washington: American Psychiatric Publishing, Inc., 1994); APA, *DSM-IV-TR,* 282.

60. Feighner et al., "Diagnostic Criteria."

61. A. V. Horwitz, *Creating Mental Illness* (Chicago: University of Chicago Press, 2002), 82.

62. B. T. Walsh, S. N. Seidman, R. Sysko, and M. Gould, "Placebo Response in Studies of Major Depression: Variable, Substantial, and Growing," *Journal of the American Medical Association,* 287 (2002): 1840–1847.

63. R. D. Marshall, R. A. Bryant, L. Amsel, E. J. Suh, J. M. Cook, and Y. Neria, "The Psychology of Ongoing Threat: Relative Risk Appraisal, the September 11 Attacks, and Terrorism-Related Fears," *American Psychologist,* 62 (2007): 304–316.

64. P. D. Kramer, *Against Depression* (New York: Penguin, 2005), 8.

2. Are We Pathologizing Everyday Life?

1. D. Summerfield, "Proposals for Massive Expansion of Psychological Therapies Would Be Counterproductive across Society," *British Journal of Psychiatry,* 192 (2008): 329.

2. A. V. Horwitz, *Creating Mental Illness* (Chicago: University of Chicago Press, 2002); A. Young, *The Harmony of Illusions: Inventing Post-Traumatic Stress Disorder* (Princeton, NJ: Princeton University Press, 1995); J. Acocella, *Creating Hysteria: Women and Multiple Personality Disorder* (San Francisco: Jossey-Bass, 1999); H. Kutchins and S. A. Kirk, *Making Us Crazy: DSM: The Psychiatric Bible and the Creation of Mental Disorders* (New York: Free Press, 1997).

3. K. Mannheim, "The Problem of a Sociology of Knowledge," in *From Karl Mannheim,* ed. K. H. Wolff (New York: Oxford University Press, 1971), 65. Original work published in 1925.

4. A. Young, "A Time to Change Our Minds: Anthropology and Psychi-

atry in the 21st Century," *Culture, Medicine, and Psychiatry,* 32 (2008): 298–300, quotation p. 299.

5. S. A. Kirk and H. Kutchins, *The Selling of DSM* (New York: Aldine de Gruyter, 1992).

6. A. Spiegel, "The Dictionary of Disorder: How One Man Revolutionized Psychiatry," *New Yorker,* 80, January 3, 2005, 56–63.

7. R. L. Spitzer, "An Outsider-Insider's Views about Revising the *DSMs,*" *Journal of Abnormal Psychology,* 100 (1991): 294–296, quotations from p. 294.

8. A. C. Houts, "Discovery, Invention, and the Expansion of the Modern *Diagnostic and Statistical Manuals of Mental Disorders,*" in *Rethinking the DSM: A Psychological Perspective,* ed. L. E. Beutler and Mary L. Malik (Washington: American Psychological Association, 2002), 17–65.

9. Kutchins and Kirk, *Making Us Crazy.*

10. J. J. Block, "Issues for DSM-V. Internet Addiction," *American Journal of Psychiatry,* 165 (2008): 306–307; E. Hollander and A. Allen, "Is Compulsive Buying a Real Disorder, and Is It Really Compulsive?" *American Journal of Psychiatry,* 163 (2006): 1670–1672; C. Bell, "Racism: A Mental Illness?" *Psychiatric Services,* 55 (2004): 1343.

11. N. D. Volkow and C. P. O'Brien, "Issues for DSM-V: Should Obesity Be Included as a Brain Disorder?" *American Journal of Psychiatry,* 164 (2007): 708–710.

12. B. A. Bruno, "Obesity and Brain Disorder," *American Journal of Psychiatry,* 165 (2008): 138.

13. R. E. Kendell, "Relationship Between the *DSM-IV* and the *ICD-10,*" *Journal of Abnormal Psychology,* 100 (1991): 297–301; M. Zimmerman, "Why Are We Rushing to Publish *DSM-IV?*" *Archives of General Psychiatry,* 45 (1988): 1135–1138.

14. M. Zimmerman, "Is *DSM-IV* Needed at All?" *Archives of General Psychiatry,* 47 (1990): 974–976.

15. A. V. Horwitz and J. C. Wakefield, *The Loss of Sadness: How Psychiatry Transformed Normal Sorrow into Depressive Disorder* (Oxford: Oxford University Press, 2007), 82.

16. C. Lane, *Shyness: How Normal Behavior Became a Sickness* (New Haven, CT: Yale University Press, 2007), 114.

17. E. B. Foa, M. R. Liebowitz, M. J. Kozak, S. Davies, R. Campeas, M. E. Franklin, J. D. Huppert, et al., "Randomized, Placebo-Controlled Trial of Exposure and Ritual Prevention, Clomipramine, and Their Combination in the Treatment of Obsessive-Compulsive Disorder," *American Journal of Psychiatry*, 162 (2005): 151–161.

18. T. Tungaraza and R. Poole, "Influence of Drug Company Authorship and Sponsorship on Drug Trial Outcomes," *British Journal of Psychiatry*, 191 (2007): 82–83. The journals were the *American Journal of Psychiatry*, the *Archives of General Psychiatry*, and the *British Journal of Psychiatry*.

19. E. H. Turner, A. M. Matthews, E. Linardatos, R. A. Tell, and R. Rosenthal, "Selective Publication of Antidepressant Trials and Its Influence on Apparent Efficacy," *New England Journal of Medicine*, 358 (2008): 252–260.

20. J. C. Fournier, R. J. DeRubeis, S. D. Hollon, S. Dimidjian, J. D. Amsterdam, R. C. Shelton, and J. Fawcett, "Antidepressant Drug Effects and Depression Severity: A Patient-Level Meta-Analysis," *Journal of the American Medical Association*, 303 (2010): 47–53.

21. I. Kirsch, B. J. Deacon, T. B. Huedo-Medina, A. Scoboria, T. J. Moore, and B. T. Johnson, "Initial Severity and Antidepressant Benefits: A Meta-Analysis of Data Submitted to the Food and Drug Administration," *PLoS Medicine*, 5 (2008): 0260–0268.

22. G. Harris and B. Carey, "Researchers Fail to Reveal Full Drug Pay," *New York Times*, June 8, 2008, www.nytimes.com/2008/06/08/us/08conflict.html (accessed 6/24/08).

23. J. R. Lacasse and J. Leo, "Serotonin and Depression: A Disconnect Between the Advertisements and the Scientific Literature," *PLoS Medicine*, 2, no. 12 (2005): 1211–1216.

24. Lane, *Shyness*, 123.

25. E. S. Valenstein, *Blaming the Brain: The Truth about Drugs and Mental Health* (New York: Free Press, 1998).

26. R. Whitaker, *Anatomy of an Epidemic: Magic Bullets, Psychiatric Drugs, and the Astonishing Rise of Mental Illness in America* (New York: Crown Publishers, 2010), 159–176.

27. Foa et al., "Randomized, Placebo-Controlled Trial Exposure"; M. W. Otto, M. H. Pollack, and K. M. Maki, "Empirically Supported Treat-

ments for Panic Disorder: Costs, Benefits, and Stepped Care," *Journal of Consulting and Clinical Psychology,* 68 (2000): 556–563.

28. P. R. Breggin, *Toxic Psychiatry* (New York: St. Martin's Press, 1991), 293–315.

29. P. R. Breggin and G. R. Breggin, *Talking Back to Prozac: What Doctors Aren't Telling You about Today's Most Controversial Drug* (New York: St. Martin's Press, 1995), 261.

30. D. A. Karp, *Is It Me or My Meds? Living with Antidepressants* (Cambridge, MA: Harvard University Press, 2006), 15.

31. Ibid., 214.

32. J. Moncrieff, "Psychiatric Drug Promotion and the Politics of Neoliberalism," *British Journal of Psychiatry,* 188 (2006): 301–302.

33. C. H. Sommers and S. Satel, *One Nation under Therapy: How the Helping Culture Is Eroding Self-Reliance* (New York: St. Martin's Press, 2005).

34. P. D. Kramer, *Listening to Prozac* (New York: Viking, 1993), x, 246.

35. Sommers and Satel, *One Nation under Therapy.*

36. Ibid., 5.

37. G. L. Klerman, "Psychotropic Hedonism *vs.* Pharmacological Calvinism," *The Hastings Center Report,* 2 (1972): 1–3.

38. Karp, *Is It Me or My Meds?* 15–16.

39. World Health Organization, 1948, quoted in "Health," http://en.wikipedia.org/wiki/Health (accessed 3/28/09).

40. Karp, *Is It Me or My Meds?*

41. W. H. Masters and V. E. Johnson, *Human Sexual Inadequacy* (New York: Bantam, 1970).

42. R. Moynihan, "The Making of a Disease: Female Sexual Dysfunction," *BMJ,* 326 (2003): 45–47; R. Moynihan and A. Cassels, *Selling Sickness: How the World's Biggest Pharmaceutical Companies Are Turning Us All into Patients* (New York: Nation Books, 2005); L. Tiefer, "Female Sexual Dysfunction: A Case Study of Disease Mongering and Activist Resistance," *PLoS Medicine,* 3 (2006): 0436–0440.

43. E. O. Laumann, A. Paik, and R. C. Rosen, "Sexual Dysfunction in the United States: Prevalence and Predictors," *Journal of the American Medical Association,* 281 (1999): 537–544.

44. Horwitz and Wakefield, *The Loss of Sadness.*

45. J. C. Wakefield, M. F. Schmitz, M. B. First, and A. V. Horwitz, "Extending the Bereavement Exclusion for Major Depression to Other Losses: Evidence from the National Comorbidity Survey," *Archives of General Psychiatry*, 64 (2007): 433–440.

46. American Psychiatric Association (APA), *Diagnostic and Statistical Manual of Mental Disorders*, 4th ed., text revision [DSM-IV-TR.] (Washington: American Psychiatric Publishing, Inc., 2000), 356.

47. R. C. Kessler, S. Zhao, D. G. Blazer, and M. Swartz, "Prevalence, Correlates, and Course of Minor Depression and Major Depression in the National Comorbidity Survey," *Journal of Affective Disorders*, 45 (1997): 19–30.

48. Ibid.

49. L. L. Judd, H. S. Akiskal, and M. P. Paulus, "The Role and Clinical Significance of Subsyndromal Depressive Symptoms (SSD) in Unipolar Major Depressive Disorder," *Journal of Affective Disorders*, 45 (1997): 12.

50. Ibid.

51. Ibid., 2.

52. R. C. Kessler, K. R. Merikangas, P. Berglund, W. W. Eaton, D. S. Koretz, and E. E. Walters, "Mild Disorders Should Not Be Eliminated from the *DSM-V*," *Archives of General Psychiatry*, 60 (2003): 1117–1122.

53. Horwitz and Wakefield, *The Loss of Sadness*, 142.

54. S. M. Monroe and K. L. Harkness, "Life Stress, the 'Kindling' Hypothesis, and the Recurrence of Depression: Considerations from a Life Stress Perspective," *Psychological Review*, 112 (2005): 417–445.

55. R. W. Pies, "Depression and the Pitfalls of Causality: Implications for DSM-V," *Journal of Affective Disorders*, 116 (2009): 1–3.

56. S. M. Monroe, G. M. Slavich, and K. Georgiades, "The Social Environment and Life Stress in Depression," in *Handbook of Depression*, 2nd ed., ed. I. H. Gotlib and C. L. Hammen (New York: Guilford, 2009), 340–360.

57. Pies, "Depression and the Pitfalls of Causality."

58. G. R. Henriques, "The Harmful Dysfunction Analysis and the Differentiation Between Mental Disorder and Disease," *Scientific Review of Mental Health Practice*, 1 (2002): 157–173.

59. K. S. Kendler, "Review of the Book *The Loss of Sadness*," *Psychological Medicine*, 38 (2008): 148–150.

60. Horwitz and Wakefield, *The Loss of Sadness*, 222.

61. American Psychiatric Association (APA), *Diagnostic and Statistical Manual of Mental Disorders*, 3rd ed. [DSM-III.] (Washington: American Psychiatric Publishing, Inc., 1980), 228.

62. R. C. Kessler, P. Berglund, O. Demler, R. Jin, K. R. Merikangas, and E. E. Walters, "Lifetime Prevalence and Age-of-Onset Distributions of *DSM-IV* Disorders in the National Comorbidity Survey Replication," *Archives of General Psychiatry*, 62 (2005): 593–602; M. B. Stein, J. R. Walker, and D. R. Forde, "Setting Diagnostic Thresholds for Social Phobia: Considerations from a Community Survey of Social Anxiety," *American Journal of Psychiatry*, 151 (1994): 408–412. In their community phone survey of social anxiety, Stein et al. found that the estimates of the point prevalence of social phobia vary dramatically depending on the threshold for diagnosing a case. By varying its strictness by excluding cases that entail only public speaking fear and by requiring definite interference with one's life or distress about the phobia, the prevalence can vary from 1.9 to 18.7 percent of the population.

63. M. Talbot, "The Shyness Syndrome: Bashfulness Is the Latest Trait to Become a Pathology," *New York Times*, 24 June 2001.

64. Lane, *Shyness*.

65. J. C. Wakefield, A. V. Horwitz, and M. F. Schmitz, "Are We Overpathologizing the Socially Anxious? Social Phobia from a Harmful Dysfunction Perspective," *Canadian Journal of Psychiatry*, 50 (2005): 317–319.

66. L. Campbell-Sills and M. B. Stein, "Justifying the Diagnostic Status of Social Phobia: A Reply to Wakefield, Horwitz, and Schmitz," *Canadian Journal of Psychiatry*, 50 (2005): 320–323.

67. D. F. Klein, "Harmful Dysfunction, Disorder, Disease, Illness, and Evolution," *Journal of Abnormal Psychology*, 108 (1999): 421–429.

68. R. G. Heimberg, M. R. Liebowitz, D. A. Hope, F. R. Schneier, C. S. Holt, L. A. Welkowitz, H. R. Juster, et al., "Cognitive Behavioral Group Therapy vs. Phenelzine Therapy for Social Phobia: 12-Week Outcome," *Archives of General Psychiatry*, 55 (1998): 1133–1141.

69. R. J. McNally, "Progress and Controversy in the Study of Posttraumatic Stress Disorder," *Annual Review of Psychology*, 54 (2003): 229–252;

R. J. McNally, "Can We Fix PTSD in DSM-V?" *Depression and Anxiety,* 26 (2009): 597–600.

70. N. Breslau and R. C. Kessler, "The Stressor Criterion in DSM-IV Posttraumatic Stress Disorder: An Empirical Investigation," *Biological Psychiatry,* 50 (2001): 699–704; quotation p. 703.

71. R. D. Marshall, R. A. Bryant, L. Amsel, E. J. Suh, J. M. Cook, and Y. Neria, "The Psychology of Ongoing Threat: Relative Risk Appraisal, the September 11 Attacks, and Terrorism-Related Fears," *American Psychologist,* 62 (2007): 304–316.

72. A. Young, "Posttraumatic Stress Disorder of the Virtual Kind: Trauma and Resilience in Post-9/11 America," in *Trauma and Memory: Reading, Healing, and Making Law,* ed. A. Sarat, N. Davidovitch, and M. Alberstein (Stanford, CA: Stanford University Press, 2007), 21–48, quotation p. 71.

73. M. A. Schuster, B. D. Stein, L. H. Jaycox, R. L. Collins, G. N. Marshall, M. N. Elliott, et al., "A National Survey of Stress Reactions after the September 11, 2001, Terrorist Attacks," *New England Journal of Medicine,* 345 (2001): 1507–1512. The quotations appear on pages 1507, 1512, and 1511, respectively.

74. W. E. Schlenger, J. M. Caddell, L. Ebert, B. K. Jordan, K. M. Rourke, D. Wilson, L. Thalji, et al., "Psychological Reactions to Terrorist Attacks: Findings from the National Study of Americans' Reactions to September 11," *Journal of the American Medical Association,* 288 (2002): 581–588.

75. N. Breslau and R. J. McNally, "The Epidemiology of 9-11: Technical Advances and Conceptual Conundrums," in Y. Neria, R. Gross, R. Marshall, and E. Susser, eds., *9/11: Mental Health in the Wake of Terrorist Attacks* (Cambridge, UK: Cambridge University Press, 2006), 521–528; R. J. McNally, *Remembering Trauma* (Cambridge, MA: Belknap Press of Harvard University Press, 2003), 88; R. J. McNally and N. Breslau, "Does Virtual Trauma Cause Posttraumatic Stress Disorder?" *American Psychologist,* 62 (2008): 282–283.

76. S. Galea, J. Ahern, H. Resnick, D. Kilpatrick, M. Bucuvalas, J. Gold, and D. Vlahov, "Psychological Sequelae of the September 11 Terrorist Attacks," *New England Journal of Medicine,* 346 (2002): 982–987.

77. S. Galea, D. Vlahov, H. Resnick, J. Ahern, E. Susser, J. Gold, M. Bucuvalas, and D. Kilpatrick, "Trends of Probable Post-Traumatic

Stress Disorder in New York City after the September 11 Terrorist Attacks," *American Journal of Epidemiology,* 158 (2003): 514-524.

78. R. J. McNally, R. A. Bryant, and A. Ehlers, "Does Early Psychological Intervention Promote Recovery from Posttraumatic Stress?" *Psychological Science in the Public Interest,* 4 (2003): 45-79.

79. J. Stuber, S. Galea, J. Boscarino, and M. Schlesinger, "Was There Unmet Mental Health Need after the September 11, 2001 Terrorist Attacks?" *Social Psychiatry and Psychiatric Epidemiology,* 40 (2006): 1-11.

80. Marshall et al., "The Psychology of Ongoing Threat."

81. E. Olde, O. van der Hart, R. Kleber, and M. van Son, "Posttraumatic Stress Disorder Following Childbirth: A Review," *Clinical Psychology Review,* 26 (2006): 1-16; J. J. McDonald, Jr., "Posttraumatic Stress Dishonesty," *Employee Relations Law Journal,* 28 (2003): 93-111.

82. A. de Jongh, M. Olff, H. van Hoolwerff, I. H. A. Aarman, B. Broekman, R. Lindaur, and F. Boer, "Anxiety and Post-Traumatic Stress Symptoms Following Wisdom Tooth Removal," *Behaviour Research and Therapy,* 46 (2008): 1305-1310.

83. D. G. Kilpatrick, "Final Editorial," *Journal of Traumatic Stress,* 18 (2005): 589-593.

84. B. Shephard, "Risk Factors and PTSD: A Historian's Perspective," in *Posttraumatic Stress Disorder: Issues and Controversies,* ed. G. M. Rosen (Wiley, 2004), 39-61. The quotations appear on pages 57 and 58.

85. R. J. McNally, "Can We Fix PTSD in DSM-V?" *Depression and Anxiety,* 26 (2009): 597-600; R. L. Spitzer, M. B. First, and J. C. Wakefield, "Saving PTSD from Itself in DSM-V," *Journal of Anxiety Disorders,* 21 (2007): 233-241.

86. APA, *DSM-IV-TR,* 468.

87. J. C. Wakefield, M. F. Schmitz, and J. C. Baer, "Does the DSM-IV Clinical Significance Criterion for Major Depression Reduce False Positives? Evidence from the National Comorbidity Survey Replication," *American Journal of Psychiatry,* 167 (2010): 302.

88. R. A. Kulka, W. E. Schlenger, J. A. Fairbank, R. L. Hough, B. K. Jordan, C. R. Marmar, and D. S. Weiss, *Trauma and the Vietnam War Generation: Report of Findings from the National Vietnam Veterans Readjustment Study* (New York: Brunner/Mazel, 1990), 52-53.

89. E. Jones and S. Wessely, *Shell Shock to PTSD: Military Psychiatry from 1900 to the Gulf War* (Hove, UK: Psychology Press, 2005), 133-134; D. H.

Marlowe, *Psychological and Psychosocial Consequences of Combat and Deployment: With Special Emphasis on The Gulf War* (Santa Monica, CA: RAND, 2001), 99–101; B. Shephard, *A War of Nerves: Soldiers and Psychiatrists in the Twentieth Century* (Cambridge, MA: Harvard University Press, 2001), 392; D. W. King and L. A. King, "Validity Issues in Research on Vietnam Veteran Adjustment," *Psychological Bulletin,* 109 (1991): 107–124; E. T. Dean, Jr., *Shook over Hell: Post-Traumatic Stress, Vietnam, and the Civil War* (Cambridge, MA: Harvard University Press, 1997).

90. R. J. McNally, "Can We Solve the Mysteries of the National Vietnam Veterans Readjustment Study?" *Journal of Anxiety Disorders,* 21 (2007): 192–200.

91. B. P. Dohrenwend, J. B. Turner, N. A. Turse, B. G. Adams, K. C. Koenen, and R. Marshall, "The Psychological Risks of Vietnam for U.S. Veterans: A Revisit with New Data and Methods," *Science,* 313 (2006): 379–982.

92. R. J. McNally, "Psychiatric Casualties of War," *Science,* 313 (2006): 923–924.

93. R. J. McNally, "Revisiting Dohrenwend et al.'s Revisit of the National Vietnam Veterans Readjustment Study," *Journal of Traumatic Stress,* 20 (2007): 481–486.

94. I. M. Engelhard, M. A. van den Hout, J. Weerts, A. Arntz, J. J. C. M. Hox, and R. J. McNally, "Deployment-Related Stress and Trauma in Dutch Soldiers Returning from Iraq: Prospective Study," *British Journal of Psychiatry,* 191 (2007): 140–145.

95. N. Breslau and G. F. Alvarado, "The Clinical Significance Criterion in DSM-IV Post-Traumatic Stress Disorder," *Psychological Medicine,* 37 (2007): 1437–1444.

3. Can Evolutionary Psychology Make Sense of Mental Disorder?

1. W. H. Masters and V. E. Johnson, *Human Sexual Inadequacy* (New York: Bantam, 1970), 218; B. L. Andersen, "Primary Orgasmic Dysfunction: Diagnostic Considerations and Review of Treatment," *Psychological Bulletin,* 93 (1983): 105–136; quotation p. 105; L. G. Barbach, "Group Treatment of Preorgasmic Women," *Journal of Sex and Marital*

Therapy, 1 (1974): 139-145; J. LoPiccolo and W. C. Lobitz, "The Role of Masturbation in the Treatment of Orgasmic Dysfunction," *Archives of Sexual Behavior*, 2 (1972): 163-171; D. H. Wallace and L. G. Barbach, "Preorgasmic Group Treatment," *Journal of Sex and Marital Therapy*, 1 (1974): 146-154.

2. J. C. Wakefield, "Female Primary Orgasmic Dysfunction: Masters and Johnson versus DSM-III-R on Diagnosis and Incidence," *Journal of Sex Research*, 24 (1988): 363.

3. J. C. Wakefield, "The Concept of Mental Disorder: On the Boundary Between Biological Facts and Social Values," *American Psychologist*, 47 (1992): 373-388; J. C. Wakefield, "Disorder as Harmful Dysfunction: A Conceptual Critique of *DSM-III-R*'s Definition of Mental Disorder," *Psychological Review*, 99 (1992): 232-247; J. C. Wakefield, "Mental Disorder as a Black Box Essentialist Concept," *Journal of Abnormal Psychology*, 108 (1999): 465-472; J. C. Wakefield, "Limits of Operationalization: A Critique of Spitzer and Endicott's (1978) Proposed Operational Criteria for Mental Disorder," *Journal of Abnormal Psychology*, 102 (1993): 160-172.

4. Wakefield, "The Concept of Mental Disorder," 373.

5. R. G. Millikan, "In Defense of Proper Functions," *Philosophy of Science*, 56 (1989): 288-302; K. Neander, "Functions as Selected Effects: The Conceptual Analyst's Defense," *Philosophy of Science*, 58 (1991): 168-184; L. Wright, "Functions," *Philosophical Review*, 82 (1973): 139-168.

6. R. E. Kendell, "The Concept of Disease and Its Implications for Psychiatry," *British Journal of Psychiatry*, 127 (1975): 305-315.

7. P. D. Kramer, *Against Depression* (New York: Penguin, 2005), 155-156.

8. American Psychiatric Association (APA), *Diagnostic and Statistical Manual of Mental Disorders*, 4th ed., text revision [DSM-IV-TR.] (Washington: American Psychiatric Publishing, Inc., 2000), 356.

9. D. F. Klein, "False Suffocation Alarms, Spontaneous Panics, and Related Conditions: An Integrative Hypothesis," *Archives of General Psychiatry*, 50 (1993): 306-317.

10. D. M. Clark, "A Cognitive Approach to Panic," *Behaviour Research and Therapy*, 24 (1986): 461-479.

11. R. J. McNally, *Panic Disorder: A Critical Analysis* (New York: Guilford, 1994), 113-115.

12. Wakefield, "Mental Disorder as a Black Box Essentialist Concept."

13. J. C. Wakefield, K. J. Pottick, and S. A. Kirk, "Should the DSM-IV Diagnostic Criteria for Conduct Disorder Consider Social Context?" *American Journal of Psychiatry,* 159 (2002): 380–386.

14. J. E. Richters and D. Cicchetti, "Mark Twain Meets DSM-III-R: Conduct Disorder, Development, and the Concept of Harmful Dysfunction," *Development and Psychopathology,* 5 (1993): 5–29.

15. J. H. Barkow, L. Cosmides, and J. Tooby, eds., *The Adapted Mind* (New York: Oxford University Press, 1992); S. Pinker, *How the Mind Works* (New York: Norton, 1997).

16. E. Sober, *Philosophy and Biology* (Boulder, CO: Westview Press, 1993), 83.

17. J. C. Wakefield, "Evolutionary versus Prototype Analyses of the Concept of Disorder," *Journal of Abnormal Psychology,* 108 (1999): 376.

18. E. Mayr, "Cause and Effect in Biology: Kinds of Causes, Predictability, and Teleology Are Viewed by a Practicing Biologist," *Science,* 134 (1961): 1501–1506.

19. N. Chomsky, *Language and Mind,* enlarged ed. (San Diego: Harcourt Brace Jovanovich, 1972), 97.

20. R. C. Lewontin, "The Evolution of Cognition: Questions We Will Never Answer," in *An Invitation to Cognitive Science,* Volume 4: *Methods, Models, and Conceptual Issues,* 2nd ed., ed. D. Scarborough and S. Sternberg (Cambridge, MA: MIT Press, 1998), 120, 130.

21. Barkow et al., *The Adapted Mind,* esp. J. Tooby and L. Cosmides, "The Psychological Foundations of Culture," 19–136; and Pinker, *How the Mind Works.*

22. G. V. Lauder, "The Argument from Design," in *Adaptation,* ed. M. R. Rose and G. V. Lauder (San Diego: Academic Press, 1996), 55–91.

23. A. M. Leroi, M. R. Rose, and G. V. Lauder, "What Does the Comparative Method Reveal about Adaptation?" *American Naturalist,* 143 (1994): 381–402.

24. F. Jacob, "Evolution and Tinkering," *Science,* 196 (1977): 1163.

25. P. W. Andrews, S. W. Gangestad, and D. Matthews, "Adaptationism—How to Carry out an Exaptationist Program," *Behavioral and Brain Sciences,* 25 (2002): 489–553.

26. S. J. Gould and R. C. Lewontin, "The Spandrels of San Marco and the Panglossian Paradigm: A Critique of the Adaptationist Programme,"

Proceedings of the Royal Society of London, B: Biological Sciences, 205 (1979): 581–598; S. J. Gould, and E. S. Vrba, "Exaptation—A Missing Term in the Science of Form," *Paleobiology,* 8 (1982): 4–15; S. J. Gould, "The Exaptive Excellence of Spandrels as a Term and Prototype," *Proceedings of the National Academy of Sciences,* 94 (1997): 10750–10755.

27. J. G. Kingsolver and M. A. R. Koehl, "Aerodynamics, Thermoregulation, and the Evolution of Insect Wings: Differential Scaling and Evolutionary Change," *Evolution,* 39 (1985): 488–504. But for contrary data see J. H. Marden and M. G. Kramer, "Surface-Skimming Stoneflies: A Possible Intermediate Stage in Insect Flight Evolution," *Science,* 266 (1994): 427–430.

28. S. J. Gould, "Exaptation: A Crucial Tool for an Evolutionary Psychology," *Journal of Social Issues,* 47 (1991): 59.

29. S. O. Lilienfeld and L. Marino, "Mental Disorder as a Roschian Concept: A Critique of Wakefield's 'Harmful Dysfunction' Analysis," *Journal of Abnormal Psychology,* 104 (1995): 411–420; S. O. Lilienfeld and L. Marino, "Essentialism Revisited: Evolutionary Theory and the Concept of Mental Disorder," *Journal of Abnormal Psychology,* 108 (1999): 400–411.

30. H. K. Reeve and P. W. Sherman, "Adaptation and the Goals of Evolutionary Research," *Quarterly Review of Biology,* 68 (1993): 1–32.

31. Ibid.; P. E. Griffiths, "Function, Homology, and Character Individuation," *Philosophy of Science,* 73 (2006): 1–25.

32. A. S. Romer and T. S. Parsons, *The Vertebrate Body,* 5th ed. (Philadelphia: W. B. Saunders, 1977), 483.

33. Wakefield, "Evolutionary versus Prototype Analyses."

34. J. C. Wakefield, "Why Specific Design Is Not the Mark of the Adaptational," *Behavioral and Brain Sciences,* 25 (2002): 532–533.

35. Wakefield, "Mental Disorder as a Black Box Essentialist Concept," 465.

36. For evolutionary psychology, M. Barkow et al., *The Adapted Mind.* For philosophy, see R. N. Brandon, "Biological Teleology: Questions and Explanations," in *Nature's Purposes,* ed. C. Allen, M. Bekoff, and G. Lauder (Cambridge, MA: MIT Press: 1998), 79–97; Millikan, "In Defense of Proper Functions"; Neander, "Functions as Selected Effects"; Wright, "Functions."

37. For a review, see A. Wouters, "The Function Debate within Philosophy," *Acta Biotheoretica*, 53 (2005): 123-151.

38. R. Amundson, "Historical Development of the Concept of Adaptation," in *Adaptation*, ed. M. R. Rose and G. V. Lauder (San Diego, CA: Academic Press, 1996), 11-53; D. C. Fisher, "Evolutionary Morphology: Beyond the Analogous, the Anecdotal, and the Ad Hoc," *Paleobiology*, 11 (1985): 120-138; Reeve and Sherman, "Adaptation and the Goals of Evolutionary Research."

39. Reeve and Sherman, "Adaptation and the Goals of Evolutionary Research," 9.

40. A. L. Basolo, "Female Preference for Male Sword Length in the Green Swordtail *Xiphophorus Helleri* (Pisces: Poeciliidae)," *Animal Behaviour*, 40 (1990): 332-338; A. L. Basolo, "Female Preference Predates the Evolution of the Sword in Swordtail Fish," *Science*, 250 (1990): 808-810.

41. R. Amundson and G. V. Lauder, "Function without Purpose: The Uses of Causal Role Function in Evolutionary Biology," *Biology and Philosophy*, 9 (1994): 443-469; A. Wouters, "Viability Explanation," *Biology and Philosophy*, 10 (1995): 435-457.

42. E. H. Hagen, "Special Design's Centuries of Success," *Behavioral and Brain Sciences*, 25 (2002): 519-520. Many people have remarked that William Harvey, "An Anatomical Disquisition on the Motion of the Heart and Blood in Animals," in *Great Books of the Western World*, vol. 28, ed. R. M. Hutchins (Chicago: Encyclopedia Britannica, Incorporated, 1952), 267-304, knew nothing about evolution, yet this did not prevent him from discovering the heart's current causal role in the circulatory system. Wakefield does not believe that the Harvey case supports claims for a nonevolutionary approach to function in biology. He remarks that Harvey certainly detected "design" in the circulatory system, realizing that it could not have appeared by accident. This must surely be true, but Harvey was not trying to distinguish "designed" from accidental features of the circulatory system; he was trying to figure out how it works and how each of its components contributes to systemic function. J. C. Wakefield, "Evolutionary History versus Current Causal Role in the Definition of Disorder: Reply to McNally," *Behaviour Research and Therapy*, 39 (2001): 347-366.

43. Amundson and Lauder, "Function without Purpose"; R. Cummins,

"Functional Analysis," *Journal of Philosophy*, 72 (1975): 741-765; P. S. Davies, *Norms of Nature: Naturalism and the Nature of Functions* (Cambridge, MA: MIT Press, 2001); Wouters, "The Function Debate within Philosophy."

44. R. J. McNally, "On Wakefield's Harmful Dysfunction Analysis of Mental Disorder," *Behaviour Research and Therapy*, 39 (2001): 309-314.

45. L. M. Shin et al., "Regional Cerebral Blood Flow in the Amygdala and Medial Prefrontal Cortex during Traumatic Imagery in Male and Female Vietnam Veterans with PTSD," *Archives of General Psychiatry*, 61 (2004): 168-176.

46. D. Bolton, *What Is Mental Disorder? An Essay in Philosophy, Science, and Values* (Oxford, UK: Oxford University Press, 2008), 232; B. Gert and C. M. Culver, "Defining Mental Disorder," in J. Radden, ed., *The Philosophy of Psychiatry: A Companion* (Oxford, UK: Oxford University Press, 2004), 215-225.

47. M. C. Seto, "Pedophilia," *Annual Review of Clinical Psychology*, 5 (2009): 391-407.

48. However, psychopathic criminals whose defective empathy mechanisms lead to crime and the harms of imprisonment would qualify as disordered under the HDA.

49. L. Cosmides and J. Tooby, "Toward an Evolutionary Taxonomy of Treatable Conditions," *Journal of Abnormal Psychology*, 108 (1999): 453-464, quotation from 458.

50. R. L. Spitzer, "Brief Comments from a Psychiatric Nosologist Weary from His Own Attempts to Define Mental Disorder: Why Ossorio's Definition Muddles and Wakefield's 'Harmful Dysfunction' Illuminates the Issues," *Clinical Psychology: Science and Practice*, 4 (1997): 259-261.

51. K. W. M. Fulford, "Nine Variations and a Coda on the Theme of an Evolutionary Definition of Dysfunction," *Journal of Abnormal Psychology*, 108 (1999): 412-420; L. J. Kirmayer and A. Young, "Culture and Context in the Evolutionary Concept of Mental Disorder," *Journal of Abnormal Psychology*, 108 (1999): 446-452; R. J. McNally, "On Wakefield's Harmful Dysfunction Analysis of Mental Disorder," *Behaviour Research and Therapy*, 39 (2001): 309-314. In "Evolutionary History versus Current Causal Role in the Definition of Disorder: Reply to

McNally," *Behaviour Research and Therapy*, 39 (2001): 347–366, Wakefield points out that not all *ought*-statements concern norms. For example, he distinguishes between the *ought* of values and the *ought* of rationality. An example of the latter would be, "To get to Boston by 10 P.M., you ought to take the 4 P.M. Metroliner" (351). However, *ought*-statements about biological function do appear inescapably normative.

52. C. F. Craver, "Role Functions, Mechanisms, and Hierarchy," *Philosophy of Science*, 68 (2001): 53–74; J. R. Searle, *Mind, Language and Society: Philosophy in the Real World* (New York: Basic Books, 1998), 121–122.

53. J. C. Wakefield, M. F. Schmitz, M. B. First, and A. Horwitz, "Extending the Bereavement Exclusion for Major Depression to Other Losses: Evidence from the National Comorbidity Survey," *Archives of General Psychiatry*, 64 (2007): 433–440.

54. S. Zisook, S. R. Shuchter, P. Pedrelli, J. Sable, and S. C. Deaciuc, "Bupropion Sustained Release for Bereavement: Results of an Open Trial," *Journal of Clinical Psychiatry*, 62 (2001): 227–229, quotation 229.

55. Kramer, *Against Depression*, xii.

56. J. J. McDonald, Jr., "Posttraumatic Stress Dishonesty," *Employee Relations Law Journal*, 28 (2003): 93–111.

57. K. R. Foster and P. W. Huber, *Judging Science: Scientific Knowledge and the Federal Courts* (Cambridge, MA: MIT Press, 1999), 115–117.

58. A. V. Horwitz and J. C. Wakefield, *The Loss of Sadness: How Psychiatry Transformed Normal Sorrow into Depressive Disorder* (Oxford, UK: Oxford University Press, 2007), 190.

59. E. G. Wilson, *Against Happiness: In Praise of Melancholy* (New York: Sara Crichton Books, 2008).

60. D. Bolton, "Continuing Commentary: Alternatives to Disorder," *Philosophy, Psychiatry, and Psychology*, 7 (2000): 141–153.

61. M. K. Nock, W. B. Mendes, H. J. Dour, and T. L. Deliberto, "Self-Harm as Self-Help," manuscript submitted for publication, 2010.

62. J. Olds and R. S. Schwartz, *The Lonely American: Drifting Apart in the Twenty-First Century* (Boston, MA: Beacon Press, 2009).

63. Wakefield, "Evolutionary History versus Current Causal Role."

64. Amundson and Lauder, "Function without Purpose."

65. Craver, "Role Functions, Mechanisms, and Hierarchy"; Griffiths,

"Function, Homology, and Character Individuation"; R. Wachbroit, "Normality as a Biological Concept," *Philosophy of Science,* 61 (1994): 579–591.

66. Wachbroit, "Normality as a Biological Concept." In physics, models are simplified, ideal entities that abstract away irrelevant details of the real world phenomenon. For example, a point mass is an object that possesses mass and has a spatial location but no spatial dimensions. However, objects in the real world have spatial dimensions as well as mass. In biology, models of the heart, the amygdala, and so forth are not abstract simplifications. Moreover, unlike in physics, where talk about normal and abnormal electrons makes no sense, in the life sciences we can speak of normal and abnormal structures and functions.

67. J. M. Hooley, S. A. Gruber, H. A. Parker, J. Guillaumot, J. Rogowska, and D. A. Yurgelun-Todd, "Cortico-Limbic Response to Personally Challenging Emotional Stimuli after Complete Recovery from Depression," *Psychiatry Research: Neuroimaging,* 172 (2009): 83–91.

68. J. M. Hooley, "Expressed Emotion and Relapse of Psychopathology," *Annual Review of Clinical Psychology,* 3 (2007): 329–352.

4. Psychopathology as Adaptation?

1. M. C. Keller and G. Miller, "Resolving the Paradox of Common, Harmful, Heritable Mental Disorders: Which Evolutionary Genetic Models Work Best?" *Behavioral and Brain Sciences,* 29 (2006): 385–452.

2. S. Rosenberg, S. K. N. Marie, and S. Kliemann, "Congenital Insensitivity to Pain with Anhidrosis (Hereditary Sensory and Autonomic Neuropathy Type IV)," *Pediatric Neurology,* 11 (1994): 50–56.

3. R. M. Nesse and G. C. Williams, *Why We Get Sick: The New Science of Darwinian Medicine* (New York: Times Books, 1994), 8–9, 27–29.

4. K. Oatley and P. N. Johnson-Laird, "Toward a Cognitive Theory of Emotions," *Cognition and Emotion,* 1 (1987): 29–50.

5. E. Klinger, "Consequences of Commitment to and Disengagement from Incentives," *Psychological Review,* 82 (1975): 1–25.

6. R. C. Kessler, P. Berglund, O. Demler, R. Jin, K. R. Merikangas, and

E. E. Walters, "Lifetime Prevalence and Age-of-Onset Distributions of *DSM-IV* Disorders in the National Comorbidity Survey Replication," *Archives of General Psychiatry,* 62 (2005): 593–602.

7. B. A. Palmer, V. S. Pankratz, and J. M. Bostwick, "The Lifetime Risk of Suicide in Schizophrenia: A Reexamination," *Archives of General Psychiatry,* 62 (2005): 247–253; L. Sher, "Alcoholism and Suicidal Behavior: A Clinical Overview," *Acta Psychiatrica Scandinavica,* 113 (2006): 13–22.

8. M. A. Taylor and M. Fink, *Melancholia: The Diagnosis, Pathophysiology, and Treatment of Depressive Illness* (Cambridge, UK: Cambridge University Press, 2006), xi.

9. Centers for Disease Control, *National Center for Health Statistics: NCHS Data on Injuries,* June 30, 2006, www.cdc.gov/nchs/data/factsheets/injury.pdf (accessed 6/28/07).

10. R. W. Maris, "Suicide," *Lancet,* 360 (2002): 319–326; Taylor and Fink, *Melancholia,* 125.

11. J. K. Kiecolt-Glaser and R. Glaser, "Depression and Immune Function: Central Pathways to Morbidity and Mortality," *Journal of Psychosomatic Research,* 53 (2002): 873–876; L. R. Wulsin and B. M. Singal, "Do Depressive Symptoms Increase the Risk for the Onset of Coronary Disease? A Systematic Quantitative Review," *Psychosomatic Medicine,* 65 (2003): 201–210; G. Rajkowska, J. J. Miguel-Hidalgo, J. Wei, G. Dilley, S. D. Pittman, H. Y. Meltzer, J. C. Overholser, B. L. Roth, and C. A. Stockmeier, "Morphometric Evidence for Neuronal and Glial Prefrontal Cell Pathology in Major Depression," *Biological Psychiatry,* 45 (1999): 1085–1098.

12. Keller and Miller, "Resolving the Paradox."

13. R. Plomin, J. C. DeFries, G. E. McClearn, and M. Rutter, *Behavioral Genetics,* 3rd ed. (New York: Freeman, 1997), 169–194.

14. P. Tienari, L. C. Wynne, K. Läksy, J. Moring, P. Nieminen, A. Sorri, I. Lahti, and K.-E. Wahlberg, "Genetic Boundaries of the Schizophrenia Spectrum: Evidence from the Finnish Adoptive Family Study of Schizophrenia," *American Journal of Psychiatry,* 160 (2003): 1587–1594. Schizophrenia spectrum disorders include syndromes such as schizophrenia, schizotypal personality disorder, delusional disorder, and psychotic bipolar disorder.

15. Keller and Miller, "Resolving the Paradox."
16. Ibid.
17. Nesse and Williams, *Why We Get Sick*, 207–233.
18. A. Stevens and J. Price, *Evolutionary Psychiatry* (London: Routledge, 1996), 267.
19. R. J. McNally, "Preparedness, Phobias, and the Panglossian Paradigm," *Behavioral and Brain Sciences*, 18 (1995): 303–304.
20. L. Cosmides and J. Tooby, "Toward an Evolutionary Taxonomy of Treatable Conditions," *Journal of Abnormal Psychology*, 108 (1999): 453–464.
21. S. J. Gould and R. C. Lewontin, "The Spandrels of San Marco and the Panglossian Paradigm: A Critique of the Adaptationist Programme," *Proceedings of the Royal Society of London, B: Biological Sciences*, 205 (1979): 581–598.
22. Nesse and Williams, *Why We Get Sick*, 207–233.
23. Gould and Lewontin, "The Spandrels of San Marco."
24. S. J. Gould and E. S. Vrba, "Exaptation—A Missing Term in the Science of Form," *Paleobiology*, 8 (1982): 4–15.
25. E. Sober, *Philosophy and Biology* (Boulder, CO: Westview Press, 1993), 81–82.
26. K. R. Jamison, *Touched with Fire: Manic-Depressive Illness and the Artistic Temperament* (New York: The Free Press, 1993).
27. J. Beatty, "Random Drift," in *Keywords in Evolutionary Biology*, ed. E. F. Keller and E. A. Lloyd (Cambridge, MA: Harvard University Press, 1992), 273–281.
28. S. Pinker, *How the Mind Works* (New York: Norton, 1997), 165–166.
29. S. J. Gould, "Sociobiology: The Art of Storytelling," *New Scientist*, 80 (1978): 530–533.
30. J. Alcock, *Animal Behavior: An Evolutionary Approach*, 7th ed. (Sunderland, MA: Sinauer Associates, 2001).
31. L. Cosmides, "The Logic of Social Exchange: Has Natural Selection Shaped How Humans Reason? Studies with the Wason Selection Task," *Cognition*, 31 (1989): 187–276.
32. A. Öhman and S. Mineka, "Fears, Phobias, and Preparedness: Toward an Evolved Module of Fear and Fear Learning," *Psychological Review*, 108 (2001): 483–522.

33. F. Renner, as cited in H. Merckelbach and P. J. de Jong, "Evolutionary Models of Phobias," in *Phobias: A Handbook of Theory, Research, and Treatment,* ed. G. C. L. Davey (Chichester, UK: Wiley, 1997), 323–347.

34. R. J. McNally, "Disgust Has Arrived," *Journal of Anxiety Disorders,* 16 (2002): 561–566.

35. A. J. Longley, "Depression Is an Adaptation," *Archives of General Psychiatry,* 58 (2001): 1083.

36. E. H. Hagen, "The Function of Postpartum Depression," *Evolution and Human Behavior,* 20 (1999): 330.

37. Ibid., 348.

38. P. J. Watson and P. W. Andrews, "Toward a Revised Evolutionary Adaptationist Analysis of Depression: The Social Navigation Hypothesis," *Journal of Affective Disorders,* 72 (2002): 1–14.

39. L. B. Alloy and L. Y. Abramson, "Judgment of Contingency in Depressed and Nondepressed Students: Sadder but Wiser?" *Journal of Experimental Psychology: General,* 108 (1979): 441–485, 441.

40. Watson and Andrews, "Toward a Revised Evolutionary Adaptationist Analysis of Depression," 11.

41. Ibid.

42. J. Price, L. Sloman, J. Gardner, Jr., P. Gilbert, and P. Rohde, "The Social Competition Hypothesis of Depression," *British Journal of Psychiatry,* 164 (1994): 309–315.

43. A. T. Beck, *Depression: Causes and Treatment* (Philadelphia, PA: University of Pennsylvania Press, 1967), 333–338.

44. R. Ackermann and R. J. DeRubeis, "Is Depressive Realism Real?" *Clinical Psychology Review,* 11 (1991): 565–584.

45. D. E. Schotte, J. Cools, and S. Pavar, "Problem-Solving Deficits in Suicidal Patients: Trait Vulnerability or State Phenomenon?" *Journal of Consulting and Clinical Psychology,* 58 (1990): 562–564.

46. P. J. Cowen, "Not Fade Away: The HPA Axis and Depression," *Psychological Medicine,* 40 (2010): 1–4.

47. S. M. Monroe and K. L. Harkness, "Life Stress, the 'Kindling' Hypothesis, and the Recurrence of Depression: Considerations from a Life Stress Perspective," *Psychological Review,* 112 (2005): 417–445.

48. R. J. Gregory and R. D. Jindal, "Ethical Dilemmas in Prescribing Antidepressants," *Archives of General Psychiatry,* 58 (2001): 1085.

49. For example, Pinker, *How the Mind Works,* 52.

50. G. E. Moore, *Principia Ethica,* rev. ed. (Cambridge, UK: Cambridge University Press, 1993; originally published 1903), 98.

51. J. Colapinto, *As Nature Made Him: The Boy Who Was Raised as a Girl* (New York: Perennial, 2000).

52. Keller and Miller, "Resolving the Paradox."

53. J. M. Murphy, "Psychiatric Labeling in Cross-Cultural Perspective," *Science,* 191 (1976): 1019–1028.

54. S. Guisinger, "Adapted to Flee Famine: Adding an Evolutionary Perspective on Anorexia Nervosa," *Psychological Review,* 110 (2003): 745–761.

55. D. Nettle, "The Evolution of Personality Variation in Humans and Other Animals," *American Psychologist,* 61 (2006): 622–631; L. Penke, J. A. A. Denissen, and G. F. Miller, "The Evolutionary Genetics of Personality," *European Journal of Personality,* 21 (2007): 549–587.

56. A. C. Allison, "Notes on Sickle-Cell Polymorphism," *Annals of Human Genetics,* 19 (1954): 39–51.

57. K. L. Bubb, D. Bovee, D. Buckley, E. Haugen, M. Kibukawa, M. Paddock, A. Palmieri, et al., "Scan of Human Genome Reveals No New Loci under Ancient Balancing Selection," *Genetics,* 173 (2006): 2165–2177; M. C. Keller, "The Evolutionary Persistence of Genes That Increase Mental Disorders Risk," *Current Directions in Psychological Science,* 17 (2008): 395–399.

58. Jamison, *Touched with Fire.*

59. L. Mealey, "The Sociobiology of Sociopathy: An Integrated Account," *Behavioral and Brain Sciences,* 18 (1995): 523–599.

60. Keller and Miller, "Resolving the Paradox," 397.

5. Does Society Create (Some) Mental Disorders?

1. R. Cooper, *Classifying Madness: A Philosophical Examination of the Diagnostic and Statistical Manual of Mental Disorders* (Dordrecht, The Netherlands: Springer, 2005), 11. The group's name has since changed to the National Alliance on Mental Illness.

2. S. Bleich, D. Cutler, C. Murray, and A. Adams, "Why Is the Developed World Obese?" *Annual Review of Public Health,* 29 (2008): 273–295.

3. T. A. Glass and M. J. McAtee, "Behavioral Science at the Crossroads in Public Health: Extending Horizons, Envisioning the Future," *Social Science and Medicine,* 62 (2006): 1650–1671.

4. D. A. Kessler, *The End of Overeating: Taking Control of the Insatiable American Appetite* (New York: Rodale, 2009).

5. Quoted in A. Sokal and J. Bricmont, *Fashionable Nonsense: Postmodern Intellectuals' Abuse of Science* (New York: Picador, 1998), 96–97.

6. For example, M. Borch-Jacobsen, *Making Minds and Madness: From Hysteria to Depression* (Cambridge, UK: Cambridge University Press, 2009).

7. H. G. Pope, Jr., M. B. Poliakoff, M. P. Parker, M. Boynes, and J. I. Hudson, "Is Dissociative Amnesia a Culture-Bound Syndrome? Findings from a Survey of Historical Literature," *Psychological Medicine,* 37 (2007): 225–233.

8. Borch-Jacobsen, *Making Minds and Madness.*

9. A. V. Horwitz and J. C. Wakefield, *The Loss of Sadness: How Psychiatry Transformed Normal Sorrow into Depressive Disorder* (Oxford: Oxford University Press, 2007), 201.

10. A. Kleinman, "Neurasthenia and Depression: A Study of Somatization and Culture in China," *Culture, Medicine, and Psychiatry,* 6 (1982): 117–190.

11. Y. E. Chentsova-Dutton and J. L. Tsai, "Understanding Depression Across Cultures," in *Handbook of Depression,* 2nd ed., ed. I. H. Gotlib and C. L. Hammen (New York: Guilford, 2009), 363–385.

12. D. E. Hinton and B. J. Good, eds., *Culture and Panic Disorder* (Stanford, CA: Stanford University Press, 2009).

13. D. M. Clark, "A Cognitive Approach to Panic," *Behaviour Research and Therapy,* 24 (1986): 461–479.

14. D. E. Hinton, D. Chhean, V. Pich, K. Um, J. M. Fama, and M. H. Pollack, "Neck-Focused Panic Attacks among Cambodian Refugees: A Logistic and Linear Regression Analysis," *Journal of Anxiety Disorders,* 20 (2006): 119–138.

15. Borch-Jacobsen, *Making Minds and Madness,* 2–3.

16. I. Hacking, *Mad Travelers: Reflections on the Reality of Transient Mental Illness* (Charlottesville: University of Virginia Press, 1998).

17. I. Hacking, *The Social Construction of What?* (Cambridge, MA: Harvard University Press, 1999), 1–34.

18. P. K. Keel and K. L. Klump, "Are Eating Disorders Culture-Bound Syndromes? Implications for Conceptualizing Their Etiology," *Psychological Bulletin,* 129 (2003): 747–769.

19. R. Popenoe, "Ideal," in *Fat: The Anthropology of an Obsession,* ed. D. Kulick and A. Meneley (New York: Jeremy P. Tarcher/Penguin, 2005), 9–28.

20. American Psychiatric Association (APA), *Diagnostic and Statistical Manual of Mental Disorders,* 4th ed., text revision [DSM-IV-TR.] (Washington: American Psychiatric Publishing, Inc., 2000), 520.

21. Borch-Jacobsen, *Making Minds and Madness,* 19–36.

22. S. Freud, "The Aetiology of Hysteria," in *The Standard Edition of the Complete Psychological Works of Sigmund Freud,* vol. 3, ed. and trans. J. Strachey (London: Hogarth Press, 1962), 191–221.

23. F. Crews, *The Memory Wars: Freud's Legacy in Dispute* (New York: New York Review of Books, 1995), 216–218; R. J. McNally, "Do Certain Readings of Freud Constitute 'Pathological Science'? A Comment on Boag (2006)," *Review of General Psychology,* 11 (2007): 359–360.

24. Pope et al., "Is Dissociative Amnesia a Culture-Bound Syndrome?"

25. Ibid., 225.

26. B. Carey, "A Study of Memory Looks at Fact and Fiction," *New York Times,* February 3, 2007; P. Choderlos de Laclos, *Les Liaisons Dangereuses,* trans. P. W. K. Stone (London: Penguin, 1782), 348–349.

27. H. G. Pope, Jr., M. B. Poliakoff, M. P. Parker, M. Boynes, and J. I. Hudson, "The Authors' Reply," *Psychological Medicine,* 37 (2007): 1067–1068. The opera is J. B. Marsollier's *Nina.*

28. R. J. McNally, *Remembering Trauma* (Cambridge, MA: Belknap Press of Harvard University Press, 2003), 186–228.

29. Ibid., 229–259.

30. J. Acocella, *Creating Hysteria: Women and Multiple Personality Disorder* (San Francisco: Jossey-Bass, 1999).

31. R. J. C. Huntjens, M. L. Peters, L. Woertman, O. van der Hart, and A. Postma, "Memory Transfer for Emotionally Valenced Words Between Identities in Dissociative Identity Disorder," *Behaviour Research and Therapy,* 45 (2007): 775–789.

32. W. S. Taylor and M. F. Martin, "Multiple Personality," *Journal of Abnormal and Social Psychology,* 39 (1944): 281–300.

33. F. R. Schreiber, *Sybil* (New York: Warner Books, 1973).

34. Borch-Jacobsen, *Making Minds and Madness,* 74.

35. S. J. Ceci and E. F. Loftus, "'Memory Work': A Royal Road to False Memories?" *Applied Cognitive Psychology,* 8 (1994): 351–364; E. Loftus and K. Ketcham, *The Myth of Repressed Memory: False Memories and Allegations of Sexual Abuse* (New York: St. Martin's Griffin, 1994).

36. R. J. McNally, *Remembering Trauma,* 229–259.

37. K. V. Lanning, "A Law-Enforcement Perspective on Allegations of Ritual Abuse," in *Out of Darkness: Exploring Satanism and Ritual Abuse,* ed. D. K. Sakheim and S. E. Devine (New York: Lexington Books, 1992), 109–146.

38. Acocella, *Creating Hysteria.*

39. H. G. Pope, Jr., S. Barry, A. Bodkin, and J. I. Hudson, "Tracking Scientific Interest in the Dissociative Disorders: A Study of Scientific Publication Output 1984–2003," *Psychotherapy and Psychosomatics,* 75 (2006): 19–24.

40. Taylor and Martin, "Multiple Personality"; S. O. Lilienfeld, S. J. Lynn, I. Kirsch, J. F. Chaves, T. R. Sarbin, G. K. Ganaway, and R. A. Powell, "Dissociative Identity Disorder and the Sociocognitive Model: Recalling the Lessons of the Past," *Psychological Bulletin,* 125 (1999): 507–523; R. R. McHugh, *Try to Remember: Psychiatry's Clash Over Meaning, Memory, and Mind* (New York: Dana Press, 2008), 60–66.

41. For the case of Eve, see C. H. Thigpen and H. M. Cleckley, "A Case of Multiple Personality," *Journal of Abnormal and Social Psychology,* 49 (1954): 135–151. For the critique of MPD overdiagnosis, see C. H. Thigpen and H. M. Cleckley, "On the Incidence of Multiple Personality Disorder: A Brief Communication," *International Journal of Clinical and Experimental Hypnosis,* 32 (1984): 63–66.

42. D. H. Gleaves, M. C. May, and E. Cardeña, "An Examination of the Diagnostic Validity of Dissociative Identity Disorder," *Clinical Psychology Review,* 21 (2001): 577–608.

43. P. Boyer and S. Nissenbaum, *Salem Possessed: The Social Origins of Witchcraft* (Cambridge, MA: Harvard University Press, 1974), 1–16.

44. Borch-Jacobsen, *Making Minds and Madness,* 64–99; R. W. Rieber, *The Bifurcation of the Self: The History and Theory of Dissociation and Its Disorders* (New York: Springer, 2006), 205–287.

45. Rieber, *The Bifurcation of the Self*.

46. Ibid., 289–295.

47. R. Tandon, M. S. Keshavan, and H. A. Nasrallah, "Schizophrenia, 'Just the Facts': What We Know in 2008. 2. Epidemiology and Etiology," *Schizophrenia Research*, 102 (2008): 1–18.

48. Ibid.; R. K. McClure and J. A. Lieberman, "Neurodevelopmental and Neurodegenerative Hypotheses of Schizophrenia: A Review and Critique," *Current Opinion in Psychiatry*, 16, suppl. 2 (2003): S15–S28.

49. E. Kraepelin, *Dementia Praecox and Paraphrenia,* trans. R. M. Barclay (Edinburgh: E. & S. Livingstone, 1919).

50. J. Paris, *The Fall of an Icon: Psychoanalysis and Academic Psychiatry* (Toronto: University of Toronto Press, 2005).

51. J. Zubin and B. J. Spring, "Vulnerability—A New View of Schizophrenia," *Journal of Abnormal Psychology,* 86 (1977): 103–126.

52. K. Evans, J. McGrath, and R. Milns, "Searching for Schizophrenia in Ancient Greek and Roman Literature: A Systematic Review," *Acta Psychiatrica Scandinavica,* 107 (2003): 323–330.

53. Suetonius [Gaius Suetonius Tranquillus], *The Twelve Caesars,* trans. R. Graves, revised with an introduction by M. Grant (London: Penguin, 1979). For Caligula, see 153–184; for Nero, see 213–246.

54. E. Hare, "Schizophrenia as a Recent Disease," *British Journal of Psychiatry,* 153 (1988): 521–531.

55. Ibid.

56. R. P. Bentall, *Madness Explained: Psychosis and Human Nature* (London, UK: Penguin, 2004), 39.

57. Hare, "Schizophrenia as a Recent Disease."

58. M. J. Friedman and E. G. Karam, "Posttraumatic Stress Disorder," in *Stress-Induced and Fear Circuitry Disorders: Refining the Research Agenda for DSM-V,* ed. G. Andrews, D. S. Charney, P. J. Sirovatka, and D. A. Regier (Arlington, VA: American Psychiatric Association, 2009), 23.

59. D. Summerfield, "The Invention of Post-Traumatic Stress Disorder and the Social Usefulness of a Psychiatric Category," *BMJ,* 322 (2001): 95–98; A. Young, *The Harmony of Illusions: Inventing Post-Traumatic Stress Disorder* (Princeton, NJ: Princeton University Press, 1995).

60. D. Fassin and R. Rechtman, *The Empire of Trauma: An Inquiry into the Condition of Victimhood*, trans. R. Gomme (Princeton, NJ: Princeton University Press, 2009), 284.

61. R. Yehuda and A. C. McFarlane, "Introduction," in *Psychobiology of Posttraumatic Stress Disorder*, ed. R. Yehuda and A. C. McFarlane (New York: New York Academy of Sciences, 1997), xv.

62. For Hotspur, see R. A. Kulka, W. E. Schlenger, J. A. Fairbank, R. L. Hough, B. K. Jordan, C. R. Marmar, and D. S. Weiss, *Trauma and the Vietnam War Generation: Report of Findings from the National Vietnam Veterans Readjustment Study* (New York: Brunner/Mazel, 1990), 284-285. For Achilles, see J. Shay, *Achilles in Vietnam: Combat Trauma and the Undoing of Character* (New York: Atheneum, 1994).

63. Young, *The Harmony of Illusions*, 51, 141.

64. E. T. Dean, Jr., *Shook over Hell: Post-Traumatic Stress, Vietnam, and the Civil War* (Cambridge, MA: Harvard University Press, 1997), 91-114.

65. S. Wessely, "Risk, Psychiatry and the Military," *British Journal of Psychiatry*, 186 (2005): 459-466.

66. Dean, Jr., *Shook over Hell*, 40.

67. D. H. Marlowe, *Psychological and Psychosocial Consequences of Combat and Deployment: With Special Emphasis on the Gulf War* (Santa Monica, CA: RAND, 2001), 86.

68. Ibid., 73.

69. R. J. Lifton, *Home from the War: Vietnam Veterans: Neither Victims Nor Executioners* (New York: Touchstone, 1973); C. F. Shatan, "The Grief of Soldiers: Vietnam Combat Veterans' Self-Help Movement," *American Journal of Orthopsychiatry*, 43 (1973): 640-653.

70. L. F. Sparr and R. K. Pitman, "PTSD and the Law," in *Handbook of PTSD: Science and Practice*, ed. M. J. Friedman, T. M. Keane, and P. A. Resic (New York: Guilford, 2007), 449-468.

71. G. Nicosia, *Home to War: A History of the Vietnam Veterans' Movement* (New York: Crown Publishers, 2001), 178.

72. A. S. Blank, Jr., "Irrational Reactions to Post-Traumatic Stress Disorder and Viet Nam Veterans," in *The Trauma of War: Stress and Recovery in Viet Nam Veterans*, ed. S. Sonnenberg, A. S. Blank, Jr., and J. A. Talbott (Washington: American Psychiatric Press, 1985), 83.

73. J. E. Osterman and J. T. V. M. de Jong, "Cultural Issues and Trauma,"

in *Handbook of PTSD: Science and Practice,* ed. M. J. Friedman, T. M. Keane, and P. A. Resick (New York: Guilford, 2007), 439, 435.

74. K. de Jong, M. Mulhern, N. Ford, S. van der Kam, and R. Kleber, "The Trauma of War in Sierra Leone," *Lancet,* 355 (2000): 2067–2068.

75. C. S. North, B. Pfefferbaum, P. Narayanan, S. Thielman, G. McCoy, C. Dumont, A. Kawasaki, N. Ryosho, and E. L. Spitznagel, "Comparison of Post-Disaster Psychiatric Disorders after Terrorist Bombings in Nairobi and Oklahoma City," *British Journal of Psychiatry,* 186 (2005): 487–493.

76. P. D. Yeomans, J. D. Herbert, and E. M. Forman, "Symptom Comparison across Multiple Solicitation Methods among Burundians with Traumatic Event Histories," *Journal of Traumatic Stress,* 21 (2008): 231–234.

77. G. J. McCall and P. A. Resick, "A Pilot Study of PTSD Symptoms Among Kalahari Bushmen," *Journal of Traumatic Stress,* 16 (2003): 445–450.

78. E. Jones and S. Wessely, *Shell Shock to PTSD: Military Psychiatry from 1900 to the Gulf War* (Hove, UK: Psychology Press, 2005).

79. E. Jones, R. H. Vermaas, H. McCartney, C. Beech, I. Palmer, K. Hyams, and S. Wessely, "Flashbacks and Post-Traumatic Stress Disorder: The Genesis of a 20th-Century Diagnosis," *British Journal of Psychiatry,* 182 (2003): 158–163.

80. For a discussion of this phenomenon, see R. J. McNally and S. A. Clancy, "Sleep Paralysis, Sexual Abuse, and Space Alien Abduction," *Transcultural Psychiatry,* 42 (2005): 113–122.

81. Jones et al., "Flashbacks and Post-Traumatic Stress Disorder."

82. Ibid., 162.

83. E. Jones, R. Hodgins-Vermaas, H. McCartney, B. Everitt, C. Beech, D. Poynter, I. Palmer, K. Hyams, and S. Wessely, "Post-Combat Syndromes from the Boer War to the Gulf War: A Cluster Analysis of Their Nature and Attribution," *BMJ,* 324 (2002): 1–7.

84. C. F. Shatan, "Post-Vietnam Syndrome," *New York Times,* May 6, 1972.

85. E. Watters, *Crazy Like Us: The Globalization of the American Psyche* (New York: Free Press, 2010), 65–125.

86. D. Murphy, *Psychiatry in the Scientific Image* (Cambridge, MA: MIT Press, 2006), 262–263.

87. Hacking, *The Social Construction of What?* 100–124. For MPD, see I. Hacking, *Rewriting the Soul: Multiple Personality and the Sciences of Memory* (Princeton, NJ: Princeton University Press, 1995); for PTSD, see McNally, *Remembering Trauma,* 284.

88. B. Shephard, "Risk Factors and PTSD: A Historian's Perspective," in *Posttraumatic Stress Disorder: Issues and Controversies,* ed. G. M. Rosen (Chichester, UK: Wiley, 2004), 39–61; Summerfield, "The Invention of Post-Traumatic Stress Disorder."

89. G. M. Heyman, *Addiction: A Disorder of Choice* (Cambridge, MA: Harvard University Press, 2009), 102–114.

6. Is It in Our Genes?

1. N. Craddock, M. C. O'Donovan, and M. J. Owen, "The Genetics of Schizophrenia and Bipolar Disorder: Dissecting Psychosis," *Journal of Medical Genetics,* 42 (2005): 193–204.

2. B. Riley and K. S. Kendler, "Molecular Genetic Studies of Schizophrenia," *European Journal of Human Genetics,* 14 (2006): 669–680.

3. K. R. Merikangas and N. Risch, "Will the Genomics Revolution Revolutionize Psychiatry?" *American Journal of Psychiatry,* 160 (2003): 625–635.

4. K. S. Kendler, "Reflections on the Relationship Between Psychiatric Genetics and Psychiatric Nosology," *American Journal of Psychiatry,* 163 (2006): 1138–1146.

5. M. C. O'Donovan, N. Craddock, and M. J. Owen, "Schizophrenia: Complex Genetics, Not Fairy Tales," *Psychological Medicine,* 38 (2008): 1697–1699.

6. K. S. Kendler, 'A Gene for . . .': The Nature of Gene Action in Psychiatric Disorders," *American Journal of Psychiatry,* 162 (2005): 1243–1252.

7. P. E. Griffiths and J. Tabery, "Behavioral Genetics and Development: Historical and Conceptual Causes of Controversy," *New Ideas in Psychology,* 26 (2008): 332–352.

8. J. M. McClellan, E. Susser, and M.-C. King, "Schizophrenia: A Common Disease Caused by Multiple Rare Alleles," *British Journal of Psychiatry,* 190 (2007): 194–199.

9. T. Walsh, S. Casadei, K. H. Coats, E. Swisher, S. M. Stray, J. Higgins,

K. C. Roach, et al., "Spectrum of Mutations in *BRCA1, BRCA2, CHEK2,* and *TP53* in Families at High Risk of Breast Cancer," *Journal of the American Medical Association,* 295 (2006): 1379-1388.

10. E. Shorter, *Before Prozac: The Troubled History of Mood Disorders in Psychiatry* (Oxford: Oxford University Press, 2009).

11. Merikangas and Risch, "Will the Genomics Revolution Revolutionize Psychiatry?"

12. Ibid.

13. L. R. Cardon and L. J. Palmer, "Population Stratification and Spurious Allelic Association," *Lancet,* 361 (2003): 598-604.

14. J. P. A. Ioannidis, "Why Most Published Research Findings Are False," *PLoS Medicine,* 2 (2005): 696-701.

15. Riley and Kendler, "Molecular Genetic Studies of Schizophrenia."

16. McClellan et al., "Schizophrenia."

17. A. R. Sanders, J. Duan, D. F. Levinson, J. Shi, D. He, C. Hou, G. J. Burrell, et al., "No Significant Association of 14 Candidate Genes with Schizophrenia in a Large European Ancestry Sample: Implications for Psychiatric Genetics," *American Journal of Psychiatry,* 165 (2008): 497-506.

18. J. P. A. Ioannidis, E. E. Ntzani, T. A. Trikalinos, and D. G. Contopoulos-Ioannidis, "Replication Validity of Genetic Association Studies," *Nature Genetics,* 29 (2001): 306-309.

19. I. I. Gottesman and T. D. Gould, "The Endophenotype Concept in Psychiatry: Etymology and Strategic Intentions," *American Journal of Psychiatry,* 160 (2003): 636-645.

20. J. Flint and M. K. Munafò, "The Endophenotype Concept in Psychiatric Genetics," *Psychological Medicine,* 37 (2007): 163-180.

21. A. R. Hariri, V. S. Mattay, A. Tessitore, B. Kolachana, F. Fera, D. Goldman, M. F. Egan, and D. R. Weinberger, "Serotonin Transporter Genetic Variation and the Response of the Human Amygdala," *Science,* 297 (2002): 400-403.

22. A. Caspi, K. Sugden, T. E. Moffitt, A. Taylor, I. W. Craig, H. Harrington, J. McClay, et al., "Influence of Life Stress on Depression: Moderation by a Polymorphism in the 5-HTT Gene," *Science,* 301 (2003): 386-389.

23. A. R. Hariri, E. M. Drabant, K. E. Munoz, B. S. Kolachana, V. S.

Mattay, M. F. Egan, and D. R. Weinberger, "A Susceptibility Locus for Affective Disorders and the Response of the Human Amygdala," *Archives of General Psychiatry*, 62 (2005): 146–152.

24. Flint and Munafò, "The Endophenotype Concept."

25. H.-Y. Tan, J. H. Callicott, and D. R. Weinberger, "Intermediate Phenotypes in Schizophrenia Genetics Redux: Is It a No Brainer?" *Molecular Psychiatry*, 13 (2008): 233–238.

26. M. R. Munafò, C. Durrant, G. Lewis, and J. Flint, "Gene × Environment Interactions at the Serotonin Transporter Locus," *Biological Psychiatry*, 65 (2009): 211–219; N. Risch, R. Herrell, T. Lehner, K.-L. Liang, L. Eaves, J. Hoh, A. Griem, M. Kovacs, J. Ott, and K. R. Merikangas, "Interaction Between the Serotonin Transporter Gene (5-HTTLPR), Stressful Life Events, and Risk of Depression: A Meta-Analysis," *Journal of the American Medical Association*, 301 (2009): 2462–2471.

27. R. Uher and P. McGuffin, "The Moderation by the Serotonin Transporter Gene of Environmental Adversity in the Etiology of Depression: 2009 Update," *Molecular Psychiatry*, 15 (2010): 18–22.

28. McClellan et al., "Schizophrenia."

29. C. Dalman and P. Allebeck, "Paternal Age and Schizophrenia: Further Support for an Association," *American Journal of Psychiatry*, 159 (2002): 1591–1592.

30. J. F. Crow, "There's Something Curious about Paternal-Age Effects," *Science*, 301 (2003): 606–607.

31. J. Haukka, J. Suvisaari, and J. Lönnqvist, "Fertility of Patients with Schizophrenia, Their Siblings, and the General Population: A Cohort Study from 1950 to 1959 in Finland," *American Journal of Psychiatry*, 160 (2003): 460–463.

32. E. Hare, "Schizophrenia as a Recent Disease," *British Journal of Psychiatry*, 153 (1988): 521–531.

33. International Schizophrenia Consortium, "Rare Chromosomal Deletions and Duplications Increase Risk of Schizophrenia," *Nature*, 455 (2008): 237–241; S. H. Stefansson, D. Rujescu, S. Cichon, O. P. H. Pietiläinen, A. Ingason, S. Steinberg, R. Fossdal, et al., "Large Recurrent Microdeletions Associated with Schizophrenia," *Nature*, 455 (2008): 232–236.

34. Stefansson et al., "Large Recurrent Microdeletions."

35. O'Donovan, Craddock, and Owen, "Schizophrenia."

36. E. Kraepelin, *Dementia Praecox and Paraphrenia,* trans. R. M. Barclay (Edinburgh: E. & S. Livingstone, 1919).

37. N. Craddock and M. J. Owen, "The Beginning of the End for the Kraepelinian Dichotomy," *British Journal of Psychiatry,* 186 (2005): 364–366.

38. Ibid.

39. Craddock et al., "The Genetics of Schizophrenia."

40. A. G. Cardno, F. V. Rijsdijk, P. C. Sham, R. M. Murray, and P. McGuffin, "A Twin Study of Genetic Relationships Between Psychotic Symptoms," *American Journal of Psychiatry,* 159 (2002): 539–545.

41. Craddock et al., "The Genetics of Schizophrenia."

42. Ibid.

43. Craddock and Owen, "The Beginning of the End."

44. Sanders et al., "No Significant Association."

45. Kendler, "Reflections on the Relationship."

46. M. F. Mehler, "Epigenetic Principles and Mechanisms Underlying Nervous System Function in Health and Disease," *Progress in Neurobiology,* 86 (2008): 305–341.

47. R. H. Perlis, S. Purcell, M. Fava, J. Fagerness, A. J. Rush, M. H. Trivedi, and J. W. Smoller, "Association Between Treatment-Emergent Suicidal Ideation with Citalopram and Polymorphisms Near Cyclic Adenosine Monophosphate Response Element Binding Protein in the STAR*D Study," *Archives of General Psychiatry,* 64 (2007): 689–697.

48. D. S. Charney, D. H. Barlow, K. Botteron, J. D. Cohen, D. Goldman, R. E. Gur, K. M. Lin, et al., "Neuroscience Research Agenda to Guide Development of a Pathophysiologically Based Classification System," in *A Research Agenda for DSM-V,* ed. D. J. Kupfer, M. B. First, and D. A. Regier (Washington: American Psychiatric Association, 2002), 31.

49. Ibid., 33.

50. R. Yehuda and A. C. McFarlane, "Conflict Between Current Knowledge about Posttraumatic Stress Disorder and Its Original Conceptual Basis," *American Journal of Psychiatry,* 152 (1995): 1705–1713.

51. A. Young, "How Narratives Work in Psychiatric Science: An Example from the Biological Psychiatry of PTSD," in *Narrative Research in Health and Illness,* ed. B. Hurwitz, T. Greenhalgh, and V. Skultans (Oxford, UK: Blackwell, 2004), 382–396.

52. S. E. Hyman, "Can Neuroscience Be Integrated into the DSM-V?" *Nature Reviews Neuroscience,* 8 (2007): 725.

53. D. Murphy, *Psychiatry in the Scientific Image* (Cambridge, MA: MIT Press, 2006), 5.

54. E. Hollander and M. Evers, "Review of Obsessive-Compulsive Spectrum Disorders: What Do We Know? Where Are We Going?" *Clinical Neuropsychiatry: Journal of Treatment Evaluation,* 1 (2004): 32–51.

55. E. Hollander, S. Kim, S. Khanna, and S. Pallanti, "Obsessive-Compulsive Disorder and Obsessive-Compulsive Spectrum Disorders: Diagnostic and Dimensional Issues," *CNS Spectrums,* 12, no. 2, suppl. 3 (2007): 5–13.

56. E. A. Storch, J. Abramowitz, and W. K. Goodman, "Where Does Obsessive-Compulsive Disorder Belong in DSM-V?" *Depression and Anxiety,* 25 (2008): 336–347.

57. Ibid.

58. J. M. Hooley, S. A. Gruber, H. A. Parker, J. Guillaumot, J. Rogowska, and D. A. Yurgelun-Todd, "Cortico-Limbic Response to Personally Challenging Emotional Stimuli after Complete Recovery from Depression," *Psychiatry Research: Neuroimaging,* 172 (2009): 83–91.

59. J. Joormann, "Cognitive Aspects of Depression," in *Handbook of Depression,* 2nd ed., ed. I. H. Gotlib and C. L. Hammen (New York: Guilford, 2009), 298–321; R. J. McNally and H. E. Reese, "Information-Processing Approaches to Understanding Anxiety Disorders," in *Oxford Handbook of Anxiety and Anxiety Disorders,* ed. M. M. Antony and M. B. Stein (Oxford, UK: Oxford University Press, 2009), 136–152.

60. International Schizophrenia Consortium, "Common Polygenic Variation Contributes to Risk of Schizophrenia and Bipolar Disorder," *Nature,* 460 (2009): 748–752.

61. International Schizophrenia Consortium, "Rare Chromosomal Deletions and Duplications Increase Risk of Schizophrenia."

62. Cross-Disorder Phenotype Group of the Psychiatric GWAS Consortium, "Dissecting the Phenotype in Genome-Wide Association Studies of Psychiatric Illness," *British Journal of Psychiatry,* 195 (2009): 97–99.

63. A. Caspi, A. R. Hariri, A. Holmes, R. Uher, and T. E. Moffitt, "Genetic Sensitivity to the Environment: The Case of the Serotonin Trans-

porter Gene and Its Implications for Studying Complex Diseases and Traits," *American Journal of Psychiatry,* 167 (2010): 509–527.

64. J. Belsky, C. Jonassaint, M. Pluess, M. Stanton, B. Brummett, and R. Williams, "Vulnerability Genes or Plasticity Genes?" *Molecular Psychiatry,* 14 (2009): 746–754.

65. B. J. Ellis and W. T. Boyce, "Biological Sensitivity to Context," *Current Directions in Psychological Science,* 17 (2008): 183–187.

66. S. G. Potkin, J. A. Turner, J. A. Fallon, A. Lakatos, D. B. Keator, G. Guffanti, and F. Macciardi, "Gene Discovery through Imaging Genetics: Identification of Two Novel Genes Associated with Schizophrenia," *Molecular Psychiatry,* 14 (2009): 416–428.

67. S. W. Cole, "Social Regulation of Human Gene Expression," *Current Directions in Psychological Science,* 18 (2009): 132–137.

68. F. A. Champagne and R. Mashoodh, "Genes in Context: Gene-Environment Interplay and the Origins of Individual Differences in Behavior," *Current Directions in Psychological Science,* 18 (2009): 127–131.

69. T.-Y. Zhang and M. J. Meaney, "Epigenetics and the Environmental Regulation of the Genome and Its Function," *Annual Review of Psychology,* 61 (2010): 439–466; S. E. Hyman, "How Adversity Gets under the Skin," *Nature Neuroscience,* 12 (2009): 241–243.

70. N. Tsankova, W. Renthal, A. Kumar, and E. J. Nestler, "Epigenetic Regulation in Psychiatric Disorders," *Nature Reviews Neuroscience,* 8 (2007): 355–367.

71. P. O. McGowan, A. Sasaki, A. C. D'Alessio, S. Dymov, B. Labonté, M. Szyf, G. Turecki, and M. J. Meaney, "Epigenetic Regulation of the Glucocorticoid Receptor in Human Brain Associates with Childhood Abuse," *Nature Neuroscience,* 12 (2009): 342–348.

7. Do Mental Disorders Differ by Kind or Degree?

1. J. P. Feighner, E. Robins, S. B. Guze, R. A. Woodruff, Jr., G. Winokur, and R. Munoz, "Diagnostic Criteria for Use in Psychiatric Research," *Archives of General Psychiatry,* 26 (1972): 57–63.

2. E. Robins and S. B. Guze, "Establishment of Diagnostic Validity in Psychiatric Illness: Its Application to Schizophrenia," *American Journal of Psychiatry,* 126 (1970): 983–987.

3. R. Cooper, *Classifying Madness: A Philosophical Examination of the Diagnostic and Statistical Manual of Mental Disorders* (Dordrecht, The Netherlands: Springer, 2005), 121.

4. M. B. First, "Clinical Utility: A Prerequisite for the Adoption of a Dimensional Approach in *DSM*," *Journal of Abnormal Psychology*, 114 (2005): 560–564.

5. R. C. Kessler, K. A. McGonagle, S. Zhao, C. B. Nelson, M. Hughes, S. Eshleman, H. U. Wittchen, and K. S. Kendler, "Lifetime and 12-Month Prevalence of *DSM-III-R* Psychiatric Disorders in the United States: Results from the National Comorbidity Survey," *Archives of General Psychiatry*, 51 (1994): 8–19.

6. C. G. Fairburn, Z. Cooper, K. Bohn, M. E. O'Connor, H. A. Doll, and R. L. Palmer, "The Severity and Status of Eating Disorder NOS: Implications for DSM-V," *Behaviour Research and Therapy*, 45 (2007): 1705–1715.

7. Ibid.; C. G. Fairburn and Z. Cooper, "Thinking Afresh about the Classification of Eating Disorders," *International Journal of Eating Disorders*, 40 (2007): S107–S110.

8. P. K. Keel, "Purging Disorder: Subthreshold Variant or Full-Threshold Eating Disorder?" *International Journal of Eating Disorders*, 40 (2007): S89–S94; H. G. Pope, Jr., J. K. Lalonde, L. J. Pindyck, T. Walsh, C. M. Bulik, S. J. Crow, S. L. McElroy, N. Rosenthal, and J. I. Hudson, "Binge Eating Disorder: A Stable Syndrome," *American Journal of Psychiatry*, 163 (2006): 2181–2183; A. Stunkard, K. Allison, and J. Lundgren, "Issues for DSM-V: Night Eating Syndrome," *American Journal of Psychiatry*, 165 (2008): 424.

9. J. J. Hudziak, T. M. Achenbach, R. R. Althoff, and D. S. Pine, "A Developmental Approach to Psychopathology," in *Dimensional Approaches in Diagnostic Classification: Refining the Research Agenda for DSM-V*, ed. J. E. Helzer, H. C. Kraemer, R. F. Krueger, H.-U. Wittchen, P. J. Sirovatka, and D. A. Regier (Arlington, VA: American Psychiatric Association, 2008), 101–113.

10. G. Parker et al., "Issues for DSM-5: Whither Melancholia? The Case for Its Classification as a Distinct Mood Disorder," *American Journal of Psychiatry*, 167 (2010): 745–747.

11. J. E. Helzer, K. K. Bucholz, and M. Gossop, "A Dimensional Option

for the Diagnosis of Substance Dependence in DSM-V," in *Dimensional Approaches in Diagnostic Classification*, 19–34.

12. L. A. Clark and D. Watson, "Tripartite Model of Anxiety and Depression: Psychometric Evidence and Taxonomic Implications," *Journal of Abnormal Psychology*, 100 (1991): 316–336; R. F. Krueger, "The Structure of Common Mental Disorders," *Archives of General Psychiatry*, 56 (1999): 921–926; S. Mineka, D. W. Watson, and L. A. Clark, "Comorbidity of Anxiety and Unipolar Mood Disorders," *Annual Review of Psychology*, 49 (1998): 377–412; D. Watson, "Rethinking the Mood and Anxiety Disorders: A Quantitative Hierarchical Model for *DSM-V*," *Journal of Abnormal Psychology*, 114 (2005): 522–536.

13. K. S. Kendler, "Major Depression and Generalised Anxiety Disorder: Same Genes, (Partly) Different Environments—Revisited," *British Journal of Psychiatry*, 168, suppl. 30 (1996): 68–75; K. S. Kendler, C. O. Gardner, M. Gatz, and N. L. Pedersen, "The Sources of Co-Morbidity Between Major Depression and Generalized Anxiety Disorder in a Swedish National Twin Sample," *Psychological Medicine*, 37 (2007): 453–462.

14. M. K. Shear, I. Bjelland, A. K. Beesdo, A. T. Gloster, and H.-U. Wittchen, "Supplementary Dimensional Assessment in Anxiety Disorder," in *Dimensional Approaches in Diagnostic Classification*, 65–84.

15. Helzer et al., "A Dimensional Option for the Diagnosis."

16. Ibid.

17. C. G. Fairburn, Z. Cooper, and R. Shafran, "Cognitive Behaviour Therapy for Eating Disorders: A 'Transdiagnostic' Theory and Treatment," *Behaviour Research and Therapy*, 41 (2003): 509–528.

18. S. A. Wonderlich, T. E. Joiner, Jr., P. K. Keel, D. A. Williamson, and R. D. Crosby, "Eating Disorder Diagnoses: Empirical Approaches to Classification," *American Psychologist*, 62 (2007): 167–180.

19. T. A. Widiger and T. J. Trull, "Plate Tectonics in the Classification of Personality Disorder: Shifting to a Dimensional Model," *American Psychologist*, 62 (2007): 71–84.

20. M. C. Zanarini, F. R. Frankenburg, J. Hennen, D. B. Reich, and K. R. Silk, "Prediction of the 10-Year Course of Borderline Personality Disorder," *American Journal of Psychiatry*, 163 (2006): 827–832.

21. J. Paris, *The Fall of an Icon: Psychoanalysis and Academic Psychiatry* (Toronto: University of Toronto Press, 2005), 145.

22. A. E. Skodol, J. G. Gunderson, M. T. Shea, T. H. McGlashan, L. C. Morey, C. A. Sanislow, D. S. Bender, et al., "The Collaborative Longitudinal Personality Disorders Study (CLPS): Overview and Implications," *Journal of Personality Disorders,* 19 (2005): 487–504.

23. C. M. Grilo, M. T. Shea, C. A. Sanislow, A. E. Skodol, J. G. Gunderson, R. L. Stout, M. E. Pagano, et al., "Two-Year Stability and Change of Schizotypal, Borderline, Avoidant, and Obsessive-Compulsive Personality Disorders," *Journal of Consulting and Clinical Psychology,* 72 (2004): 767–775.

24. T. H. McGlashan, C. M. Grilo, C. A. Sanislow, E. Ralevski, L. C. Morey, J. G. Gunderson, A. E. Skodol, et al., "Two-Year Prevalence and Stability of Individual DSM-IV Criteria for Schizotypal, Borderline, Avoidant, and Obsessive-Compulsive Personality Disorders: Toward a Hybrid Model of Axis II Disorders," *American Journal of Psychiatry,* 162 (2005): 883–889.

25. T. A. Widiger and D. B. Samuel, "Diagnostic Categories or Dimensions? A Question for the *Diagnostic and Statistical Manual of Mental Disorders—Fifth Edition*," *Journal of Abnormal Psychology,* 114 (2005): 494–504; A. S. New, J. Triebwasser, and D. S. Charney, "The Case for Shifting Borderline Personality Disorder to Axis I," *Biological Psychiatry,* 64 (2008): 653–659; P. Tienari, L. C. Wynne, K. Läksy, J. Moring, P. Nieminen, A. Sorri, I. Lahti, and K.-E. Wahlberg, "Genetic Boundaries of the Schizophrenia Spectrum: Evidence from the Finnish Adoptive Family Study of Schizophrenia," *American Journal of Psychiatry,* 160 (2003): 1587–1594.

26. L. A. Clark, "Assessment and Diagnosis of Personality Disorder: Perennial Issues and an Emerging Reconceptualization," *Annual Review of Psychology,* 58 (2007): 227–257.

27. Skodol et al., "Two-Year Prevalence and Stability."

28. Widiger and Trull, "Plate Tectonics."

29. R. Verheul and T. A. Widiger, "A Meta-Analysis of the Prevalence and Usage of the Personality Disorder Not Otherwise Specified (PDNOS) Diagnosis," *Journal of Personality Disorders,* 18 (2004): 309–319.

30. Widiger and Trull, "Plate Tectonics."

31. R. K. Blashfield and V. Intoccia, "Growth of the Literature on the Topic of Personality Disorders," *American Journal of Psychiatry,* 157 (2000): 472–473.

32. Widiger and Trull, "Plate Tectonics."

33. J. Block, "A Contrarian View of the Five-Factor Approach to Personality Description," *Psychological Bulletin,* 117 (1995): 187–215; Widiger and Trull, "Plate Tectonics."

34. P. T. Costa and R. R. McCrae, "Domains and Facets: Hierarchical Personality Assessment Using the Revised NEO Personality Inventory," *Journal of Personality Assessment,* 64 (1995): 21–50.

35. R. R. McCrae, A. Terracciano, and 78 Members of the Personality Profiles of Culture Project, "Universal Features of Personality Traits from the Observer's Perspective: Data from 50 Cultures," *Journal of Personality and Social Psychology,* 88 (2005): 547–561.

36. S. Yamagata, A. Suzuki, J. Ando, Y. Ono, N. Kijima, K. Yoshimura, F. Ostendorf, et al., "Is the Genetic Structure of Human Personality Universal? A Cross-Cultural Twin Study from North America, Europe, and Asia," *Journal of Personality and Social Psychology,* 90 (2006): 987–998.

37. First, "Clinical Utility."

38. Widiger and Lowe, "Five-Factor Model Assessment"; T. A. Widiger and S. N. Mullins-Sweatt, "Five-Factor Model of Personality Disorders: A Proposal for DSM-V," *Annual Review of Clinical Psychology,* 5 (2009): 197–220.

39. Clark, "Assessment and Diagnosis of Personality Disorder."

40. Skodol et al., "Two-Year Prevalence and Stability."

41. L. M. Saulsman and A. C. Page, "The Five-Factor Model and Personality Disorder Empirical Literature: A Meta-Analytic Review," *Clinical Psychology Review,* 23 (2004): 1055–1085.

42. S. Epstein, "Trait Theory as Personality Theory? Can a Part Be as Great as the Whole?" *Psychological Inquiry,* 5 (1994): 120–122; L. A. Pervin, "A Critical Analysis of Current Trait Theory," *Psychological Inquiry,* 5 (1994): 103–113.

43. J. Kagan, "Validity Is Local," *American Psychologist,* 45 (1990): 294–295; J. Kagan, "A Time for Specificity," *Journal of Personality Assessment,* 85 (2005): 125–127.

44. J. Kagan, "Three Pleasing Ideas," *American Psychologist,* 51 (1996): 901–908.

45. G. Claridge and C. Davis, "What's the Use of Neuroticism?" *Personality and Individual Differences,* 31 (2001): 383–400.

46. S. Shifman et al., "A Whole Genome Association Study of Neuroticism Using DNA Pooling," *Molecular Psychiatry,* 13 (2008): 302–312.

47. J. Ormel, J. Rosmalen, and A. Farmer, "Neuroticism: A Non-Informative Marker of Vulnerability to Psychopathology," *Social Psychiatry and Psychiatric Epidemiology,* 39 (2004): 906–912.

48. D. Borsboom and C. V. Dolan, "Why *g* Is Not an Adaptation: A Comment on Kanazawa (2004)," *Psychological Review,* 113 (2006): 433–437.

49. W. Bechtel, "Mechanisms in Cognitive Psychology: What Are the Operations?" *Philosophy of Science,* 75 (2008): 983–994.

50. P. W. Bridgman, *The Logic of Modern Physics* (New York: Macmillan, 1927), 5.

51. E. Sober, *Philosophy and Biology* (Boulder, CO: Westview Press, 1993), 39.

52. D. Borsboom, *Measuring the Mind: Conceptual Issues in Contemporary Psychometrics* (Cambridge: Cambridge University Press, 2005), 161.

53. H. Putnam, "What Is Realism?" in *Scientific Realism,* ed. J. Leplin (Berkeley, CA: University of California Press, 1984), 140–153.

54. B. Ellis, *The Philosophy of Nature: A Guide to the New Essentialism* (Chesham, UK: Acumen, 2002), 12.

55. E. Mayr, *Toward a New Philosophy of Biology: Observations of an Evolutionist* (Cambridge, MA: Harvard University Press, 1988), 204–209.

56. J. S. Wilkins, *Species: A History of the Idea* (Berkeley, CA: University of California Press, 2009), 231–234.

57. D. Murphy, *Psychiatry in the Scientific Image* (Cambridge, MA: MIT Press, 2006), 334–341.

58. R. Boyd, "Realism, Anti-Foundationalism and the Enthusiasm for Natural Kinds," *Philosophical Studies,* 61 (1991): 127–148.

59. Cooper, *Classifying Madness,* 54.

60. Ibid., 46, 50, 149.

61. K. H. Teigen, "One Hundred Years of Laws in Psychology," *American Journal of Psychology,* 115 (2002): 103–118; L. Darden, "Thinking Again

about Biological Mechanisms," *Philosophy of Science,* 75 (2008): 958–969; Bechtel, "Mechanisms in Cognitive Psychology."

62. R. A. Wilson, ed., *Species: New Interdisciplinary Essays* (Cambridge, MA: MIT Press, 1999).

63. Wilkins, *Species,* 198.

64. J. Dupré, *The Disorder of Things: Metaphysical Foundations of the Disunity of Science* (Cambridge, MA: Harvard University Press, 1993).

65. First, "Clinical Utility"; M. B. First, H. Pincus, J. Levine, J. Williams, B. Ustun, and R. Peele, "Clinical Utility as a Criterion for Revising Psychiatric Diagnoses," *American Journal of Psychiatry,* 161 (2004): 946–954.

66. P. E. Meehl, "Clarifications about Taxometric Method," *Applied and Preventive Psychology,* 8 (1999): 166.

67. P. E. Meehl, "Bootstraps Taxometrics: Solving the Classification Problem in Psychopathology," *American Psychologist,* 50 (1995): 266–275; Meehl, "Clarifications about Taxometric Method"; P. E. Meehl, "What's in a Taxon?" *Journal of Abnormal Psychology,* 113 (2004): 39–43.

68. N. G. Waller, F. W. Putnam, and E. B. Carlson, "Types of Dissociation and Dissociative Types," *Psychological Methods,* 1 (1996): 300–321.

8. So What Is Mental Illness Anyway?

1. L. Wittgenstein, *Philosophical Investigations,* trans. G. E. M. Anscombe (New York: Macmillan, 1953), 32–33.

2. S. O. Lilienfeld and L. Marino, "Mental Disorder as a Roschian Concept: A Critique of Wakefield's 'Harmful Dysfunction' Analysis," *Journal of Abnormal Psychology,* 104 (1995): 411–420; S. O. Lilienfeld and L. Marino, "Essentialism Revisited: Evolutionary Theory and the Concept of Mental Disorder," *Journal of Abnormal Psychology,* 108 (1999): 400–411. J. C. Wakefield, "Evolutionary versus Prototype Analyses of the Concept of Disorder," *Journal of Abnormal Psychology,* 108 (1999): 374–399, is unconvinced by Lilienfeld and Marino's prototype approach to mental disorder. He argues that the occurrence of ambiguous cases does not undermine the concept of mental disorder as having necessary and sufficient criteria. Indeed, he says, the classi-

cal concept of *bachelor* has two necessary and sufficient criteria: being unmarried and being a man, but each criterion itself has fuzzy boundaries. When does an adolescent boy qualify as a man? Is an unmarried eighteen-year-old a bachelor? How many years of common-law living must elapse before we no longer call a man a *bachelor?* "The existence of necessary and sufficient defining criteria is one thing; the precision of the criteria is another," as Wakefield says (378). However, clarifying the boundaries for the criteria that define the concept of *bachelor* differs from doing so for the criteria that define *mental disorder.* In the first case, we stipulate what these boundaries are, whereas in the second case we aim to discover what they are. Moreover, the conceptual breadth of *bachelor* is far more restrictive than that of *mental disorder.* The cases that fall under the rubric of *mental disorder* are far more diverse and complex than candidates for the label *bachelor.*

3. P. R. McHugh, "Striving for Coherence: Psychiatry's Efforts over Classification," *Journal of the American Medical Association,* 293 (2005): 2526–2528.

4. For reviews and critiques of this model of addiction, see G. M. Heyman, *Addiction: A Disorder of Choice* (Cambridge, MA: Harvard University Press, 2009); S. L. Satel and F. K. Goodwin, *Is Drug Addiction a Brain Disease?* (Washington, DC: Ethics and Public Policy Center, 1998); S. Satel and S. O. Lilienfeld, "Singing the Brain Disease Blues," *American Journal of Bioethics Neuroscience,* 1 (2001): 46–54.

5. S. T. Higgins, S. H. Heil, and J. P. Lussier, "Clinical Implications of Reinforcement as a Determinant of Substance Use Disorders," *Annual Review of Psychology,* 55 (2004): 431–461.

6. B. J. Rounsaville, R. D. Alarcón, G. Andrews, J. S. Jackson, R. E. Kendell, and K. Kendler, "Basic Nomenclature Issues for DSM-V," in D. J. Kupfer, M. B. First, and D. A. Regier, eds., *A Research Agenda for DSM-V* (Washington, DC: American Psychiatric Association, 2002), 1–29.

7. J. A. Greene, *Prescribing by Numbers: Drugs and the Definition of Disease* (Baltimore, MD: Johns Hopkins University Press, 2007), 7.

8. R. M. Kaplan and M. Ong, "Rationale and Public Health Implica-

tions of Changing CHD Risk Factor Definitions," *Annual Review of Public Health*, 28 (2007): 321–344.

9. T. B. Baker, R. M. McFall, and V. Shoham, "Current Status and Future Prospects of Clinical Psychology: Toward a Scientifically Principled Approach to Mental and Behavioral Health Care," *Psychological Science in the Public Interest*, 9 (2009): 67–103.

Acknowledgments

I am very grateful to Donna (Valliere) McNally and Jerome Kagan for their incisive comments on early drafts of this book. Two peer reviewers provided excellent reviews of the manuscript, and one of them, Dominic Murphy, signed his critique, enabling me to thank him by name. Finally, Elizabeth Knoll and Christine Thorsteinsson of Harvard University Press provided superb editorial guidance and comments.